The Art and Science of Tennis

Bruce Elliott, Ph.D., Dip.P.E.
Lecturer in Biomechanics and Tennis
University of Western Australia

Rob Kilderry, Dip.P.E.
Western Australian State
Tennis Coach

SAUNDERS COLLEGE PUBLISHING
Philadelphia New York Chicago
San Francisco Montreal Toronto
London Sydney Tokyo Mexico City
Rio de Janeiro Madrid

Address orders to:
383 Madison Avenue
New York, NY 10017

Address editorial correspondence to:
West Washington Square
Philadelphia, PA 19105

Text Typeface: 10/12 Baskerville
Compositor: Bi-Comp, Inc.
Acquisitions Editor: John Butler
Project Editors: Janis Moore, Don Reisman
Copyeditor: Monica Wysong
Managing Editor & Art Director: Richard L. Moore
Design Assistant: Virginia A. Bollard
Text Design: Caliber Design Planning, Inc.
Cover Design: Christine Nardello
Production Manager: Tim Frelick
Assistant Production Manager: Maureen Iannuzzi

Cover credit: Photograph supplied by Four by Five.

Library of Congress Cataloging in Publication Data

Elliott, Bruce, Ph.D.
  The art and science of tennis.

  Bibliography: p.
  Includes index.
  1. Tennis. I. Kilderry, Rob. II. Title.
GV995.E38 1983   796.342'2   82-61050
ISBN 0-03-062501-7

THE ART AND SCIENCE OF TENNIS   ISBN 0-03-062501-7

© 1983 by CBS College Publishing. All rights reserved. Printed in the United States of America.
Library of Congress catalog card number 82-61050.

345 038 987654321

CBS COLLEGE PUBLISHING
Saunders College Publishing
Holt, Rinehart and Winston
The Dryden Press

Preface

The Art and Science of Tennis was written to offer a comprehensive evaluation of the needs of the tennis player. The topics pertinent to these needs have been presented in a way that will provide a greater understanding of tennis for the player, coach, and teacher.

Selected topics have been included that will have specific appeal to players, coaches, or teachers. The chapters titled Stroke Production, Tennis Strategy, Sports Psychology and the Tennis Player, Training for Tennis, and Equipment Design should be of interest to both beginning and advanced players. Teachers, who should also find those chapters beneficial, have been further catered to with sections on Tennis Administration and Unit Structure, which are applicable to both school and community settings. Coaches just entering the field should find the entire book of value; experienced coaches can learn from the high-speed photographs and the chapters on the Coaching and Teaching of Tennis, Player Evaluation for Improved Performance, and Controversy in Tennis.

The theory of the game of tennis has been linked to the applied problems of coaching and teaching so that new concepts can be easily adopted. We hope that our approach will provide an understanding of tennis that will help coaches and teachers to increase their effectiveness, and players to improve their performance.

Acknowledgments

We are grateful to the many tennis players who have raised the questions that helped motivate us to write this book, to Tibor von Karlowitz for his photography, to Jenny Porter for her art work, to Freda Maguire for her help with the typing, to Ray Neuling for his help with the editing of some of the early manuscripts, to the Department of Human Movement and Recreation Studies at the University of Western Australia, and to our wives who have contributed time and patience in the preparation of this book. Special thanks must go to Alan Brien, whose help with the psychological aspects of tennis influenced the content of Chapter 3.

Finally, we want to thank the following people, who gave us valuable advice in preparing our final manuscript: Bob Gensemer, University of Denver; Bob McEvoy, Pembroke State University; Jeff Moore, University of Colorado; Bill Richards, Ball State University; and Dave Snyder, University of Texas.

Bruce Elliott
Rob Kilderry

Contents

1 Stroke Production   1
    Grips   1
    Ready Position   5
    The Forehand Drive   6
    The Backhand Drive   19
    The Service   25
    Return of Service   34
    Approach Shot   36
    The Volley   40
    The Smash   49
    The Lob   53
    The Drop-shot   57
    The Half-volley   59

2 Tennis Strategy   64
    Concentration   64
    Singles Strategy   67
    Specific Singles Preparation and Tactics   73
    Doubles Strategy   77

3 Sports Psychology and the Tennis Player   83
    Introduction   83
    Factors Influencing Performance   84

4 The Coaching and Teaching of Tennis   91
The Basis of Coaching/Teaching   91
Teaching Strategies in a Coaching or Teaching Program   93
Planning the Coaching Program   95

5 Player Evaluation For Improved Performance   98
Analysis of Stroke Production   99
Game Analysis   99
Tennis Test Battery   103

6 Training For Tennis   110
Energy Systems Involved in the Game   110
Tennis: A Training Program in Itself   111
Squad Preparation: General Training Principles   112
Squad Organization: Physiological Development   114
Tournament Preparation   132

7 Controversy In Tennis   136

8 Junior Development in Tennis   149
Principles For the Design of a Children's Tennis Program   149
Physical Effects of Tennis Training   152
Psychological Effects of Tennis Training   152
Talent Identification and Development   154

9 Tennis Administration   155
Social and Competitive Club Play   155
Tournament Organization   163

10 Unit Structure   165
School Program for Children Eight to Nine Years Old   165
School Program for Children 13 to 14 Years Old   170
Adult Tennis Program: Preparation for Intermediate Club Play   175
Adult Tennis Program: Preparation for Advanced Club Play   183
Tennis Camp for Children 10 to 16 Years of Age   184

11 Equipment Design 188
    Racket Weight, Balance, and Grip Size   189
    String Type, Tension, and Racket Flexibility   191

Appendix A Rules of Tennis   193

Appendix B Glossary of Terms   207

Appendix C Tennis Etiquette   212

Index   215

1

Stroke Production

Good strokes last a lifetime and as such are important to players of all skill levels. This chapter is aimed at providing players, coaches, and teachers with an understanding of the techniques involved in each tennis stroke. High-speed photographs enable these techniques to be both identified and explained.

The causes of many of the common errors involved in stroke production are also included, along with appropriate cures. Drill sequences for each stroke then allow development of stroke production for both beginners and advanced players.

Grips

For reasons of anatomical advantage, most of the hand should be behind the grip to ensure firm contact between the player's body and the racket at impact. Although coaches present a number of different grip techniques for different strokes, it is important to realize that the grip, as well as providing a link between the racket and the player's body, will also determine the point of contact with the ball in relation to the body. The grip should be such that the racket is close to horizontal at impact, with the racket face vertical (perpendicular) to the court.

The Eastern Forehand (Figure 1.1)

This is the most universally taught forehand grip because it facilitates hitting balls of all heights while also allowing them to be hit off the front foot.

2 Stroke Production

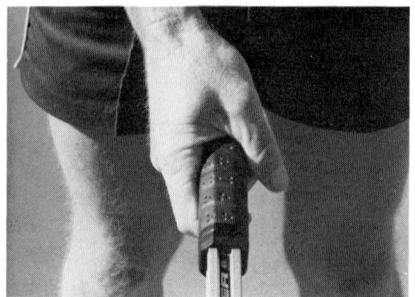

Figure 1.1 Eastern forehand grip.

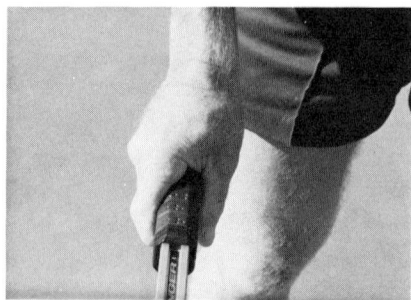

Figure 1.2 Eastern backhand grip.

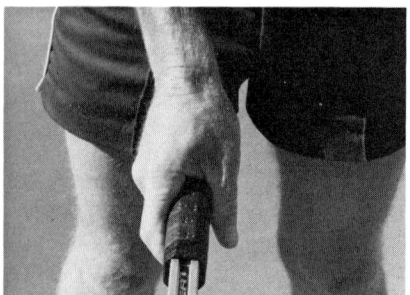

Figure 1.3 Continental grip.

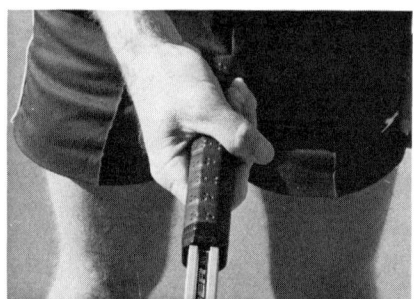

Figure 1.4 Western grip.

(A low ball will sometimes present a problem.) To make this grip, place the palm directly behind the racket strings, with the flat of the hand perpendicular to the ground. Slide the hand down the shaft and wrap it around the handle with the fingers spread comfortably. Check that

1. The base knuckle of the thumb is centered on the top of the grip.
2. The palm is behind the handle. (The hand is thus basically behind the handle.)
3. The thumb overlaps and is next to the middle finger, with the index finger spread.
4. The fingers are evenly spread.
5. The butt end just protrudes from the hand.

Analogies

This grip is often known as the "shake hands grip," because the position of the hand around the handle is similar to the grip used to shake hands.

The following analogy helps explain the correct finger position: "make a trigger finger." The first finger is slightly separated and crooked, as in pulling the trigger of a pistol. Ensure that the finger is wrapped around the handle, as shown in Figure 1.1.

Eastern Backhand (Figure 1.2)

This is the most universally taught backhand grip because it places the wrist behind the racket, allowing the wrist to be kept straight when the ball is played forward of the front foot. This backhand grip is the result of turning the hand a quarter of a turn toward the back of the handle from the eastern forehand grip. This means that the base knuckle of the index finger moves toward the top of the handle. Check that

1. The "V" formed by the thumb and forefinger is slightly to the left of the top of the handle (for a right-handed player) or slightly to the right of the top of the handle (for a left-handed player).
2. The palm of the hand is approximately parallel to the ground.
3. The tip of the thumb should cross the end of the second finger.

Analogies

"Draw the sword": If the racket is positioned under the nonplaying arm, with the handle protruding forward, and then gripped and drawn in a flourish, as a sword fighter does, this backhand grip will be adopted.

"Remove the lump": A lump is formed at the wrist if an eastern forehand grip is made and the hand flexed. If the hand is then turned toward the back of the grip, the backhand grip will be correct when "the lump" disappears.

Continental (Figure 1.3)

This is a grip between the eastern forehand and backhand grips which may be used for all strokes. The "V" formed by the forefinger and the thumb is located on top of the handle. There are both advantages and disadvantages in using this grip.

Advantages

1. It is not necessary to change grips between forehand and backhand strokes. (This is a great advantage for quick volley exchanges.)
2. It permits maximum wrist flexion, very important to service technique.
3. It opens the racket face to enable easy stroking of low bouncing balls.
4. It produces a natural slice on the ball. This often improves control during serving.

Disadvantages

1. It is difficult to hit high groundstrokes.
2. It requires a strong forearm, because the wrist is not behind the

racket at impact. This also makes the racket more difficult to control when the hand sweats.
3. It often causes the ball to be played behind the front foot, with a consequent lack of power.
4. It is more difficult to hit through the ball using this grip, causing most balls to be played across the court.

Analogy

"Hammer grip": The grip adopted to hammer an imaginary nail into the court surface usually will be a continental grip.

Western (Figure 1.4)

This extreme forehand grip is achieved by laying the racket flat on the ground and then picking it up. It provides a firm hitting position for the forehand drive as the wrist is positioned behind the handle; however, it closes the racket face, making a low bouncing ball hard to play. This grip also has a tendency to cause the ball to be hit after it has reached the height of its bounce and is on the way down as in a topspin forehand drive. The follow-through then tends to be more vertical as the player lifts the racket to permit maximum racket face contact with the ball. This movement has contributed to the bent arm follow-through so common among professionals.

Analogy

"Frying pan grip": A western forehand grip will result if a racket handle is grasped in the same way as a frying pan from a position in which the racket lies flat on the court.

Minor changes to the four grips mentioned are, of course, common. Many players use grips between some of the more commonly accepted techniques. Many Australian players use a forehand grip described by Metzler[6] as the Australian grip. This has the palm and wrist toward the top surface of the handle, and so lies between the eastern forehand and continental grips.

Good wrist control and timing have permitted many players to overcome the inherent disadvantages associated with a particular grip. John McEnroe has emphasized the importance of the *correct* racket face angle at impact regardless of the grip used.

Recommended Progressions

Forehand drive   The eastern forehand grip. This permits the player to experience the "feel" of hitting a ball with both power and control with a minimum of effort.

Backhand drive   The eastern backhand grip, for the same reasons as the forehand.

Figure 1.5 The ready position.

Service The eastern forehand grip, followed by the continental grip. Beginners should be taught with an eastern forehand grip. The added wrist movement possible with the continental grip can be introduced when the player is ready to learn the approach shot.

Volley The eastern forehand or backhand grip.

Ready Position

A player who is balanced between strokes requires less effort to establish a sound technique. In tennis, a player requires only a momentary stability to allow sudden movement in any direction in response to the opponent's stroke. This dictates that

1. The feet should be placed at shoulder width to provide balanced posture for subsequent movement.
2. The legs should be slightly bent and the trunk inclined forward. This moves the body weight closer to the toes, which also aids in subsequent sudden movement.
3. The racket should be held in both hands, the second hand lightly supporting the shaft.
4. The racket should be at waist level, straight out in front, with the racket head slightly above the wrist. Some players may prefer a low

racket position when waiting for the ball. On completion of a backhand (using an eastern backhand grip), the racket may angle slightly to the backhand side as it is uncomfortable to point the racket forward with this grip.
5. The racket should not be spun in the hand when waiting for the ball.
6. At the completion of each return adopt a ready position with reference to (a) a central court location, (b) the position where the ball has been played, and (c) the general strategy being used by the opponent.
7. The racket should be held in an eastern forehand grip thus equalizing the preparation time for other groundstrokes. Natural body rotation together with the use of the free hand in aiding backswing preparation and grip change make the backhand easier to prepare for more quickly. The ready position should be such that orientation of the body and racket can be quickly prepared for the oncoming ball.

The Forehand Drive

Although the topspin forehand drive is now favored by many tournament professionals, both the flat and topspin stroke techniques are discussed. The flat forehand drive is discussed first.

The Stroke

The backswing, forward swing, and follow-through phases of the forehand stroke must all be fluently integrated for an efficient drive.

The Grip
An eastern forehand grip is recommended in teaching the forehand drive. This grip (which has the hand behind the racket) permits the ball to be hit in line with the front foot more easily than any other grip.

The Backswing
The preparation to hit the ball will determine the effectiveness of the stroke ("as the preparation goes, so goes the stroke"). Since the key to the forehand drive is to hit the ball in line with the front foot, the length of the backswing will be affected by the speed of the oncoming ball and the position of the player on the court. A fast approaching ball will therefore dictate a shorter backswing (as on service return). A correctly timed backswing allows time to develop optimal racket-head speed at impact. Preparing too early can also have a detrimental effect on the fluency of the stroke.

7 The Forehand Drive

Figures 1.6 to 1.16 *The Mechanics of the Flat Forehand Drive.* The mechanics of the forehand drive were analyzed by filming with a high-speed camera at 200 frames per second. Not all frames have been included here, but the relative movement sequence is clearly illustrated.

Figure 1.6

Figure 1.7

Figure 1.8

Figure 1.9

Figure 1.10

Figure 1.11

Figure 1.12

Figure 1.13

Figure 1.14

Figure 1.15

Figure 1.16

The following techniques ensure that both the body and the racket are prepared for the forward swing:

1. The player should begin the stroke by moving as quickly as possible into position after the opponent has hit the ball.
2. In moving to the ball, the player should turn both shoulders and pivot the hips so that the forward shoulder is pointing in the direction of the flight of the ball (Figure 1.7).
3. The racket should be drawn back as the player moves toward the ball, so that the racket is approximately parallel to the player's body and between waist and knee height (below the intended point of contact with the ball).
4. A straight-back technique with the racket allows a player to limit the length of the backswing, to ensure a smooth forward swing. This technique should not be rushed, since any sudden stopping of the racket arm at the completion of the backswing may cause excessive wrist and racket movement.
5. A semicircular backswing may also be used, provided excessive movement is eliminated. Such excessive movement can be caused by having a fully cocked racket head (racket at a 90° angle to the arm). A semicircular backswing, which is superior for returning a wide ball, must be completed in two parts. In the first part the racket should be taken back and held above waist level. The second section is characterized by the racket continuing to a low position with a fixed wrist and then moving forward as the forward foot moves to meet the ball.
6. The racket should be at a comfortable length from the body with the grip hand just hidden from the player's opponent (Figures 1.8 and 1.9).

Coaches and players should not attempt to groove all backswings into a definite pattern, but excessive movements (which cause a rushed forward swing or late point of impact) should be eliminated.

Forward Swing

The body and racket preparation of the backswing are coordinated during the forward swing in an attempt to produce an optimal racket speed and alignment at impact. The following points can be used as a guide to an efficient forward swing:

1. The player should dictate body and racket position at impact by "going after" the ball; the ball should not dictate the stroke.
2. As the player's forward foot hits the ground his/her front knee should be bent so that the eyes are closer to the line of flight of the ball. This position aids the development of power by enabling the lifting action from the player's legs to coordinate with the rotation

of the hips during the forward swing (Figure 1.9 to Figure 1.14). Movement onto the front foot coincides with the commencement of the forward swing (Figure 1.10).
3. The arm and racket move forward as a unit with the racket head trailing the player's wrist during the early stages of this movement (Figures 1.10 and 1.11). Before contact the racket head catches up with the wrist and is ready for impact. Remember that the racket moves both forward and upward (at approximately a 14 to 17° angle) for a flat forehand drive hit at about 3 feet (1 meter) from the ground (Figures 1.10 to 1.13).
4. At impact the racket does not form a natural extension of the forearm, but is laid back (hyperextended) so that the ball can be struck in line with, or slightly in front of, the leading foot. Ideally, the ball should be at the top of its bounce-height (Figure 1.13), although many players today hit the ball after it has passed this height.
5. Balls that bounce to different heights can be hit at a relatively constant level when correct footwork and legwork are used.
6. To produce a vertical racket head that is in line with the wrist at impact, the wrist must be kept firm and must not change its original position during the forward swing. The racket control at impact must, however, be achieved without a "stiff muscular swing" that would result from a completely locked elbow and wrist.
7. The player using a closed or semiopen stance is able to flatten the "arc of the swing," thus maximizing the chance of the ball following the intended direction of travel. Any impact that occurs at the positions shown in Figures 1.12 to 1.14 will follow the intended direction of the stroke. A semiopen stance is often used to play the ball that is approaching either down the middle of the court or very wide on the court. With a backswing and back foot placement oriented to the line of the ball, the player's front foot then moves forward toward the ball prior to impact. This ensures that the weight is going forward at impact, prevents excess running by playing the ball earlier, and permits a quick return to a central court position.
8. The cross-court forehand drive requires minor modification to the technique taught for the straight drive:
    a. Hit the ball further forward of the foot than for a straight drive.
    b. Hit around the ball, particularly if playing the ball behind the line of the front foot.
    c. Use a semiopen stance.
9. The relative pathways of the racket and the ball dictate the rotation imparted to the ball at impact. The ball is in contact with the strings for such a brief period that no purposeful movement is possible once the ball has contacted the strings.

Follow-through

The follow-through allows the player to develop an optimal racket velocity at impact (the player would unconsciously slow the racket down before impact if there were no follow-through in the stroke). It also helps to avoid muscle and joint injury by allowing the racket to decelerate gradually. An efficient follow-through is characterized by the following:

1. The early stages of the follow-through have the racket following the intended direction of travel of the ball. The wrist and racket should stay together as a unit for a short time during this early follow-through. The player must "push" the racket through the ball.
2. Some players benefit by watching the spot where contact was made to avoid pulling their eyes off the ball. This should not be continued for too long or it will hamper recovery for the next shot.
3. The player's head should remain in precisely the same position during the follow-through as when the ball was contacted. The stroke is completed with a full sweep of the arm close to the chin, with the body balanced ready to move for the next shot (Figure 1.16).

The forehand previously discussed is a flat drive with a low-to-high hitting action through the ball. The path traced out by the racket during the forward swing is similar if the player wishes to hit a topspin forehand drive.

Topspin Forehand Drive

This stroke requires basically the same preparation as the flat drive. A steeper low-to-high hitting action (Figures 1.17 to 1.23) will impart topspin to the ball. The racket should be close to knee level at the commencement of the forward swing (Figure 1.17) and move to approximately shoulder height at the end of the follow-through (Figure 1.23). The racket is "brushed-up" through the ball with a vertical or slightly closed racket face at impact (Figure 1.21).

Analogies

For integrating the phases of the forehand drive:

"Open and close the door": The arm movement is like a door as it swings open (backswing) and closes (forward swing).

"Climb the hill": Visualize the racket gradually going upward as if climbing a hill.

Forehand Tips

1. Most forehands that go wrong do so at the very beginning of the backswing. Concentrate on achieving an early backswing that is rhythmical and allows adequate time for a good forward swing.

11 The Forehand Drive

Figures 1.17 to 1.23 *The Mechanics of the Topspin Forehand Drive.*

Figure 1.17

Figure 1.18

Figure 1.19

Figure 1.20

Figure 1.21

Figure 1.22

Figure 1.23

2. Start moving to the ball the moment the opponent hits the ball. Players often move too slowly to the ball and do not achieve the momentary pause prior to playing the shot.
3. Bend the knees and step forward into the ball (as with a half-volley). An arm swing with no forward movement of body weight reduces the power of the drive.
4. Play the ball in line with the front foot when possible. Hit out in front by going after the ball.
5. Learn to bend the knees and use footwork so that the ball can always be hit at about the same height and distance from the body. In other words, develop a good "strike zone."
6. Always be aware of the position of the ball and the racket.

Corrective Techniques for Forehand Errors

Error The player continuously hits the ball off the back foot.
Correction Have another player feed a succession of balls so that a half-volley can be hit close to the baseline. This ensures that the racket is forward of the front foot at impact (see Figures 1.13 and 1.21).
Error The player remains upright during the stroke, thus neglecting to lean into the ball.
Correction This is usually the result of a late backswing or the player stepping too early without the racket coming forward. Ensure during practice that the step forward on the front foot is coordinated with the beginning of the forward swing of the racket. The ball is then impacted in line with the forward foot. At the end of the stroke ensure that the front knee is over the toe. A ball dropped from the forehead should land in front of the forward foot.
Error The player does not rotate the hips and shoulders, thus reducing the effective power of the drive.
Correction As the racket is taken back in the backswing, move the non-racket arm back to a comfortable position in line with the front leg, thus ensuring body rotation.
Error The player hits the forehand with too much wrist movement.
Correction Sweep the ball with the entire arm, keeping the wrist locked during the stroke. Practice the forward swing against a wall (forward toe touching the wall) to determine the wrist position that produces a vertical racket head at impact.
Error The player tends to open the face of the racket and chop the ball at impact.
Correction The end of the backswing must be characterized by a low racket position. In the forward swing keep the elbow relatively close to the body and hit up through the ball with the racket face vertical to the court at impact.
Error The player opens the body, turning the shoulders so they are parallel to the net at impact.
Correction Ensure that the shoulders are perpendicular to the net for as long as possible during the stroke. The shoulders will inevitably turn from this ideal position during the forward swing of the stroke.
Error The player cuts short the follow-through phase of the stroke.
Correction Ensure that the player reaches out with the arm and racket following impact.

Teaching Drills

Demonstration of the complete stroke and then of the drill to be used should precede all on-court practice.

1. *Shadow drill.* Some coaches may favor using the format shown in Figure 1.24 to look quickly at a forehand drive played without a

13 The Forehand Drive

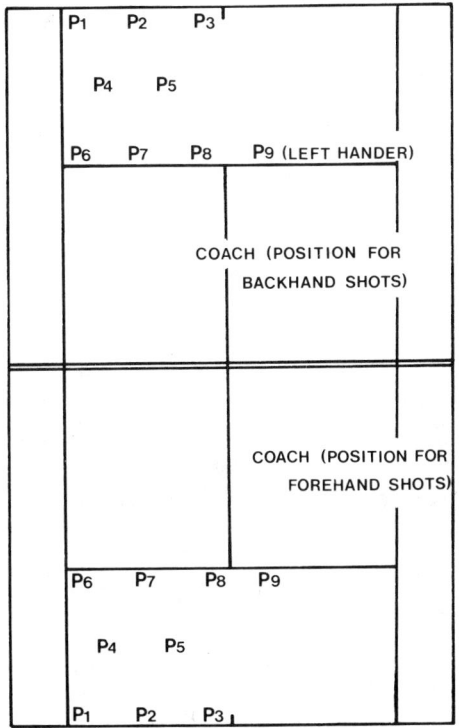

Figure 1.24 Shadow drill formation.

ball. It is better to try and teach the stroke in its entirety. Then just check racket positions at the completion of the backswing, at impact, and at the finish of the stroke.

2. *Bounce, step, and hit.* The player throws the ball to approximately shoulder height in front of the forward foot so that he/she can move into the stroke after the ball has bounced. This drill, which should initially be practiced on the service line, can be played from further back in the court as skill develops. This drill can also be used with advanced players. They can play against themselves by trying to hit to a specific area of the court.

3. Use the same drill formation as in (2) but have the ball fed to the player (Figure 1.25).

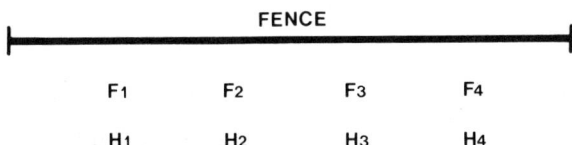

Figure 1.25 Feeding and hitting positions for a forehand drive.

4. Use the same drill formation as in (3) but practice control by having the hitter play the ball so it can be caught by the feeder.
5. Use the same drill as in (4) except the ball should now be hit over the net (Figure 1.26). Work in threes with a feeder (F), a hitter (H), and a collector (C). Players rotate after hitting ten forehands. The position of the hitter can be gradually moved toward the baseline as skill improves.
6. *Full-court forehand.* The ball is now fed to a player standing on the baseline, who must hit it to a collector at the far end of the court.
7. *Forehand from a hit.* This drill should be used sparingly because it creates a situation in which only one player is hitting a ball at any time. It does, however, allow each person to play a forehand from a hit that is well directed. The coach can vary the direction of the ball to ensure that it is played either straight to or away from the hitter (Figure 1.27).
8. *Service line rally.* Players in pairs (four players to a court at a time) strive to achieve the most consecutive hits over the net.

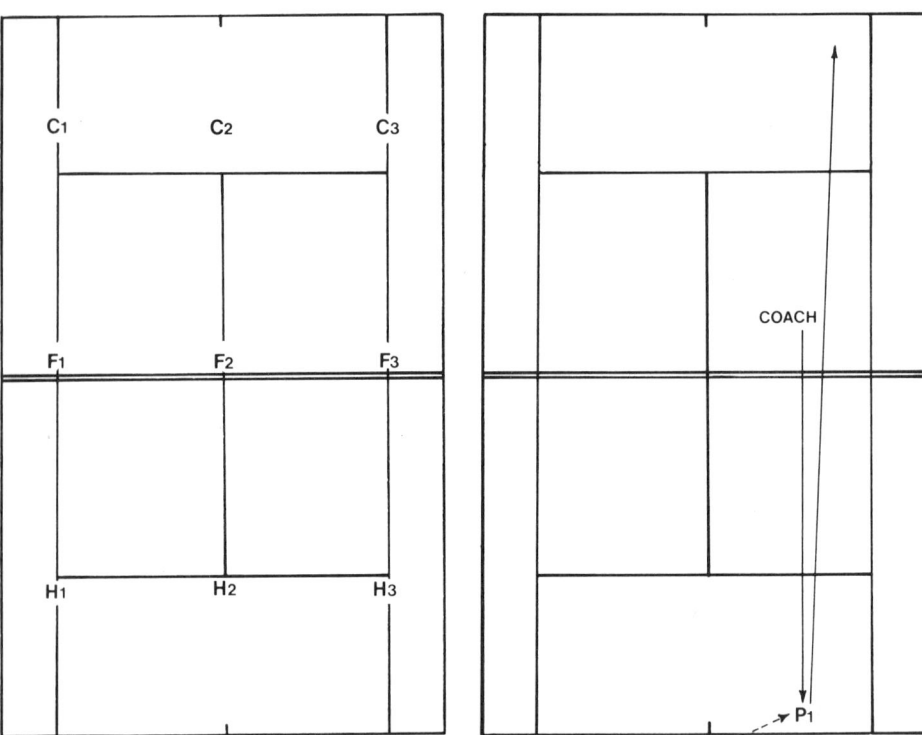

Figure 1.26 Court positions for a forehand from the service line.

Figure 1.27 Court positions for a forehand drive from a hit.

15 The Forehand Drive

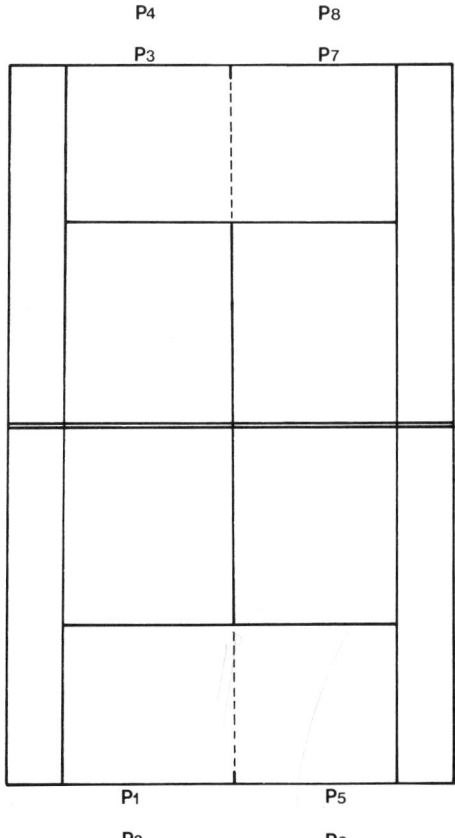

Figure 1.28 Court positions for a half-court drill.

9. *Baseline rally (half-court drill).* Players use half the doubles court to rally with forehand drives. At the end of five rallies, players can change over with those waiting. All rallies start with a bounce-hit forehand drive (Figure 1.28).

Culmination Games

1. *One-on-one cooperative.* The coach hits a ball to player 1 who plays a forehand drive to player 5. Player 5 then returns the ball to player 2. Players 1 and 5 then change ends. The goal of the drill is to hit the most consecutive shots over the net (Figure 1.29).
2. *One-on-one competition.* The same as the preceding drill, but each player competes against an opponent. The winner of each rally scores one point. These points are either totaled for a team if the players remain at the same ends of the court, or kept individually if

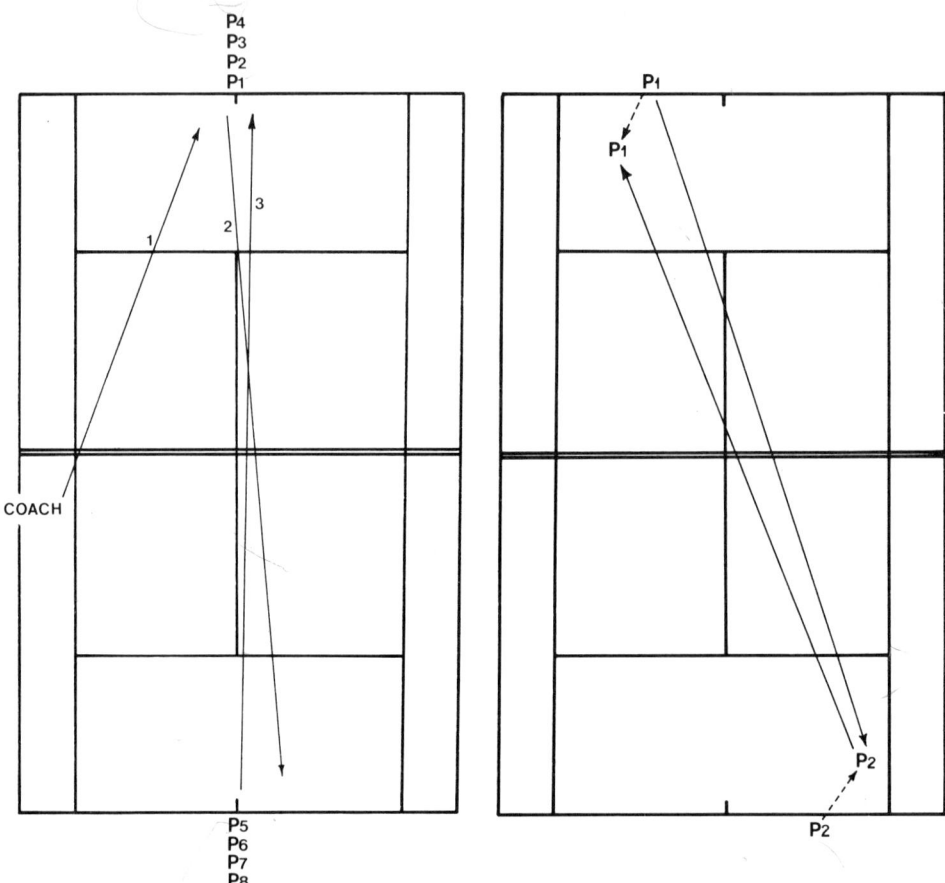

Figure 1.29 Court positions for a one-on-one drill.

Figure 1.30 Court positions for a cross-court rally.

the players change ends. When one player gets to five points, restart the drill with different opponents.

3. *Cross-court to cross-court.* This drill may be used to see how many consecutive shots can be played (Figure 1.30).
4. *Two-on-one (forehands).* Players 1 and 2 are required to hit forehands into the shaded area (Figure 1.31), while player 3 may hit a forehand to any part of the opponent's court.
5. *Eleven-up.* Player 1 starts a rally with a bounce-hit forehand. The rally is then completed using forehands, with the winning pair scoring a point. Player 3 starts the next rally in the same way. The game continues with the "service" changing until one team reaches eleven points. This format can be used in the "king of the mountain" concept, where pairs change courts in a direction dictated by their last result (Figure 1.32).

6. *Champion.* The coach hits the ball to each player in turn. Every successful forehand results in a letter: C, H, A, and so on. The first person to spell the word *champion* is the winner.
7. *Mug's Alley.* All pupils line up on the outer sideline of the right court. A coach, standing close to the net, acts as the feeder. In turn, each player comes out onto the baseline and attempts to return a forehand "fed" by the coach. Each return must land in the singles court, or that player "loses a life" (gains a letter: M, U, G). Once the word *mug* has been spelled out, the player moves into the alley behind the coach (shaded area) and attempts to catch any forehand returns. If a catch is taken, the catcher regains a life, removes a letter from his/her tally (G), and returns to the end of the playing line. Any subsequent error causes this player to again join those players in the alley.
8. *Baseball Tennis.* This game is played according to the following rules:
    a. Six players comprise a team (one team batting, one team fielding).

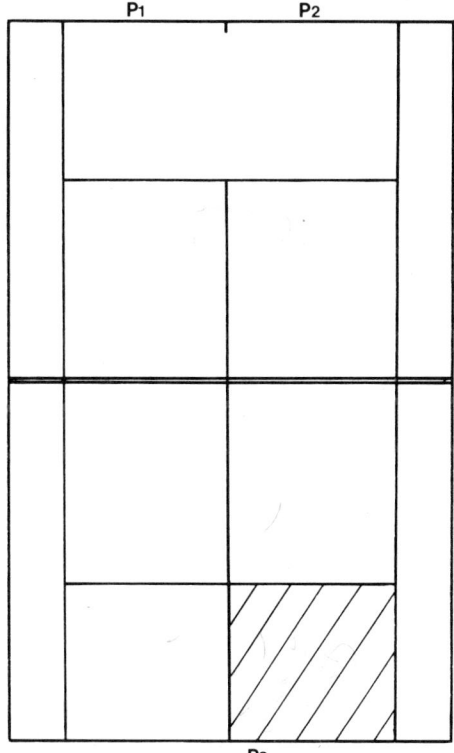

Figure 1.31 Court positions for a two-on-one drill (forehand drive).

18 Stroke Production

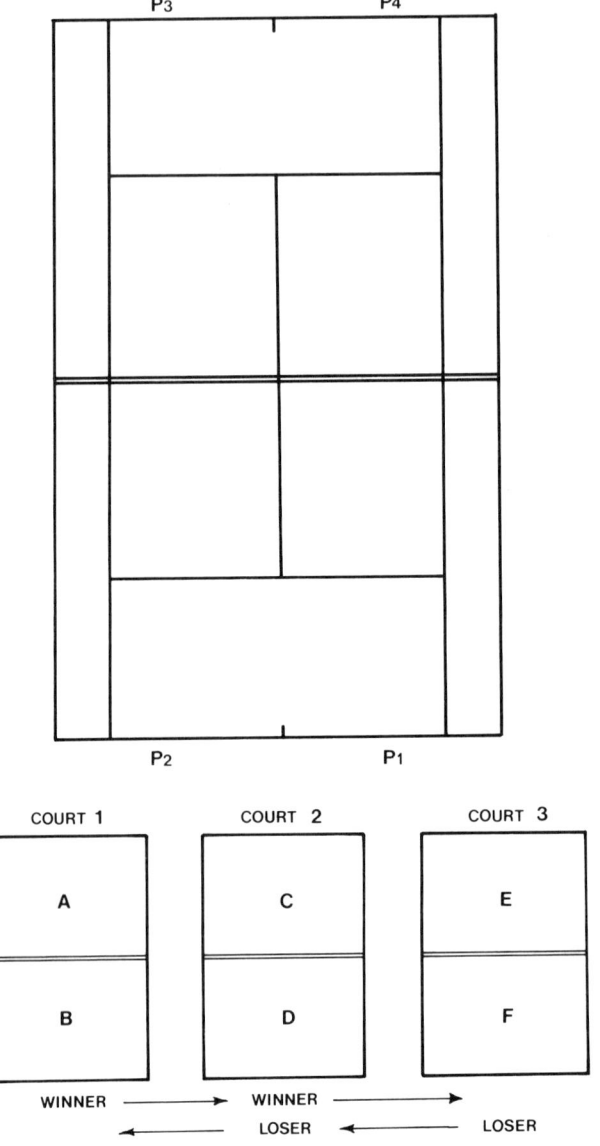

Figure 1.32 Court positions for an 11-up drill.

      b. A dropped catch could cost six runs (optional).
      c. The feeder (pitcher) must throw underarm cooperatively.
      d. A player is out if the ball is hit out of court, into the net, or is caught on the fly.

19 The Backhand Drive

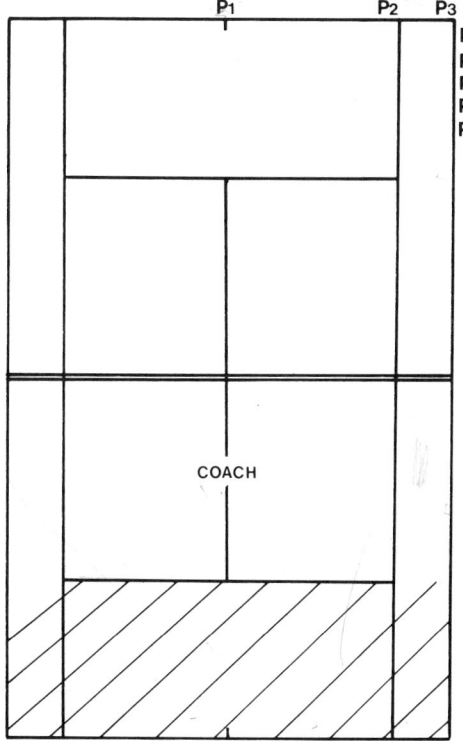

Figure 1.33 Court positions for Mug's Alley drill.

e. Beginners should usually be given four hits each for the whole team prior to changing batting and fielding sides. Advanced players may prefer to allow each batter to continue hitting until out (struck out, ball caught, or ball landing in the net or out of court).

Note the scoring areas in Figure 1.34.

The Backhand Drive

The backhand is, surprisingly, a more natural movement than the forehand because the ball is played just in front of the forward shoulder with the head closer to the point of impact.

The Stroke

An efficient backhand stroke will result only if the component parts of the stroke flow smoothly together.

20 Stroke Production

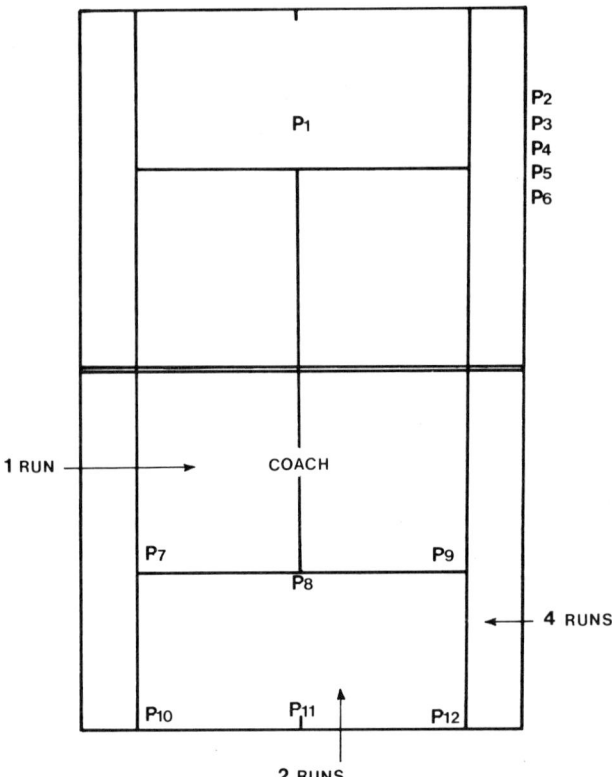

Figure 1.34 Court positions for baseball tennis.

The Grip
An eastern backhand grip is recommended for the backhand drive. The wrist is positioned behind the racket so that control and power are both possible at impact.

The Backswing
This preparation phase provides a stable hitting position from which the forward swing can occur.

1. The shoulders and hips pivot as the ball leaves the opponent's racket and the player moves to the ball (Figure 1.35). If a player needs to cover an extreme distance to hit a shot, then quick movement to the vicinity of the ball will occur prior to this pivot.
2. The racket is taken back with the racket arm tucked against the abdomen. The knees are bent and the racket is held below the intended point of ball contact. The other hand is used to rotate the racket into the eastern backhand grip position.

21 The Backhand Drive

Figures 1.35 to 1.45 *The Mechanics of the Backhand Drive.* The mechanics of the backhand drive were analyzed by filming with a high-speed camera at 200 frames per second. Not all frames have been included here, but the relative movement sequence is clearly illustrated.

Figure 1.35

Figure 1.36

Figure 1.37

Figure 1.38

Figure 1.39

Figure 1.40

Figure 1.41

Figure 1.42

Figure 1.43

Figure 1.44

Figure 1.45

3. The back foot pivot occurs simultaneously with the initial movement of the racket (Figure 1.35).
4. The player looks over his/her forward shoulder while moving to the ball.
5. If backspin is required, the racket should be held higher than the hip so that it can move in a downward path to the ball.
6. The wrist is in a locked position and not cocked (unless backspin is desired).

Coaches and players should not attempt to standardize all backswings, but excessive movements of the racket that cause a rushed forward swing or a late point of impact should be eliminated.

Analogy
"Pull the sword from the scabbard": The racket goes back on the backswing to about the same position as a sword fighter would reach to draw the sword from the scabbard.

Forward Swing
During the forward swing the body weight is shifted to the front foot by stepping into the ball and bringing the racket forward. The following points can help the player develop an efficient forward swing:

1. The body and the racket must move forward and upward together. This is accomplished by beginning the forward movement simultaneously with the step of the front foot and the push of the back leg (Figure 1.37).
2. The player should step across the body and forward, attacking the ball. It is important to adopt a closed stance to enable the racket path to be flattened in the area of ball contact (Figure 1.38). A player using a two-handed backhand should adopt a more open stance to allow the racket to hit through the line of the ball.
3. The direction of the hips and shoulders will generally dictate the direction of the hit.
4. The arm should be kept straight and the wrist fixed. Some professionals, however, have adopted a multiple-segment approach to the backhand using the wrist to add greater velocity to the swing.
5. Much of the hitting power comes from the hips, thighs, and the rotation of the trunk (Figures 1.37 to 1.42).
6. The player should hit up onto the ball at a point about 12 to 15 inches (30 to 40 centimeters) in front of the body, with a vertical racket head. The angle of the racket head is constant through the hitting zone (Figures 1.41 to 1.43).
7. A low-to-high hitting action is required for both the flat and topspin backhand drives. A steeper angle in the forward swing produces the topspin drive.

8. The body should be maintained in the hitting position throughout the hit and for part of the follow-through.
9. The player's head should be held in a fixed position to aid stability.

Analogies

"Throw the arm across the net": Pretend to throw the racket arm over the net as the ball is struck.

"The backhand slap": Unwind the racket arm as in a backhand slap.

"Ball under the arm": The backhand should be capable of being hit with a tennis ball held under the armpit of the racket arm. The ball should fall to the court only near the end of the follow-through section of the stroke.

Follow-through

An efficient follow-through is characterized by the following components:

1. The racket should continue on a path from low to high, with the racket head at a constant angle (Figures 1.38 to 1.45).
2. The head should be kept down during the forward swing and early follow-through (Figures 1.38 to 1.44).
3. The knuckles should be turned out and upward toward the target as if lifting (Figures 1.41 to 1.45).

The stroke should end with a full follow-through so that the body is balanced ready to move for the next shot.

Analogy

"Air the armpit":[2] This reminds the player to extend the hitting arm upward after contacting the ball until it is pointed toward the sky.

Backhand Tips

1. The racket must move from low to high (the legs aid in this action).
2. The knuckles on the hitting hand dictate the success of the backhand.
3. There should be no long pause at the completion of the backswing—prepare soon enough to hit the ball at the desired position.
4. Lean forward into the stroke—a backward lean causes the racket face to open at impact.
5. Use the legs and hips to gain power in the stroke (this is a "corkscrew" action emphasizing upper body rotation).
6. Tuck the elbow into the body during the backward swing and move the body next to and inside the line of the ball for impact.

Corrective Techniques for Backhand Errors

Error   The player continually hits the ball with an underspin action, imparting backspin to the ball.
Correction   Encourage a low backswing position with a forward swing that attempts to "lift" the ball over the net. (*Remember:* the knuckles lead the stroke.)
Error   The backhand drive is led by the elbow (elbow push).
Correction   The arm should be swung forward as a unit, with the elbow close to the stomach.
Error   The body turns to be parallel with the net too early in the stroke.
Correction   The player should look over the front shoulder at the ball, maintaining a shoulder position that is perpendicular to the net (this ensures a side-on stance).
Error   The ball seems to impact low on the racket face (the ball "falls off the racket").
Correction   The player should move up to the ball and simulate a lifting action, with the racket and the body moving as a unit.
Error   The player tends to push the ball.
Correction   At the completion of the preparation the racket arm should be comfortably extended backward so that it is relatively straight. A lack of power is usually associated with poor preparation.
Error   The player always impacts the ball at a position between the feet.
Correction   The racket should move forward simultaneously with the front foot. A closed stance and early preparation will usually correct this fault.
Error   The player hits the ball with too much wrist movement.
Correction   Using the other hand at the throat of the racket during the backswing phase helps eliminate this habit. The forward swing starts at the shoulder, and the arm should be rotated forward as a unit.
Error   The stroke is characterized by excessive head movement.
Correction   Place a tennis hat upside down on the head. Insist that this hat be balanced on the head throughout the stroke.

Teaching Drills

The same sequence of drills can be used for the backhand drive as was used for the forehand drive. The "bounce, step, hit" drill will often prove more difficult on the backhand side and may therefore play a less prominent role in the teaching of this stroke. The coach can use the groundstroke drills discussed earlier, first to practice the backhand drive and then in drills using a combination of both forehand and backhand drives.

Culmination Games

The same games may be played as for the forehand drive. A combination of backhand and forehand strokes will naturally follow the practice of a backhand drive. With advanced players, it is often better to start games such as "Eleven-up" with a backhand drive rather than a forehand drive so that both pairs begin the rally with equal chances of success.

The Service

This is the most important stroke in the game and, as such, should be practiced to ensure its effectiveness. It is also the only stroke that is always controlled by the player. Because it is so controllable, it can be made consistently effective by practicing the correct technique.

The primary consideration in any service technique is rhythm. The arms (including the racket) and the body must be synchronized so that a rhythmical serve results. The action begins with the legs, flows through the body, and finishes with the racket. Rhythm that integrates the body and the arms enables a player to serve for long periods without a dramatic drop in power. It also ensures that little strain is placed on the shoulder and the elbow of the hitting arm. This service rhythm should be maintained for both the first and second serves.

What are the things that differ between a first and a second serve? A flat, hard serve with no forward rotation must be hit from approximately 12 feet (3.5 meters) above the ground if the ball is to land in the service area.[2] The speed of the ball, the height of the net, and the size of the court dictate this hitting position. The path of the ball is affected by gravity (pulling the ball down), air resistance (slowing the ball), and spin (curving the flight path). The height of most tennis players dictates that a hard first serve must be hit with an "up and out" action, to impart a small amount of forward rotation to the ball. This technique permits the downward trajectory of the forward rotation to help bring the ball down into the court. Such an action is certainly necessary for children who must utilize spin to advantage, enabling the ball hit with power to climb over the net and then land in the service area.

The slice and kicker serves have a greater chance of success because they are hit with less speed than the power serve and because of the spin imparted to the ball. This is why these serves (particularly the slice serve) have become the standard for most players as second serves.

Each type of serve has its own advantages. The blistering power of the first serve may terrify an opponent, but it will also produce the greatest percentage of service errors. The safer slice serve can be used to move a player off the court or to bring the ball back into the opponent's body. The kicker serve, which is so effective in doubles play, causes the ball to jump and move away from an opponent. The player with a rhythmical serve who can vary service type and direction will always be the one whose service is hardest to "break."

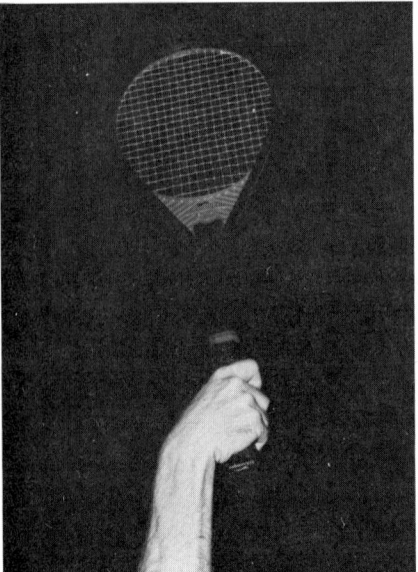 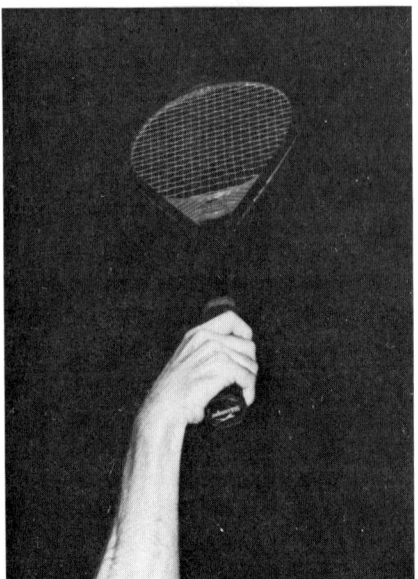

Figure 1.46 Amount of wrist flexion possible with an eastern forehand grip (*left*) and a continental grip (*right*).

The Stroke

The Grip
The eastern forehand grip should be used by all beginners. Players should, however, change to a continental grip (which allows for maximum use of wrist flexion) as quickly as is practicable. This change should precede the development of a game plan where the serve is "followed" to the net.

The Stance
1. Stand so that a line drawn through the heels will point in the direction of the serve (Figures 1.47, 1.58, and 1.62). The feet should be a comfortable distance apart with the racket pointed along the line of the service.
2. When serving to the forehand/deuce court in singles, the player should stand close to the centerline (about one racket's length) so that the serve will pass over the lowest height of the net. Similarly, when serving to the backhand/advantage court in singles, the player should stand about two racket's lengths from the center mark.
3. Body weight may be over one foot or evenly distributed.
4. The player must be relaxed to ensure a rhythmical swing.

29 The Service

Figure 1.58

Figure 1.59

Figure 1.60

Figure 1.61

Figures 1.58 to 1.67 *The Mechanics of the Serve (continued).* Sequences taken from high-speed film show both an adult man and a seven-year-old child serving.

Figure 1.62

Figure 1.63

Figure 1.64

Figure 1.65

Figure 1.66

Figure 1.67

Ball Toss

As was stated in the discussion of the swing, the ball hand moves down to a position close to the front thigh and then moves upward in unison with the racket.

The upward arm movement should be smooth, then the fingers open to release the ball. The following points should aid the server in achieving a well-positioned ball toss:

1. The arm continues upward (carrying the ball as long as is practical) to a position where the fingers point toward the ball, so that the eye, fingertips, and ball are in a straight line.
2. The heel of the hand should be kept pointing upward to ensure that the ball moves both upward and slightly forward.
3. The ball should be pushed to a position slightly to the right and forward of the serving shoulder. The height should be just above where the racket will reach at the top of its swing.

Impact

In making contact with the ball, the player should watch for the following:

1. The ball should be contacted with a vertical racket face in an "up and out" action (Figures 1.55, 1.61, and 1.66).
2. Contact should occur about 12 inches (30 centimeters) in front of the forward toe and about 6 inches (15 centimeters) to the right of the head.
3. The body weight should be on the front foot.

Flat Serve The ball should rotate forward, even on a flat hard service. The "up and out" action, together with the natural rotation of the body and the movement of the racket from inside out, causes the ball to be hit as shown in Figure 1.68.

Slice The movement of the body and racket in respect to the ball, as described for the flat serve, makes the slice-service action almost natural. For this action the racket strikes near the center of the back of the ball, while the racket moves across, as shown in Figure 1.68.

Kicker In this serve the racket is moved across and over the ball. The ball is pushed from above or slightly behind the head over the left shoulder (for a right-handed player). The ball is hit from behind and to the left of the server's head, thus facilitating the high trajectory over the net, which is the key factor in generating rebound.

Follow-through

The completion of the weight transfer onto the right foot (for a right-handed player) moves the body into the court as part of the follow-through (the racket appears to drag the body forward).

Flat *Slice* *Kicker*

Figure 1.68 Racket positions for flat, slice, and kicker service actions.

The hitting face of the racket continues an outward rotation after impact to reduce the strain on the shoulder joint[5] (Figure 1.56).

The racket then moves across the body so that it can be gradually slowed down while the body rebalances in preparation for the next stroke (Figure 1.57) or movement toward the net.

Service Tips

1. Hold the ball in the fingers (thumb and first two or three fingers), not in the palm of the hand. This allows finer touch and greater control.
2. On the downswing, let the arms extend fully before they move upward (Figures 1.48, 1.59, and 1.63).
3. Have the racket arm relaxed to add fluency to the swing and to allow greater wrist snap prior to impact.
4. Keep the head up until after the hit (chin up).
5. Think *up* and *out* when hitting the serve.
6. Don't rush the serve; start slowly and build up racket head speed gradually. It is more difficult but still possible to develop a good service technique from a fast swing (Roscoe Tanner).

Corrective Techniques for the Service

Error The player continually rushes the swing. The player does not have time to achieve a full loop in the swing.

Correction These errors are usually caused by the ball moving upward too quickly, leaving the racket trailing behind. Work toward moving both arms in unison.

Error The player serves from the elbow without using the body to help add power to the serve.

Correction This error is usually caused by not using a full loop in the swing or by standing too square to the net. The loop can be added to the swing by having the player close his/her eyes and swing while concentrating on a full loop. If the shoulders are parallel to the net, have the player practice maintaining a more side-on position to the net during the downward swing. This is often achieved by holding the right hip (for a right-handed player) back so that rotation takes place in the correct sequence: first legs, then hips, then shoulders.

Error The player allows the ball to fall to such an extent that it is hit with a bent racket arm and flexed body (bottom out).

Correction The player must hit up and out so that the body and arm are extended. The ball must be pushed higher in the air so that a rhythmic swing can be maintained and an optimal hitting height achieved.

Teaching Drills

The serve must be taught using a combination of the whole and the part teaching techniques. Emphasis must be placed on achieving a rhythmical swing and then fitting the ball toss to this swing.

Development of the Swing

Use the following sequence of steps to develop the swing:

Point the rifle (Figure 1.62)
Brush your foot (past the feet) (Figure 1.63)
Win the fight (Figure 1.64)
Scratch your back (Figure 1.65)
Rotate into and hit up to the ball (Figure 1.66)
Follow through (Figure 1.67).

Integrating the Ball Toss

1. Perform the preceding drill, pushing the ball into the air without attempting to hit it.
2. Repeat the preceding drill, attempting to hit the ball.
3. If the swing "breaks down," close the eyes and attempt the full serve.

A further description of service-teaching drills is given in Chapter 4.

Culmination Games

Eleven-up Swing

1. The first team or player to get eleven points wins.
2. The server must use a full swing from behind the baseline.
3. A point is scored when the ball goes over the net and lands in the court.

This game can then be modified so that the ball must land in the appropriate half of the court, followed by a progression to land in a specific service area.

Service Golf

The score is the total number of serves required to place one serve in the appropriate court locations, as shown in Figure 1.69.

Twenty-one-up

This game can be modified to suit the level of the players. Beginners may score two points for a correct first service and one point for a

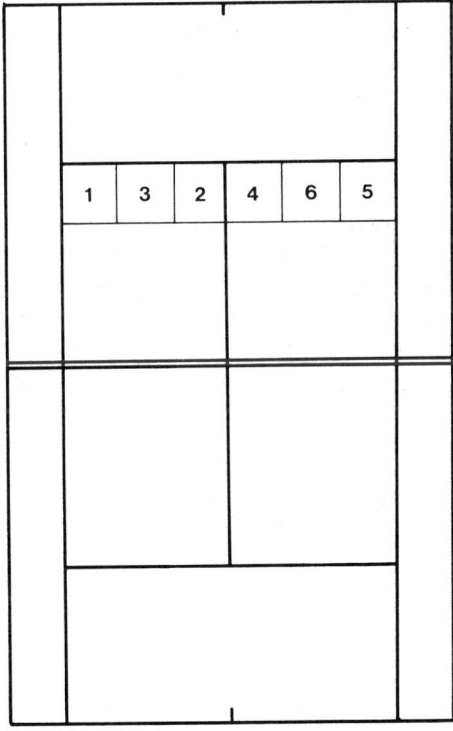

Figure 1.69 Target locations in service-golf.

correct second serve. More advanced players may use the following format:

First Service

Score two points for a hard service into the appropriate area, and one point for a slower service.

Second Service

Score one point for either a flat service or a spin service into the appropriate area.

The first player to total 21 points is the winner.

Return of Service

The most neglected shot in tennis, in terms of the time devoted to its practice, is the return of service. It is, however, probably second only to the serve in its influence on the result of a match.

The Stroke

The Grip

Generally the eastern forehand or backhand grip would be used to return the service with either a forehand or a backhand stroke. If the player's opponent has a particularly fast serve, it may become necessary to adopt the eastern forehand grip for both groundstrokes or to use a continental grip.

The Swing

There is no universally accepted ready position for the return of serve; however, the racket should be kept in front of the body with the weight forward on the balls of the feet so that the player can move forward to hit the ball. Remember that anticipation is the greatest ally a player can call upon in this stroke. It is necessary to develop attributes that encourage the player to remain alert, watchful, and ready to move to the ball.

The technique used in a return of serve is characterized by

1. A pronounced shoulder turn that helps compensate for the semiopen stance that is often adopted when returning a fast serve.
2. A shortened backswing.
3. A step forward at the ball, after the bounce. This ensures that the ball is hit in front of the body with the body weight moving forward at the right time. This technique also cuts down the angle of the serve, thus making it easier to return.
4. Hitting up and through the ball, particularly with the forehand return. The high-to-low-to-high action often is preferred on the

backhand return and causes the ball to be hit with underspin. Remember that the ball bounces off the court at a greater angle from the serve than from a groundstroke, causing a higher rebound from the racket. The aim for the service return should therefore be lower than for a normal groundstroke.
5. A firm grip at impact.
6. Reducing the follow-through enables quick movement to cover the anticipated volley or subsequent groundstroke.

Where to Stand

The person returning service will normally stand in the center of the "service angle." Tactics or a clear preference for a selected type of return may modify this position.

Tips for the Service Return

Reduce the length of the backswing and always step forward as in a volley so that the body weight is moving toward the ball at impact.

Hit through the line of the oncoming ball. Always remember that the most difficult volley the opponent will have to play is that volley following the serve. Therefore, the player should allow some margin for error in the service return.

Corrective Techniques for the Return of Serve

Error The player continually hits the opponent's serve too early.
Correction Watch the ball bounce and take a forward swing, timing from this bounce. This will ensure the correct forward motion of the body for impact. This is particularly valuable against an opponent who varies the pace of the service.
Error The player does not get enough penetration with the return of serve.
Correction Check that the body weight is moving diagonally forward rather than simply across the baseline and that, at impact, the player is contacting the ball at a comfortable height.

Teaching Drills

1. Practice returning a service from a ball hit by the coach from the service line. The coach should use a normal action with reduced speed.
2. *Target returns.* Have somebody serve to particular places and practice hitting returns to different positions using targets such as "witches hats," balls, or racket covers.

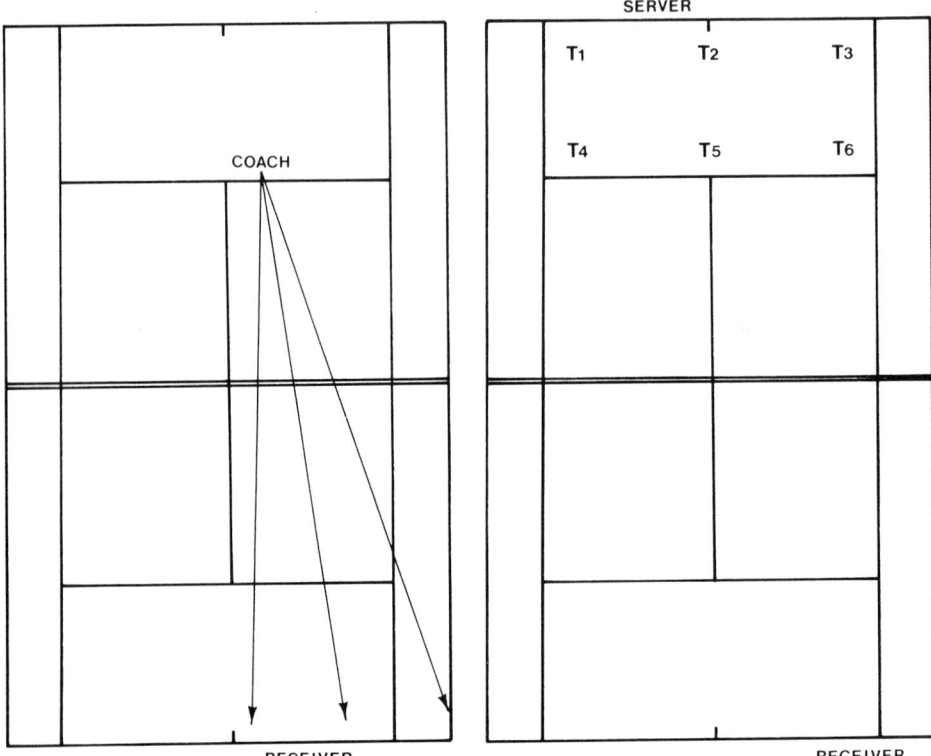

Figure 1.70 Return of service practice.

Figure 1.71 Target (T) returns.

Approach Shot

The approach shot is a forehand or a backhand, hit in such a way that the player may progress to the net ready to volley the opponent's return. In hitting this stroke emphasis must be placed on when and where to hit it (Figure 1.72).

If an approach shot was played from positions 1 or 2, the next shot would be hit either off balance or from "no man's land" in the center of the court. A ball played from position 3 should be an approach shot. But if the level of play dictates a different strategy, then a case could be made for playing a drive and *returning* to the *back section* of the court. A ball at position 4 should be made into an approach shot. Otherwise the next shot will be a half-volley, difficult volley, or a groundstroke played with the weight moving backward. Most shots should be played to the area of the court shown shaded in Figure 1.73 on the same side of the court. But diagonal shots to the center or across the court are often required, depend-

37 Approach Shot

ing on the movement of the opponent. The player who understands when and where to hit an approach shot, as well as the correct court position for the subsequent volley, places pressure on the opponent who must attempt to play a passing shot or a lob. (The aim is always to make the opponent play the most difficult return.)

The Stroke

The Grip
The approach shot grip is the same as for the forehand and backhand drives.

Preparation for the Stroke
Think positively during a match, and always be eager for a short return. When this occurs, move quickly into position ready to play an approach shot. As the player moves to the ball, he/she should turn sideways in preparation for a deliberate stroke. Continue the forward motion of the body during the stroke.

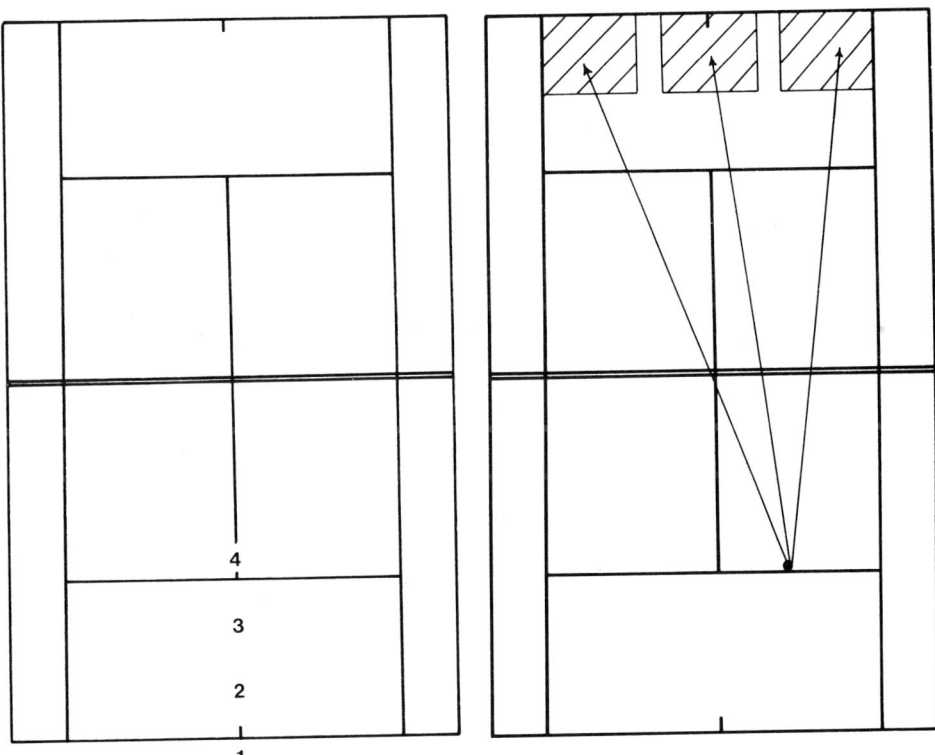

Figure 1.72 Court positions for an approach shot.

Figure 1.73 Hitting areas for an approach shot.

The Backswing

Use a short backswing, because most power comes from the forward motion of the body.

The Forward Swing

There are two basic forward swing techniques in the approach shot. The aggressive technique of hitting the ball with topspin is used by some players, while the safer technique of using underspin is favored by the more percentage-conscious players.

A high-to-low-to-high forward swing action produces backspin on the ball, thus helping it to clear the net.

A low-to-high forward swing action will produce topspin on the ball. This stroke gives the opponent less time to attempt a passing shot. (This technique is more commonly used on the forehand approach shot.)

The wrist should be firm at impact, and the legs should also be used in the stroke to help lift the ball, particularly if the ball is relatively low.

Follow-through

The racket must hit through the line of the ball, as with groundstroke technique.

The racket must travel *up* and *out* toward the intended hitting area.

Limit the follow-through, since quick movement to the volley position is imperative.

Approach Shot Tips

1. A deep groundstroke is usually required to produce the ball from which an approach shot can be played.
2. Modify the forehand approach shot hit with underspin, so that it is a mirror image of the backhand slice return.
3. The side-on position of the shoulders is essential for good balance and effective disguise on approach shots.

Corrective Techniques for the Approach Shot

Error The player is not getting into position quickly enough to hit the approach shot.

Correction Be eager to approach the net on short balls. Know that the short ball will eventuate, and concentrate on moving quickly into position to play it.

Error The player tends to move slowly toward a high short ball, with the result that the ball is continually played below the peak of its bounce.

Approach Shot

Correction Move quickly to the ball, ensuring a balanced position before impact.

Error The player seems to be continually unbalanced in running to the ball. (Experience has shown this occurs more on the backhand side.)

Correction Run to the vicinity of the ball carrying the racket in front of the body. Then take the racket back with a turn of the shoulders to prepare for the stroke.

Error Two common faults with social players when hitting approach shots are (1) hitting the ball over the baseline and (2) hitting the ball into the net.

Correction To correct these faults (1) get into a balanced hitting position and reduce the backswing and (2) open the racket face slightly to lift the ball over the net.

Teaching Drills

1. In the drill shown in Figure 1.74, the player moves in from the baseline to hit an approach shot down the line to a target area in

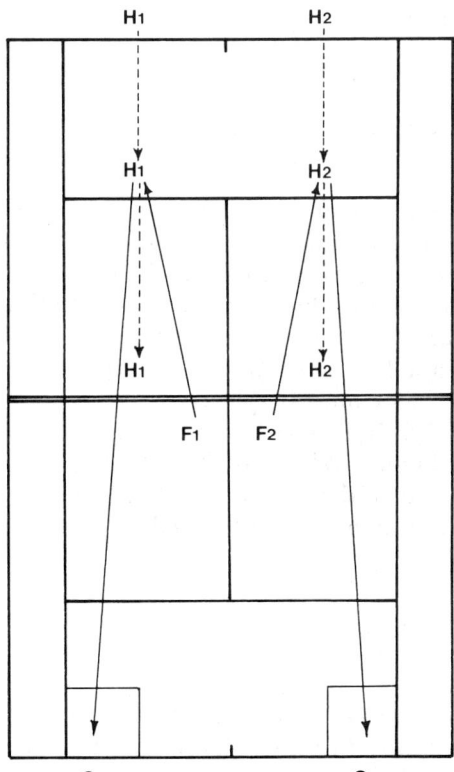

Figure 1.74 Approach shot drill.

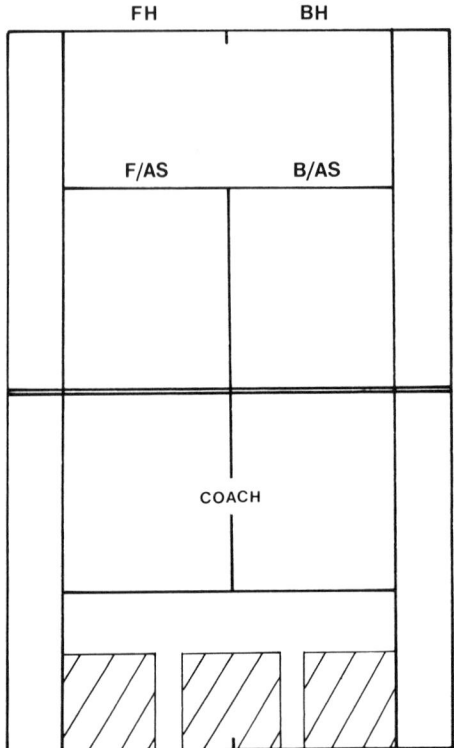

Figure 1.75 Combination drill.

front of the collector. The player then moves forward and adopts the volley position prior to rejoining the end of the other line.

2. *Approach shot practice within a game structure.* If the ball lands in the player's service area he/she must hit an approach shot and move to the net. Although there are a number of options on the subsequent return, it is often desirable to encourage the opponent to hit a passing shot so that a volley must be played.
3. *Combination drill.* In this drill the coach or a feeder hits the following sequence of shots (Figure 1.75): a forehand drive (FH), a backhand drive (BH), a forehand drive, and a backhand approach shot (B/AS). The coach may nominate selected targets for the approach shots.

The Volley

The volley, often the favorite shot of the advanced player, will often be a problem to the recreational player. But any player who has developed sound groundstrokes should find that with minor modification to stroke technique, the volley develops into an effective attacking weapon.

The Stroke

The Grip
There is time in all but volley-to-volley rallies to change grips for the backhand and forehand strokes. The eastern forehand and backhand grips, with the hand primarily behind the grip, are often preferred for volleys. The continental grip (which would be used for the service) is an alternative grip that can be used for both forehand and backhand volleys. Many players prefer to use the same continental grip for both volleys so that they can then concentrate on the other aspects of volley technique. These players should be careful of high forehand volleys, as this grip causes the racket face to be opened slightly, increasing the possibility of volleying the ball out of court. It is also more difficult to change the direction of the ball using a continental grip than it is using the eastern grips.

The Preparation
It is imperative to move quickly into position in preparation for a volley. The racket should be carried farther out in front of the body, and the trunk should be angled farther forward than for the ready position used on the baseline. As the opponent hits the ball (Figure 1.76), effective preparation is facilitated by the following:

1. The player should adopt a balanced position with his/her weight on the balls of the feet ready to move into the volley.
2. The player should turn his/her shoulders (Figures 1.77 and 1.78).
3. The racket should not be taken back further than the back shoulder for a forehand or backhand volley (Figure 1.79).
4. The nonracket hand may assist this preparation phase for the backhand volley.

Forward Swing
The power in a volley is obtained from a combination of the short backswing and the forward movement of the body. A firm hitting position out in front of the body then "takes" the power from the preceding shot. The following technique ensures that this firm volley position is developed:

1. The racket face should be positioned so that it is always in line with the oncoming ball.
2. The player should move forward diagonally by stepping both across the body and forward (Figures 1.78 and 1.79).
3. The player should always move forward to meet the ball, bending the knees as he/she steps (Figures 1.79 to 1.81). (*Remember:* most volleying power comes from this forward movement of the body.)

42 Stroke Production

Figures 1.76 to 1.83 *The Mechanics of the Forehand Volley.* The mechanics of the forehand volley were analyzed by filming with a high-speed camera at 100 frames per second. Not all frames have been included here, but the relative movement sequence is clearly illustrated.

Figure 1.76

Figure 1.77

Figure 1.78

Figure 1.79

Figure 1.80

Figure 1.81

Figure 1.82

Figure 1.83

4. The forward movement of the racket, led by the palm of the hand in a forehand volley and by the knuckles in a backhand volley, is a "punching action" (Figures 1.80 to 1.82).
5. The whole arm and racket move forward as a unit. (There should be no movement at the wrist in an attempt to generate extra power.)
6. The ball must be watched right onto the racket, and a firm grip must be adopted in preparation for the impact.

Impact/Follow-through
The impact positions for the forehand and backhand volleys differ slightly, so they will be treated separately.

Forehand Volley (Figure 1.82)
The ball is hit at about eye level. The angle of the racket with the court will vary depending on the height of the volley, however, the racket should always be in line with or higher than the wrist. (This means that the knees must be bent to move the body down in preparation for a low volley.)

The arm-racket unit resembles an "L" formation. (Notice how the wrist is laid back as in the forehand drive.)

The follow-through, which is in the intended direction of the volley, is reduced when compared with other strokes (Figure 1.83).

Backhand Volley (Figure 1.84)
The volley is hit forward of the front shoulder 6 to 8 inches (15 to 20 centimeters) when possible.

Again the ball is hit at about eye level and the angle of the racket face with the court will vary, depending on the height of the volley. But again, the racket should always be in line with, or higher than, the wrist.

The arm-racket unit resembles a "V" formation (Figure 1.84).

Analogy
"Punch the ball": The small backswing and forward movement may be likened to a boxer's punch. The reduced follow-through should be in the direction of the volley.

Tips for the Volley

1. Do not take the racket back past the shoulder in preparation for a volley.

Figure 1.84 Impact position for a backhand volley.

2. Always "attack" the volley. Hit the ball in front of the body before it drops. This helps the player impact the ball higher, increasing the number of possible returns.
3. Keep the eyes on the ball right onto the racket.
4. Arm and racket should move forward as a unit. Never use the wrist to "add power" to a volley.
5. Keep the racket head in line with or above the wrist.
6. Have a firm grip at impact.
7. When moving to the volley keep the arm and racket up so that the swing can go forward onto the ball.
8. Coordinate the forward movement of the body with ball impact. The forward step and impact should coincide.
9. Continue advancing toward the net after each volley.
10. Always assume another volley will be necessary to win the point (be prepared).

Corrective Techniques for the Volley

Error The player continually hits the volley behind the line of the body.
Correction Have the player carry the racket further forward than normal and keep the racket out in front during the entire stroke. The following drills 1 and 2 can be used initially to achieve this feeling of always attacking the ball out in front.
Error The player swings at the volley.
Correction Have the player perform a "shadow volley," standing with the heels against a fence. An excessive backswing has taken place if the racket hits the fence.
Error The player uses the wrist during the volley in an attempt to achieve greater power.
Correction Emphasize that the arm-racket combination swings forward (in a punching action) as a unit. If the whole arm is tensed in preparation for impact, the tendency to use the wrist is often removed.
Error The player drops the racket head below the wrist when volleying.
Correction This is usually the result of allowing the ball to come to the player, often resulting in the ball being hit as it is dropping. Have the player practice moving forward to the ball. This will require bending the knees for a volley that must be played close to the ground.

Teaching Drills

All teaching drills for the volley should be aimed at ensuring that the ball is hit out in front of the body.

1. The forehand volley progressions begin with players in pairs throwing the ball underarm from one to the other. The person

45 The Volley

catching the ball must extend the catching arm forward with the fingers pointing to the sky in an attempt to simulate the blocking action of the volley. (This drill should not be carried out over the net.)

2. The preceding drill except that one player "punches" the ball back to the partner with the racket held by the throat.
3. The preceding drill except that one player holds the racket in the hitting position (held at the handle) and "punches" the ball back to the partner. This drill can be used in the form of a competition where the total number of hits and catches are used as the score.
4. The preceding drill but throwing to a partner who is in the ready position.
5. The preceding drill but over a net.
6. The player now adopts the ready position in anticipation for a volley hit from the coach. Initially the player is told that the stroke will be a forehand or a backhand volley, but the drill progresses to where either a forehand or backhand volley may be required.
7. *Forehand/backhand volley drill* (Figure 1.85). The coach feeds to

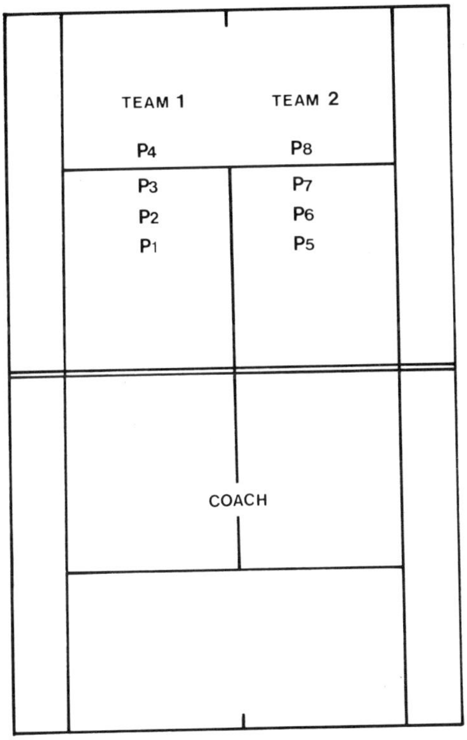

Figure 1.85 Court positions for forehand/backhand volley drill.

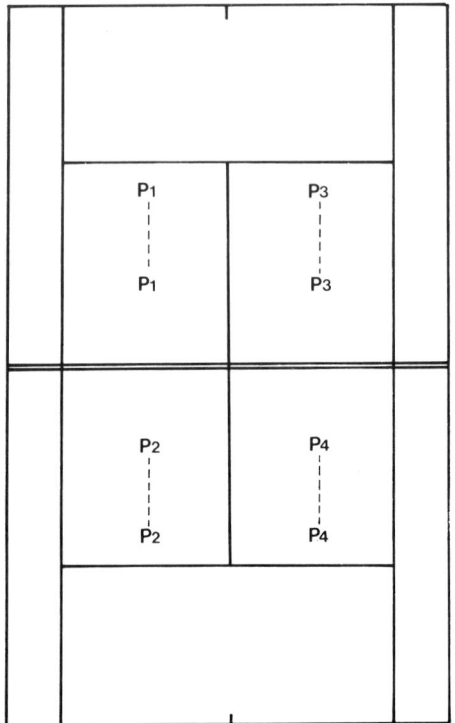

Figure 1.86 Volley-to-volley drill.

alternate players. Each player has three or four volleys, then runs and picks up a corresponding number of balls and returns to the end of the other line.

8. *Volley to volley* (Figure 1.86). This drill can be used for volley control. As players move further back and continue to volley, added depth is required for each volley. (This can be used as a competitive game, such as cooperative volleying as a pair to see which pair can get the most volleys in two minutes.)

9. *Combination drill* (Figure 1.87). Players hit a sequence of strokes that culminate in a series of volleys. The coach, who controls the drills, may vary the sequence in an effort to add variety. Each player must collect and return as many balls as were hit in the hitting sequence.

10. *Rapid volley–pressure drill.* The coach hits a series of volleys to the player in rapid succession, emphasizing the ready position after each volley.

11. *Stretch volleys.* The coach hits a series of balls to the player so that each ball can be volleyed only while at full stretch. The feeder has the responsibility of making this drill successful through controlled feeding.

47 The Volley

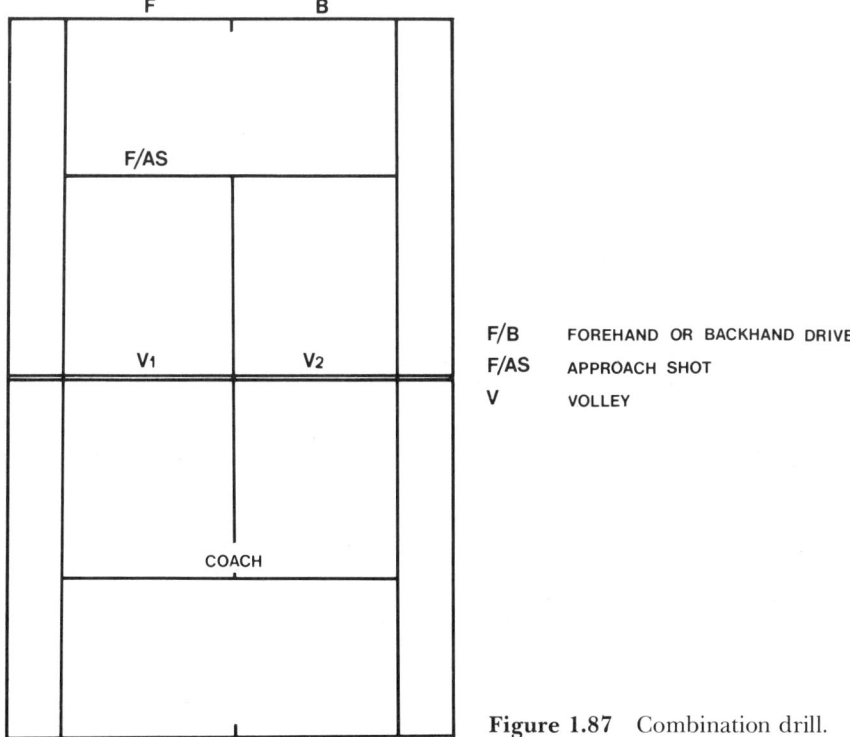

Figure 1.87 Combination drill.

12. *Approach volleys* (Figure 1.88). A player serves a ball and moves to the net in anticipation of a volley at the service line. The coach disregards the service and hits a ball to the server who has now progressed to the service line for a volley. This player then collects the balls and rejoins the end of the line ready to serve again.
13. *Volley for balance.* The coach feeds a short ball. The player advances from the baseline, hits an approach shot, and intercepts the resultant passing shot. The player then returns to the baseline and repeats the process.

Culminating Games

The "two-on-one" drills and the half-court drills may both be used so that the volley is incorporated as part of the practice.

1. *Volley to volley.* The total number of consecutive volleys that can be hit between two players is used as a score in a competition.
2. The coach stands behind the net player and hits a ball to the next player in sequence at the back of the court. This player then attempts to pass the volleyer with a groundstroke hit either cross-

court or down-the-line (Figure 1.89). The subsequent rally is then played to completion, with the winner receiving one point. The net and baseline players then move to the end of the other line. A winner is declared when a player has ten points. This game may be varied by having three rallies between players before changing positions. The coach may hit the ball so that the first rally is started with a forehand, the second with a backhand, and the third with an approach shot (that is, the ball is fed so that an approach shot can be played from the service line.

3. *Four-person controlled volley* (Figure 1.90). The ball is volleyed to either of the two players on the other side of the net. Each team of four players is required to change court positions after a rally. The total number of consecutive volleys represents the team's score.

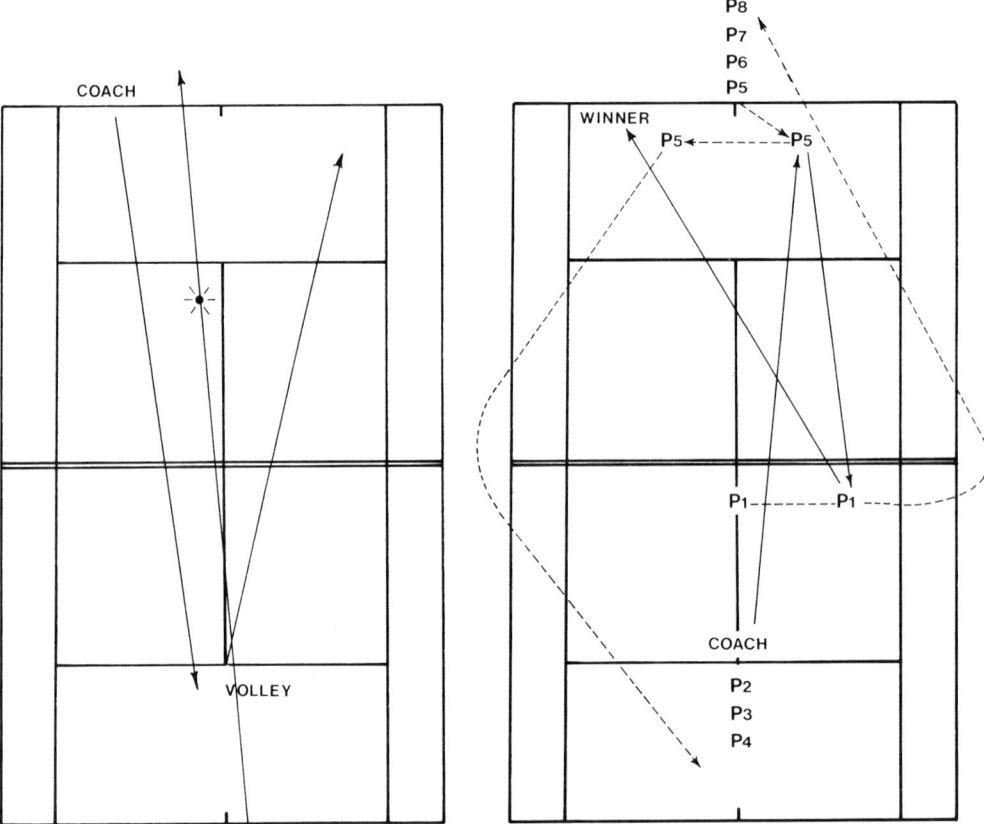

Figure 1.88 Approach volley drill following a serve.

Figure 1.89 One-on-one drill emphasizing groundstrokes and volleys.

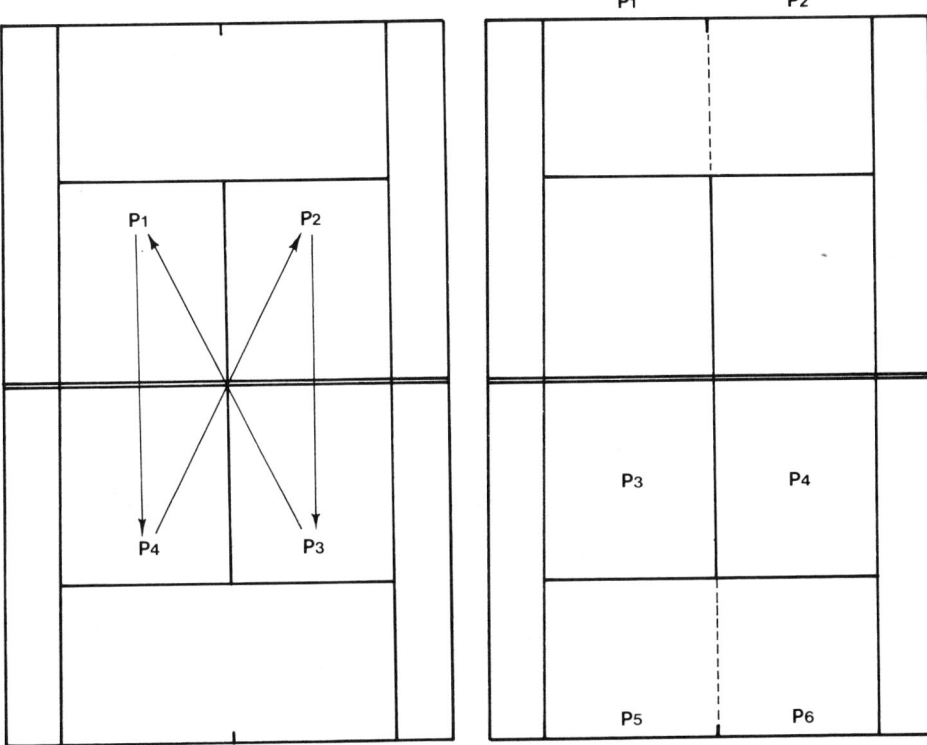

Figure 1.90 Four-person controlled volley drill.

Figure 1.91 Half-court drill for practicing groundstrokes and volleys.

4. *Groundstroke volley.* The class is divided into groups of six players. Using a half-court drill format the net player feeds a ball to the player on the baseline, who attempts to pass the net player with a groundstroke. Any number of rallies, each worth one point, may be played in this formation prior to the teams changing positions (Figure 1.91).

The Smash

The smash requires a very similar stroking action to that of the serve. The major difference between the two is that one (the serve) is controlled by the player, while the other is always the choice of the opponent. A player with a good smash, therefore, immediately limits the number of viable options that an opponent may select during a rally.

The Stroke

The Grip
The continental grip allows for optimal usage of the wrist as in the service action.

Preparation
From the ready position, the body moves under the path of the ball while turning side-on to the net with the eyes on the ball. The following points will aid preparation for a smash:

1. The index finger of the nonracket hand points at the ball. This helps to ensure that the player is both under the ball and side-on to the net (Figures 1.92 and 1.93).
2. While moving to the ball, the racket head stays above the hand and is lifted over the shoulder to initiate the racket loop behind the back (Figures 1.92 to 1.96). The elbow should be positioned in line with the shoulder to enable the racket to move down the back and then up at the ball without excessive shoulder movement. This facilitates better timing.
3. If a jump is required, it should be initiated by the back foot to help the body stay side-on to the net until the swing to the ball.

The Swing
This action is virtually the mirror image of the service swing, as follows:

1. The rotation of the hips and shoulders is combined with the transfer of body weight onto the front foot for optimal power.
2. The nonhitting arm should be tucked into the body prior to impact (Figures 1.94 to 1.97).
3. The wrist should play a role in increasing the racket head speed at impact.
4. The ball should be struck out in front of the body at the optimum height (Figure 1.99). (*Remember:* The *up* and *out* swing of the serve should be used when hitting a smash from between the service line and the baseline.)
5. The back leg drives the body off the ground if a jump smash is required.

Follow-through
A natural follow-through along the line of the shot and then across the body should occur, followed by a quick movement to the correct court location for the next return (Figures 1.100 and 1.101).

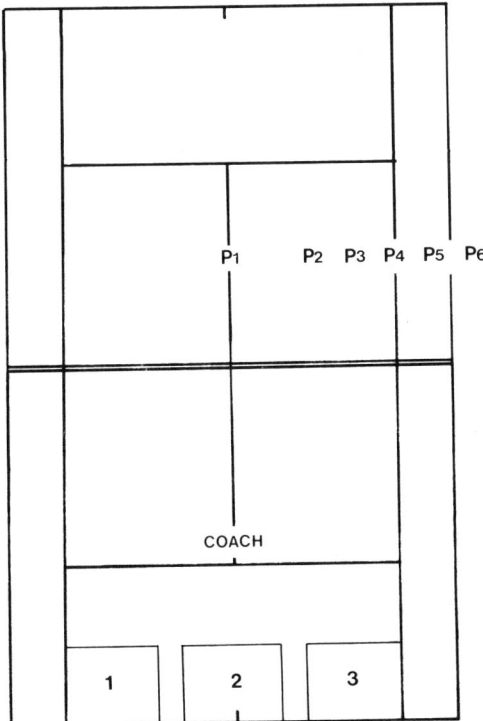

Figure 1.102 Court positions for a smash drill to designated court areas (1, 2, 3).

Culminating Games

Any half-court one-on-one or two-on-one drills may be used, incorporating the smash.

The Lob

The lob is probably the most underrated shot in tennis. If played at the right time it can provide a player with an extremely effective offensive or defensive weapon. Examples include (1) if the opponent is weak overhead, (2) if the opponent plays too close to the net, (3) when in extreme trouble and there is a need to "buy time," and (4) to add variety to passing shots.

The Stroke

The Grip
An eastern forehand or backhand grip can be used. The continental grip may also be used for the lob because it helps produce an open racket face.

54 Stroke Production

Figures 1.103, 1.104, and 1.105 The lob.

The Swing

The stroke technique is similar to that for the forehand and backhand drives, except that the angle of the racket face is changed. The following differences in technique from the groundstroke should be noted:

1. A shortened backswing positions the racket face below the height of the ball (Figure 1.103).
2. There should be an upward swing in the direction of the ball flight, with the racket face perpendicular to the flight of the ball (Figures 1.103 and 1.104).
3. Variations in the angle of the racket face depend on the type of spin required and upon the flight and bounce of the ball from the court. An open racket face imparts backspin on the ball, whereas a relatively vertical racket face is used to impart topspin.
4. The follow-through should be along the intended line of the hit.

Tips for the Lob

1. Use the legs to help lift the ball over the net player and use the shoulders to help disguise the shot.
2. Players who lob defensively are usually under extreme pressure, so it becomes even more essential to watch the ball closely and to hit with a firm wrist.
3. Always follow through along the intended flight path of the ball.
4. The air space is there to be used, so experiment in practice by hitting lobs at varying heights.
5. When an opponent continually approaches the net following a short approach shot, it is advisable for the player to mix in offensive lobs of varying trajectories with passing shots.
6. When lobbing defensively with the wind, aim to lob high with maximum height above the net.

7. When lobbing into the breeze, aim to get maximum height above the opponent's service line.
8. When hitting attacking lobs, aim to hit the ball at a height of about 2 feet (60 centimeters) above where the opponent's outstretched racket would be. The speed of the hit is critical. If it is too slow the opponent will be able to move into position to play a smash.

Corrective Techniques for the Lob

Error The player hits the lob from the back foot (weight moving backward).

Correction Early preparation will usually help to remove this fault. Pushing the racket through a little farther than normal will help compensate if the player cannot avoid leaning back during the stroke.[3]

Error The player drops the racket head and plays the stroke like a pendulum, thus making it extremely difficult to control the power imparted to the ball.

Correction Keep the racket head as nearly in line with the wrist as possible at impact. Use the legs to help hit up through the line of flight of the stroke with an open racket face.

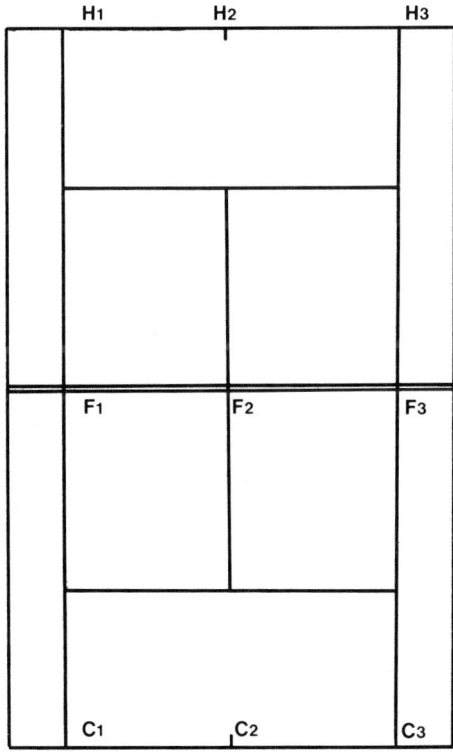

Figure 1.106 Court positions for practicing the lob.

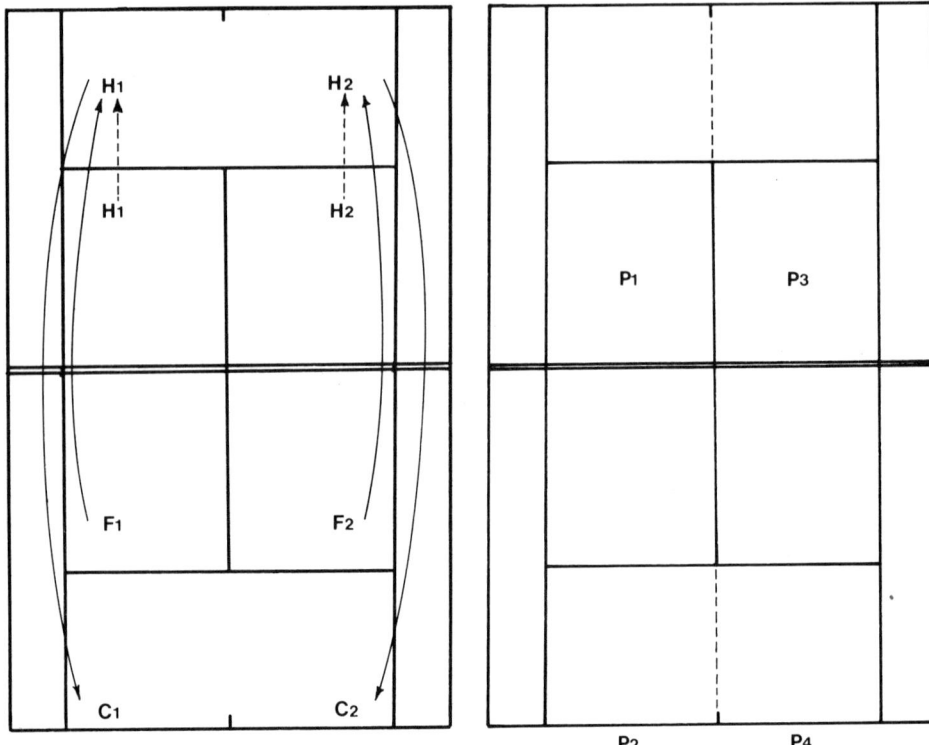

Figure 1.107 Lob retrieval drill.

Figure 1.108 A half-court drill emphasizing the lob.

Teaching Drills

1. A feeder (F) throws the ball to a hitter (H), who attempts to play a lob over the outstretched racket of the feeder. The collector (C) gathers the balls and after a specified number of hits, the players rotate.
2. The preceding drill, but the lob is played from a ball hit by the feeder.
3. *Lob retrieval.* The feeder hits the ball over the head of player H1, who runs back and retrieves the ball with a lob. This player then returns to the start position and the drill is repeated.

Culminating Games

Half-court drill. This drill follows the normal half-court format with player 1 hitting the ball to player 2, who tries to win the rally by passing or lobbing player 1. Players change positions when one has scored five points.

The Drop Shot

This is a delicately hit shot that must land just over the net. It can be used to earn a point, to tire an opponent, to force a weak return, to hit an approach shot from a short return, to break up the rhythm of the game, or to draw the defensive opponent to the net. The drop shot should be considered only when a player is balanced and capable of hitting a variety of shots.

The Stroke

The Grip
The drop shot grip is the same as for a backhand or forehand drive. The continental grip, which provides an open racket face at impact and is not favored for groundstrokes, is of assistance when hitting a drop shot.

The Backswing
The body should be bent to allow the player to get closer to the height of the ball (Figure 1.109).

A full backswing should be used to disguise the shot. Social players might wish to use a reduced backswing to improve the control of the stroke.

Forward Swing
A downward path of the racket with an open face will impart backspin to the ball (Figures 1.109 to 1.111).

Follow-through
The follow-through, which is reduced, completes the high-to-low-to-high hitting action (Figures 1.113 to 1.116).

Tips for the Drop Shot

1. A drop shot hit when the opponent is not out of position must be disguised. The drop shot using a full backswing should preferably be hit from the backhand side of the body. The stroke should appear to possess the characteristics of a normal slice backhand (including the follow-through).
2. It is important that players do not hit too many drop shots because they should be used as surprise shots.
3. It is preferable to hit the drop shot when ahead of the opponent in a particular game.

58 Stroke Production

Figures 1.109 to 1.116
The Mechanics of the Drop Shot. The mechanics of the backhand drop shot were analyzed by filming with a high-speed camera at 100 frames per second. Not all frames have been included here, but the relative movement sequence is clearly illustrated.

Figure 1.109

Figure 1.110

Figure 1.111

Figure 1.112

Figure 1.113

Figure 1.114

Figure 1.115

Figure 1.116

Corrective Techniques for the Drop Shot

Error The player tends to chop at the ball in an attempt to produce backspin.

Correction Encourage a smoother approach to the stroke, hitting through the ball with an open racket face (high-to-low movement).

Error The player hits the net too often with the ball.

Correction Given that the drop shot is well disguised, the hitter should take advantage of this fact and make sure that there is sufficient elevation in the trajectory (Figure 1.117).

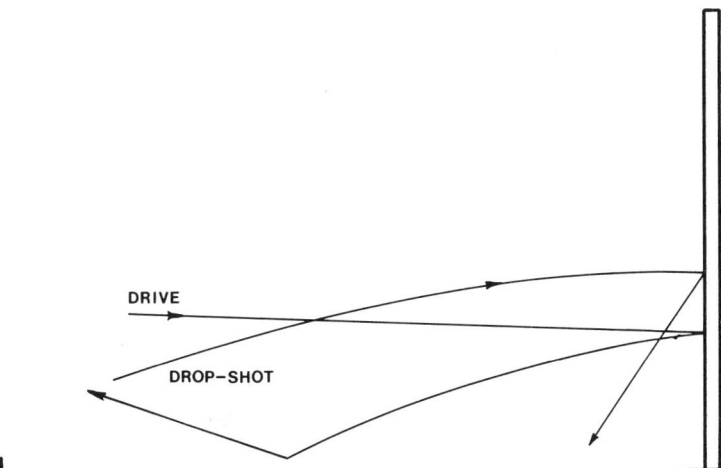

Figure 1.117 Ball trajectory for a drop shot compared with that for a drive.

Teaching Drills

1. Practice hitting a drop shot into a fence from a ball tossed by the hitter.
2. Practice hitting a drop shot from a ball tossed by a partner.
3. Practice hitting a drop shot after a drive against a hit-up wall.
4. Practice hitting drop shots from a groundstroke played by the opponent. This drill is best begun with one player hitting a drive to the opposite service line. The opponent then returns a drop shot.

The Half-volley

This more advanced stroke often proves to be difficult, since players are required to play it from a great variety of court locations. Sound court tactics ensure that this stroke can be mastered.

The Stroke

The Grip
The half-volley grip is the same grip as would be used for the volley.

The Backswing
This stroke has a shorter backswing than a groundstroke (Figure 1.118).

60 Stroke Production

Figures 1.118 to 1.125
The Mechanics of the Half-Volley. The mechanics of the backhand half-volley were analyzed by filming with a high-speed camera at 100 frames per second. Not all frames have been included here, but the relative movement sequence is clearly illustrated.

Figure 1.118

Figure 1.119

Figure 1.120

Figure 1.121

Figure 1.122

Figure 1.123

Figure 1.124

Figure 1.125

The Forward-swing

This follows a low-to-high hitting pattern, as outlined here:

1. Step forward into the ball as with a forehand or backhand drive (Figure 1.119).
2. Bend the knees and have the trunk forward to get close to the level of the ball at impact.
3. Watch the ball closely onto the racket.
4. Swing the racket forward and upward so that impact can occur soon after the ball has bounced (Figures 1.120 to 1.123).

Impact (Figure 1.122)

At impact, the racket face should usually be perpendicular to the court.

The grip should be firm, although "touch" half-volleys are often hit with a moderate grip pressure.

Follow-through

The racket should follow a low-to-high position (Figures 1.122 to 1.125) along the intended flight path of the ball.

Half-volley Tips

1. Contact the ball soon after it bounces on the court.
2. Use the knees to help "lift" the shot.
3. Keep the racket head in line with the wrist.
4. Hold the racket face close to vertical at impact.
5. Keep the head down, looking at the ball.
6. It is important that the body be balanced, with a momentary pause in the forward movement prior to impact.
7. Decide as early as possible that a half-volley is the shot that must be played. (Do not "get trapped" into playing it as a last resort—play it with purpose.)

Corrective Techniques for the Half-volley

Error The player tends to lift his/her head prior to hitting the ball.
Correction Keep the eyes on the ball throughout the stroke (Figure 1.119 to Figure 1.124).
Error The player drops the racket head when hitting the ball.
Correction The knees must be bent and the body inclined forward so that the player is down close to the ball. Lazy legs usually produce a dropped racket head. (Also ensure that the shoulders are perpendicular to the line of the ball.)
Error The player hits the half-volley behind the line of the front foot.
Correction Shorten the backswing and step forward so that the weight and the racket are moving forward at impact.
Error The player never balances prior to hitting the half-volley.
Correction Have the player serve and move toward the net so that a half-volley (fed by the coach) must be hit at the service line.

Teaching Drills

1. Hit a series of half-volleys from balls fed by the coach or a feeder. These should be hit from near the service line.

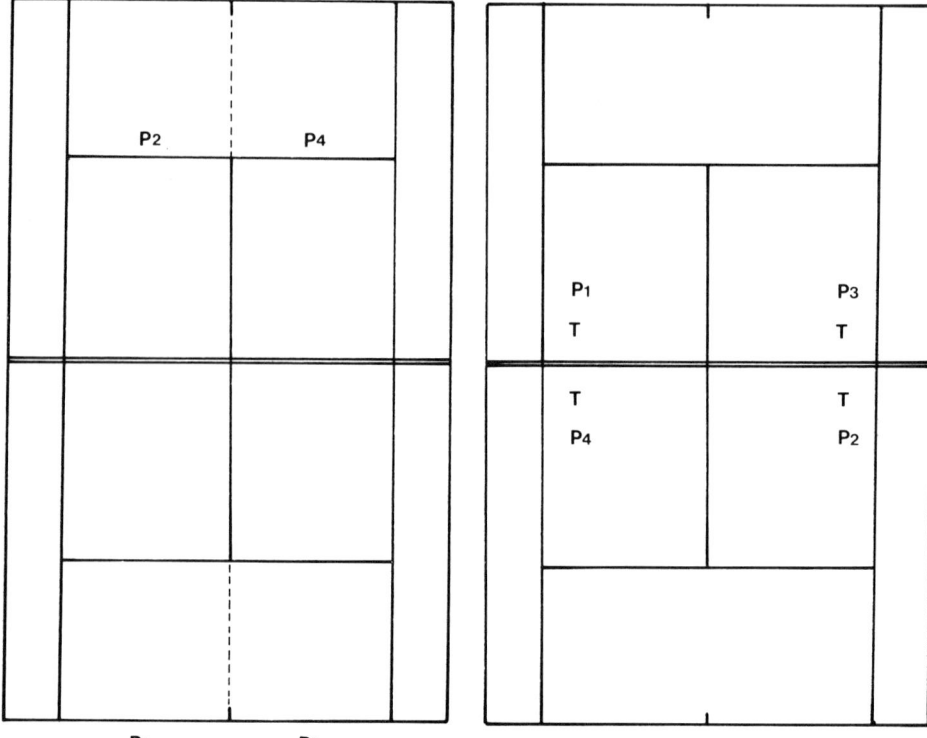

Figure 1.126 Half-court drill emphasizing half-volleys.

Figure 1.127 Cross-court half-volley drill aiming for target (T).

2. Rally at the baseline, attempting to hit any balls that are hit deep in the court as soon as possible after the bounce. Use regular groundstroke technique (reducing backswing) but concentrate on hitting the ball just after it has bounced.
3. Hit a serve followed by a half-volley on the service line.

Culminating Games

1. *Modification of a half-court drill.* Normal rules apply as for half-court, except that players 2 and 4 must rally from positions where half-volleys can be practiced (Figure 1.126).
2. *Cross-court half-volley rally.* Players rally across the net using either forehand or backhand half-volleys. This is a "fun" game in which the players try to land the ball on a target (players rotate positions after a series of rallies; Figure 1.127).

References

1. Bergelin, L.: "How Bjorn Borg Prepares for Match Play." *World Tennis*, May 1979, pp. 82–83.
2. Braden, V. and Bruns, B.: *Vic Braden's Tennis for the Future.* Little, Brown and Company, Boston, 1977.
3. Braden, V. and Bruns, B.: *Teaching Children Tennis the Vic Braden Way.* Little, Brown and Company, Boston, 1980.
4. Faulkner, E. J. and Weymuller, F.: *Tennis: How To Play It, How to Teach It.* Dial Press, New York, 1970.
5. Krauer, J. and Sheehan, L.: *How to Play Your Best Tennis All The Time.* Hutchinson Group Pty., Australia, 1977.
6. Metzler, P.: *Tennis Weaknesses and Remedies.* Sterling Publishing Company, New York, 1973.
7. Plagenhoef, S.: *Fundamentals of Tennis.* Prentice-Hall, Englewood Cliffs, N.J., 1970.
8. Tilmanis, G.: *Advanced Tennis for Coaches, Teachers, and Players.* Australia and New Zealand Book Company, Sydney, Australia, 1975.

2

Tennis Strategy

The overriding aim in tennis is to win points from an opponent. The development of a competitive attitude by each player, incorporating a sound understanding of match strategies, is important if playing standards are to continue to rise.

Some general rules should be observed in planning tennis strategy:

1. A player should listen to advice but never accept the validity of the advice before proving its value.
2. When planning specific strategies a player must consider his/her personal strengths as well as the opponent's weaknesses.
3. A player must be flexible enough to adjust match strategies to suit match conditions.
4. Mastery of the full array of tennis strokes provides a player with more flexibility in varying strategies.

This chapter, which has been written for players and teachers of tennis, outlines general tennis strategies and discusses how improved concentration can aid playing effectiveness. Specific strategies for singles and doubles play are described to provide alternatives when planning tactics.

Concentration

Maintenance of concentration during a match is vital for good performance. Most players, however, cannot maintain a peak level of attentiveness for an entire match.

Players have developed different methods to sustain a high level of concentration throughout a match. Some of these are (1) to concentrate on the court and not on the surrounding environment, (2) never to look at the opponent between rallies, and (3) to change ends at the opposite side of the net to the opponent.

The best way to maintain concentration throughout a match is to limit periods of peak concentration. During a rally the player must be attentive to the cues that his/her opponent offers. However, between rallies and when changing ends of the court it is imperative to reduce concentration level without "switching off" from the main goal—winning the match. This helps the player avoid mental fatigue as the match progresses. Most stress during a match is self-imposed. The stress of worrying about stroke production multiplies if the player makes judgments about the outcome of the match between rallies, or thinks between games about the rewards of winning or the humiliation of losing. If the player thinks about future problems or the result of the match, he/she can lose touch with the task at hand—winning each rally. Concentration, like stroke production, can be improved only through practice.

The following tips can help a player improve concentration:

1. Pay special attention to the ball rather than the object or person hitting it. Try to watch the ball more closely than ever before. Try to read the brand on the ball. This "fine focus" helps aid both concentration and stroke production because it can lead to a better preparation to hit the ball.
2. At the end of each game, take a mental break. A few deep breaths, together with general body relaxation, help ensure that peak concentration can be maintained during rallies. When changing ends it may be necessary to assess match tactics; however, part of this time must be spent relaxing. Arthur Ashe used meditation to aid his relaxation when changing ends during the Wimbledon competition in 1975, when he defeated Jimmy Connors for the title.
3. Develop positive thought patterns and mentally rehearse the skills to be performed.
4. Rhythm and timing should be achieved prior to a match. Concentrate on hitting through the ball. Enjoy the feeling of hitting the ball, particularly the opponent's serve. Many good returns can be played from service faults or from balls that land out of court. This is a positive response to an opponent's stroke without any fear of the consequences of such an action. If a player can develop this positive frame of mind, he/she will be capable of playing well even when under pressure.

All players must learn to overcome situations that tend to reduce levels of concentration. Some of these situations are discussed here.

Missing an Easy Shot

During a close match, the pressure of the moment often turns easy strokes into extremely difficult ones. Rationalize a failure to hit a winner from an easy return by believing that all similar shots in the future will be dispatched for winners.

Bad Calls

Adopt the attitude that if bad calls outnumber the bad shots, then that would be reason to complain.

Harsh Environmental Conditions (Wind, Sun)

Players should practice in poor conditions as part of their mental and physical preparation for tennis. Concentration will thus be less affected when tournament matches are to be played in these conditions. Continual practice on indoor courts for an outdoor match will often lead to lapses in concentration because of the influence of the wind and sun.

Noisy Spectators

Accept that play is taking place in a noisy environment, and concentrate on watching the ball. The more mature player can often interact with and thus "win over" a crowd during the relaxation period between games. This type of player tends to enjoy the environment and so puts even more pressure on the opponent. Such interaction must be of a spontaneous nature. Deliberate efforts to "win over" the crowd will inevitably lead to a loss of concentration.

Verbal Abuse From an Opponent

It is important to win every battle on the court. The wind, bad calls, bad courts, noisy spectators, fatigue, blisters, or an overaggressive opponent must all be overcome. Ignoring the opponent's comments will usually cause him further frustration and loss of concentration. Abuse is usually effective only if a response is forced from the person at which it was directed.

A Crowd that Favors the Opponent

This is often the case when the crowd (or portion thereof) claps at a player's error, and it must be accepted. Becoming upset will often encourage the crowd further and make concentration more difficult.

Concentration will not only improve stroke production, but also will aid the development of strategy during a match. A player with good concentration learns from an opponent's style of play. This can help in anticipation and in noting minor flaws in stroke production that may be exploited in future rallies.

Concentration will be improved if just before and during a match the player's eyes and ears are attuned to the court and the ball. It is important to concentrate throughout the entire match, but peak periods of concentration should be maintained only during a rally.

Singles Strategy

Winning a match of singles requires the mastery of many facets of play. A player who is fit and has developed sound stroke production will sometimes lose to an opponent with less talent but with a greater mastery of singles strategy.

The specific singles tactics adopted should be based on the player's strengths and the opponent's weaknesses. The good tactician will ensure that both these factors are working toward the goal of victory in a particular match. The game strategy should also reflect the limitations and demands of the specific court surface.

The basic game strategy should be formulated before the match (if the opponent is known) or during the warm-up. (*Remember:* Complicated strategies run the risk of placing unnecessary demands on stroke production.) The player must maintain a flexible approach toward game tactics. It is imperative that the tactics being used in a losing game be changed, whereas those working effectively in a winning game should be retained. If a good game strategy is combined with appropriate court movement and the right level of concentration, then the likelihood of success will be enhanced.

Singles strategy, up to the level of an advanced player, evolves from a few basic principles, outlined here.

Consistent Play

The ball must be kept in play. Since approximately 75 to 80 per cent of points end with an error,[4] it is obvious that a game strategy built around forcing the opponent into error should provide the cornerstone for game strategy. Remember that statistics also show that the winner of a singles match also is usually the player who hits the most winning strokes. The following will help to improve consistency:

1. Hit more cross-court drives from the baseline. The longer diagonal length of the court and the lower height of the net in the center both permit a greater margin for error. Most players also prefer this stroke because it is usually played from the more easily adopted semiopen stance.

2. Hit the majority of drives with topspin (particularly forehand drives). The forward rotation of the ball allows it to be hit well clear of the net, yet still land in the court.
3. Be patient when setting up a winner. This is particularly important when playing the first volley after following a serve to the net. When returning service, the first priority should be to get the ball into play.
4. Develop the ability to hit offensive as well as defensive lobs. Practice drills that incorporate hitting the ball to different parts of the court while under pressure.
5. Shorten the backswing if necessary when playing against a hard hitter of the ball. It is also important to move the feet quickly when playing against hard hitters to ensure that the body is in the best possible position at impact.
6. Slow the ball down a little when serving with the wind.
7. Aim the ball to about 6 feet (2 meters) past the service line when hitting with the wind and to an area close to the baseline when hitting into the wind.

Shot Selection

Many errors are made in singles because of poor shot selection. Although Figure 2.1 is only a guide to stroke selection, it offers a starting point for beginners and intermediate players.

Balls that land in the "defensive area" at the back of the court should be treated with respect. The player should try to regain the offensive, using groundstrokes played from this area, by hitting the ball deep to the opponent's "defensive area." (*Remember:* The safest shot to hit is the cross-court drive; it offers the biggest target area and also allows the ball to pass over the lowest point of the net.)

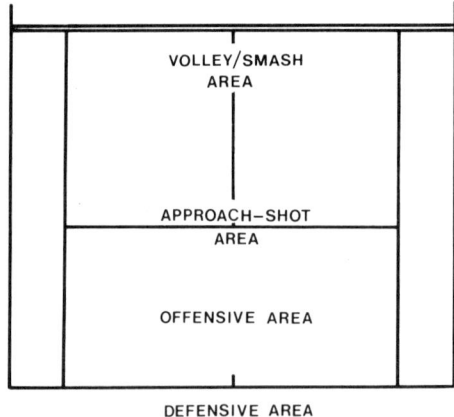

Figure 2.1 General guide to shot selection.

Any ball that lands in the offensive area should be hit firmly to force the opponent to play a short return. Attacking groundstrokes from this area of the court enable the player to dictate play.

Once the short return has been forced, an approach shot should be played from the "approach area" of the court. This area should be used to improve the player's court position and to move to the volley/smash area. Once the player is at the net he/she should try to win the point with either a volley or a smash. If forced to retreat to the defensive zone, then he/she should repeat the procedure of trying to force a short return.

Court Coverage

Many errors are also made in singles because of poor court position. Good court position means that the opponent's return can be reached with least movement.

Good court coverage begins with the service position. When serving to the forehand court, stand close to the center mark so that the ball can be hit to all parts of the service area and, in so doing, will cross the lowest part of the net. When serving to the backhand court, move further to the left so that the ball again will pass over the lowest part of the net and angle wide to the right-handed opponent's backhand. If serving to a left-handed opponent, a more central location may be adopted so that the ball can be directed to his/her backhand. Both of these service positions are close to the center of the return area of the opponent (the center of all possible returns). The player can vary his/her ready position as a means of adding disguise or variety to the serve.

When receiving service the player should stand in the center of the serving angle. Movement from this location is then determined by preference for a particular type of return or because of the server continually hitting to a particular spot. The player may also vary this position when "running around the backhand" to play an aggressive forehand return. Effective court coverage is achieved by stepping forward into the ball, and so reducing the angle of the serve. This technique can turn the relatively poor court position of the receiver into the stronger position of an offensive player.

Stepping into the ball and cutting down the angles when playing groundstrokes from the baseline will also help the player to reduce the playing area effectively. He/she should generally move to a central court location following each groundstroke, ready for the next shot.

When volleying, the player should be so placed that it is possible to hit most of the opponent's returns. The player should move slightly to the same side of the court that the approach shot has been hit. A central court location should be adopted for a ball hit down the center of the court. (*Remember:* Pay special attention to the opponent's strengths that increase the probability of a particular return.) If the player is forced to retreat from the net to hit a smash, he/she should move quickly back into the correct volley position ready for the return.

Keep the Ball Deep in the Court

The ball should be hit to the back few yards (meters) of the court. No matter whether the player is advancing to the net or playing from the baseline, a ball deep to a back corner of the court will prove the most difficult for the opponent to return. Hitting a forceful deep shot is an important method of forcing an opponent to play a lofted or weak return. Deep returns also allow the player more time to recover court position.

Play Each Stroke with Purpose

Every ball should be hit for an express purpose. The following points should help the player decide where to hit the ball:

1. If the opponent does not cover the court well, move the ball around the court.
2. If the opponent prefers that the player hit the ball hard, play shots with a variety of speed, height, and depth.
3. If the opponent doesn't like to volley and smash, then draw him to the net by hitting the ball short.
4. All opponents have preferences for certain types of shots, based on ability level, the grip used, or the hitting stance commonly adopted. These traits should be observed and acted upon when deciding on match strategies.

Play the Opponent's Weakness(es)

Consistency, the ability to play the ball deep into the court, and the accurate placement of strokes should expose deficiencies in the opponent's game. When the player sees these, he/she should place as much pressure as possible on them. (*Remember:* The player should switch his/her attack every once in a while to keep the opponent off balance and retain the initiative.) A weak backhand, which is often protected during a rally, can be "opened up" by hitting the ball wide to the opponent's forehand prior to attacking the backhand side.

Effective Service Game Strategy

To help develop a sound singles game, this section discusses service and return-of-service tactics. The following points are essential to develop an effective service game strategy:

1. The service must be capable of being hit deep into the service area.
2. The player must be capable of hitting a variety of service types and placements. A good server relies on a combination of speed, placement, disguise, and spin to keep the opponent on the defensive.
3. The serve must be supported by either a sound first volley or an effective approach shot.

These abilities can help a player become an aggressive server, ready to place immediate pressure on the opponent. A high percentage of effective first serves (approximately 65 per cent) helps keep the server on the offensive. The second serve should be hit with a similar action to the first, but with less racket power being imparted to the ball. This is often achieved by hitting the second serve with spin.

Service placement and variety on both serves also helps to keep the receiver guessing. The power serve can be hit wide to the forehand, at the body, or to the backhand of an opponent. If the opponent has a weak backhand, hit the majority of serves to that court position.

The slice service is a particularly effective weapon when serving to the forehand court (for a right-handed player). The ball can then be caused to swing away from the opponent or to move into his/her body. Although not as effective to the backhand court, the slice serve can again move the ball into the backhand of the opponent or occasionally be hit down the center (particularly if the opponent is standing wide to shelter a weak backhand).

The "kicker" serve can be used when serving to both the backhand and forehand courts. In both cases the ball should generally be directed at the backhand of the opponent.

When the player moves to the net behind a serve, he/she should follow the general line of the ball, hitting the first volley from a balanced position near the service line.

When returning service it is important to treat every ball on its merits. It is difficult to adopt anything more than a general strategy when returning serve. Try to enjoy returning the opponent's serve. This will inevitably lead to a more effective return.

The depth and type of serve determine where the receiver should stand in returning serve. The receiver should prepare to hit a hard serve by standing just behind the baseline in the center of the serving angle. If the server is missing the first serve, the receiver should move inside the court and use a variety of returns to force volley errors from the opponent. The receiver must also move inside the court to reduce the effectiveness of the slice or kicker serves (Figure 2.2).

In all service returns it is beneficial to move forward into the ball and try to play the return on the rise or at the top of its bounce.

If the opponent serves the ball to the backhand side (and if it is the receiver's weak side), it is best to show caution and generally chip the return

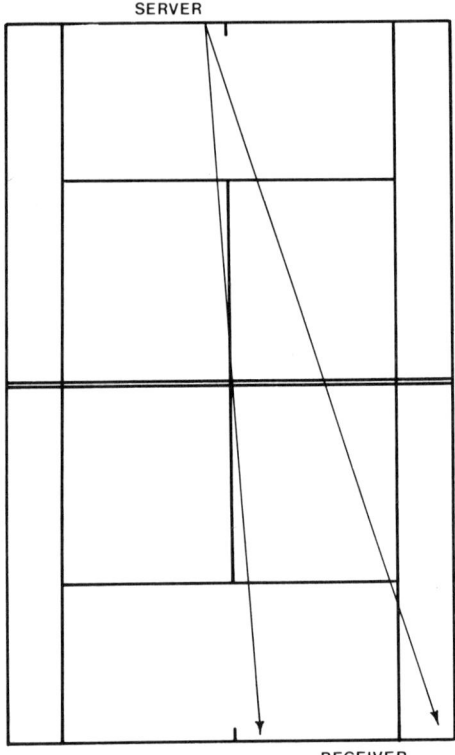

Figure 2.2 The ideal position for the receiver in the center of the service angle.

as low as possible over the net. If the ball is served to the forehand side of the body (and if it is the receiver's favorite shot), he/she should attack with a hard-hit low return or a deep drive down the line or across court. Some tournament players attempt to hit a clean winner from any forehand drive that they can play with confidence.

On the return of serve and during a rally, the player should play the angle. If forced wide on the forehand (Figure 2.3), he/she should not aim for the sideline at the level of the net post, but rather aim for a point inside the sideline behind the service line.

When returning serve the receiver should do the following:

1. Move into the serve.
2. Probe the opponent's weaknesses.
3. Show caution on good serves.
4. Hit back along the line of hard first serves.
5. Be aggressive with a slow serve that lacks depth.

The receiver should enjoy returning serve and be aggressive. The player who places pressure on an opponent's serve is one that is always hard to beat.

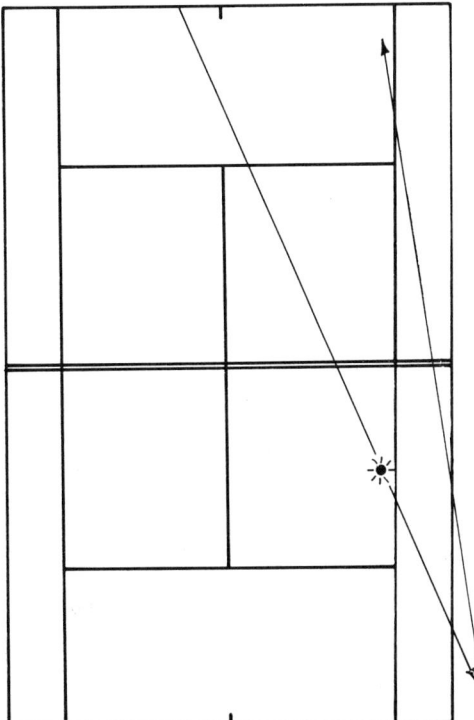

Figure 2.3 Angle of return from a wide serve.

Specific Singles Preparation and Tactics

The Warm-up

It is dangerous for a player to predict how he/she is going to perform in a match immediately following the warm-up. Always concentrate on the game, rhythm, and timing rather than paying too much attention to an opponent. The player should also practice both first and second serves during the prematch warm-up. The player should check the environmental (wind, sun) and court conditions (type and speed of bounce) during the warm-up so he/she can plan how they may help (not hinder) game tactics. This does not mean that the player should ignore potential weaknesses in his/her opponent's game. The player should check the following:

1. What type of grip does the opponent use? What effect will this grip have on stroke production?
2. Did the opponent ask for a lob to be hit that could be smashed? If so, was the smash hit with confidence?
3. Does the opponent hit topspin, backspin, or flat groundstrokes?
4. Does the opponent volley with confidence?

5. Where must the player stand to receive the opponent's serve? (Pay attention to both speed and type of serve.)

This list may seem long, but the player must attempt to develop match strategies as quickly as possible while still paying attention to stroke production.

The "Service Toss"

The player who wins the toss at the beginning of a match should generally serve first. The player must convey to the opponent that he/she *enjoys* serving. If playing a nervous opponent, the player may decide to receive service in an attempt to "break" his/her opponent's first service game.

In hot and/or humid conditions it may be advisable to receive serve. This then allows the player to "towel-down" and rest when changing ends prior to serving. This also means that the opponent must serve following the warm-up and immediately after receiving.

Court Conditions

Often certain court surfaces are suitable to a particular style of play. A player may prefer to play on fast courts where he/she can exploit a serve and volley game. Grass courts are particularly suitable to this style of play, since the opponent often finds the fast and irregular bounce difficult to return. Cement, boards, and other indoor surfaces also enhance the serve and volley style of play. Clay or some hard court surfaces may be favored if the player has built his/her game around strong groundstrokes.

Champion players, while having a favorite surface, tend to be flexible enough to play on many types of surfaces. Chris Evert Lloyd, a great clay court player, has also won two Wimbledon titles. Her defensive tactics are modified when playing on grass. She keeps the ball deep, waiting for a short return from which she can play an approach shot. Her movement to the net, ready for a volley or a smash, is the result of playing an approach shot.

Playing a Defensive Player on a Hard Court

The defensive player will usually rely on his/her opponent to make errors. The player must therefore develop the patience necessary to wait for the opportunity to attack. Such a defensive player is usually limited by the number of strokes from which he/she is capable of forcing an error. Armed with this knowledge the player should attack the strokes from which this defensive opponent is incapable of playing an aggressive return.

If the defensive opponent cannot be beaten using conventional tactics, then the player may choose to hit the ball short and bring him/her to the net. The player must then force the opponent to hit a volley or offer him/her the challenge of a smash from a high lob.

The defensive opponent often does not like being out-rallied. If the player can win a reasonable number of long rallies, particularly early in the match, then the opponent may be tempted to hit the ball harder or with more angle in an attempt to force errors. A defensive opponent may show a preference for a forehand or backhand groundstroke. If he/she prefers a forehand, play the backhand. If the opponent always uses a reduced backswing to "take the speed from the player's hit," the player should hit the ball softly to the back of the court, since it is more likely to force him/her to hit the short ball from which the player can use an aggressive stroke.

If the player adopts an aggressive attitude in playing this type of opponent and continually has the ball lobbed over his/her head, the player should vary the length, direction, and pace of the approach shot in an attempt to destroy the opponent's rhythm. If the player adopts aggressive tactics against a defensive opponent, it is imperative that he/she is capable of hitting a well-controlled smash. On hard courts it is also more important that the first serve is successful. This takes the pressure off the second serve and places more pressure on the opponent's return. However, when playing a good hard-court specialist the player may decide to follow the first serve to the net. It is probably better to remain on the baseline after the second serve.

Some tactics that a player can use against the defensive opponent are

1. To hit aggressive shots from his/her better strokes and defensive shots from his/her poorer strokes or when under pressure.
2. To keep the ball deep in the court, ensuring that the ball is well clear of the net if there is no immediate danger of the opponent volleying the return.
3. To hit approach shots down the line to reduce the angle for the opponent's passing shot.
4. To be aggressive and look for the opportunity to come to the net. Do not continually rally with a defensive opponent. The player must force the "pace of play" by being aggressive.
5. To use the lob as often as is practicable.

The key to playing such an opponent is to change the rhythm of his/her game while playing patiently but aggressively. The player must follow the basic fundamentals of consistent play while being alert for a short ball that can be attacked.

Playing an Aggressive Player

Aggressive players get most enjoyment from the game by hitting winners. The best position on the court to hit winners is the net. The aggressive player must then be kept away from the net or, alternatively, made to play difficult returns when on the net. (*Remember:* Each player serves in turn, so each has an equal chance of hitting the first volley.)

If a player continually misses his/her first serve against an aggressive player, the player may employ one of two basic strategies. He/she can reduce the speed of the first serve, thus ensuring a higher percentage of success, or he/she can hit the second serve deep into the service court and wait for a short ball to hit an approach shot at the first chance. The aggressive opponent may elect to follow his/her return of service to the net. Service variety will force a number of errors from this opponent, but if errors do not occur, the player may have to follow his/her second serve to the net.

Variation in pace and type of return is also a tactic that must be adopted against the "net rusher." The player's first priority in returning service is to hit the ball back into play, preferably at the feet or wide of the server who is approaching the net. Employ the lob return to alter the rhythm of play again so that the server is put under maximum pressure. Use as much of the court as possible in varying returns.

If this aggressive opponent does not have a particularly strong serve, the player should be aggressive and place added pressure on the opponent's first volley.

When rallying against the aggressive net player, there are two golden rules that must be followed:

1. The ball *must* be kept deep in the court so that the opponent cannot attack the net or, if he/she does, so that it will be from an incorrect court position.
2. The player must attempt to be first to the net in an attempt to take the aggressive role away from the opponent.

Tactics to use against net rushers are

1. To get to the net as much as possible. Let the net rusher know early in the match that he/she will have to share the net.
2. To aim for a high percentage of successful first serves.
3. To enjoy returning the serve. Be prepared to take some risks on returning serve, particularly with the second serve.
4. To try and keep the ball low when the opponent is on the net. The topspin return is particularly effective in forcing volley errors.
5. To move the ball around the court as much as possible. Often the net rusher is not particularly mobile.
6. To use the "air space" when lobbing the opponent. Don't lob short. Make him/her smash from behind the service line.
7. To concentrate on observing any patterns of play that the opponent adopts. The net rusher will often play conventional strokes without any disguise in an all-out attempt to get to the net.
8. To return the ball cross-court if the opponent stays back and down the line if he/she approaches the net.

Variety is still the key factor in upsetting the rhythm of such a player.

Doubles Strategy

Doubles play should be a cooperative team effort; winning should be the goal shared by both players. Each player should be aware of the strengths and weaknesses, likes and dislikes of his/her partner so that teamwork can be fostered.

Doubles play, as with singles, requires each stroke to be played with purpose. This enables the pair to be mentally alert, ready for the variety of stroke alternatives from the opposing pair. The ability to read the play comes from an understanding of stroke mechanics and match strategies.

In singles play, particularly at beginner and intermediate levels, it is possible to mold a game on a serve and on forehand and backhand groundstrokes. Doubles play at these levels, however, requires more strokes—the volley, lob, and smash. Many players at these levels are forced to play these shots under pressure because of inappropriate court positions.

Court Positions

The Server (P1)

This player serves from a position approximately 7 to 10 feet (2 to 3 meters) from the center mark towards the sideline. If the server stands too close to the center mark, then half the court is left open for an easy return. If positioned close to the "alley," then too large a gap is left between the two partners. (*Remember:* The server must move straight in to the net in preparation for the first volley.)

The Server's Partner (P2)

This player should stand approximately 7 to 12 feet (2 to 3.5 meters) from the net in a position that enables the coverage of about 50 per cent of the "alley" with a volley. More advanced players will tend to stand further toward the center of the court. This player should stand further back against the team that lobs very well. He/she may find it necessary to stand at the front of this range if the opponents are capable of hitting topspin returns that would cause very low volleys to be played if the 12-foot (3.5-meter) position was adopted. Standing too close to the net makes a reaction volley extremely difficult, particularly if the return is from a weak service.

The Receiver (P3)

This player should stand on or close to the baseline in the center of the serving angle. The court surface, speed, and type of service will all affect this initial position.

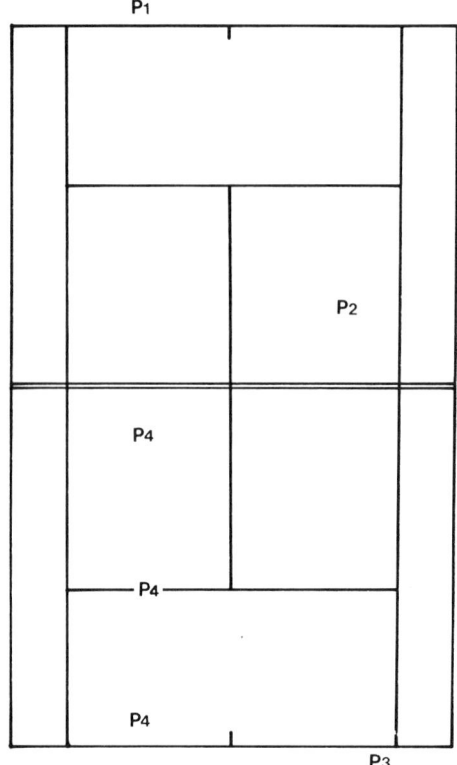

Figure 2.4 Doubles court positions.

The Receiver's Partner (P4)
This player, more than any other, is under extreme pressure during doubles play, and as such, it is crucial that he/she maintain correct court position. When the server remains on the baseline, this player may choose to stand at the net. But once a higher level of doubles play is attained, the position must be either close to the service line, in the center of the service area, or close to the baseline. The baseline position should be adopted if the receiver is having difficulty returning serve. The position on the service line (the most favored position) should quickly be changed to a volley position closer to the net when the receiver has played an effective return, either low and across court or deep to the baseline, if the server does not follow the ball to the net.

Positional Tactics

The Server
The server and partner have such a distinct advantage in doubles that they should win each service game and then concentrate on "break-

ing" an opponent's serve to win a set. The server should concentrate on placing a high percentage of first serves into the court (75 per cent). This may require him/her to reduce speed for the first serve.

Placement and the type of service action used play vital roles in doubles play. The slice and kicker serves play greater roles in doubles than in singles because they usually allow the server a higher service percentage, as well as more time to reach a better position for the first volley. The slice serve can be used tactically when serving to the forehand court (for a right-handed server) to move the receiver into the alley or off the court to play a return. When using the slice serve to the backhand court, the server must try to swing the ball into the body of the receiver. Moving the ball into the center of the court often allows the receiver to hit a forehand to the more open court area.

The kicker serve should, like the flat serve, normally be aimed at the backhand of the receiver. This serve down the center of the court, when serving to the forehand court, forces the receiver to hit one of the most difficult returns in tennis—the backhand service return.

Having hit the ball, the server must move straight toward the net and adopt a balanced position in the vicinity of the service line. This requires him/her to slow down before impact to play a balanced volley with a good transfer of weight. Then the server must move forward again to the preferred volley position.

The Server's Partner

This player should be especially alert, ready to intercept poor returns of serve and assist the server where possible. This net player *must* be "active" in a manner that adds pressure to the player attempting to return service. A poor service return should be volleyed low and wide of the opponent standing on the service line. A good service return directed at the server's partner should be volleyed as deep as is possible, back toward the player who hit the return.

The Receiver

To win a set of doubles, the pair receiving serve must be aggressive and must break the opponent's serve. The fundamental rule in returning serve is to move forward into the ball at impact. With this in mind, a priority order of types of service returns can be established.

The preferred return is to hit the ball cross-court, low to the incoming player's feet. Variation should be achieved by hitting some returns flat and others with topspin or backspin. This return forces a difficult volley from the server or, at best, forces an elevated volley that might be hit for a winner.

The ball should be lobbed over the backhand of the net player if the receiver is in difficulty or to change the pattern of service returns.

If the ball clears the net and the other player's racket, then both players at the receiving end of the court should move quickly forward to volleying positions. The receiver should remain on the baseline if the ball cannot be kept low over the net or if a follow-up drive is preferred to a volley. If it is evident that the ball is going to be smashed, the net player on the receiving end of the court should move back quickly until just before the smash when he/she should adopt a balanced posture, ready to recover the smash.

The Receiver's Partner

This player should be close to the service line and angled slightly toward the other net player. If the service return is "poached" by the net player, the receiver's partner must attempt to play a low return, probably a volley, back between the opposing pair or to the person farthest from the net. If the service return is hit across the court, the receiver's partner must focus full attention on the server, who will have moved into the first volley position close to the service line. An elevated volley by the server can then be played offensively by the receiver's partner. Any aggressive volley by the server to this player *must* be hit from a stable body position, with the racket out in front of the body. Once a rally has begun, the receiver's partner should move closer to the net in a preferred position for a volley return.

Coordinated Movement

Doubles is a team effort, and as such the movement of both players should be coordinated so that optimal court coverage is attained. The statement, "You take care of your half of the court and I'll take care of mine," although basically true, is not the essence of doubles play. There are four basic exceptions to this statement.

1. The poach. This occurs when a player (P2, Figure 2.4) moves onto the partner's section of the court to hit an offensive shot from a poor return. The person closer to the net has priority on any shot that can be volleyed or smashed. This player must therefore watch the opponent's racket very carefully so that any ball that can be poached can quickly be intercepted. As a general rule, if a player poaches past the center of the court, then players should change sides.
2. The short ball. Most short drop shots hit cross-court to the open court can be played by the net player, and partners change sides. A clear call of "mine" is essential when the net player is to take such a shot.

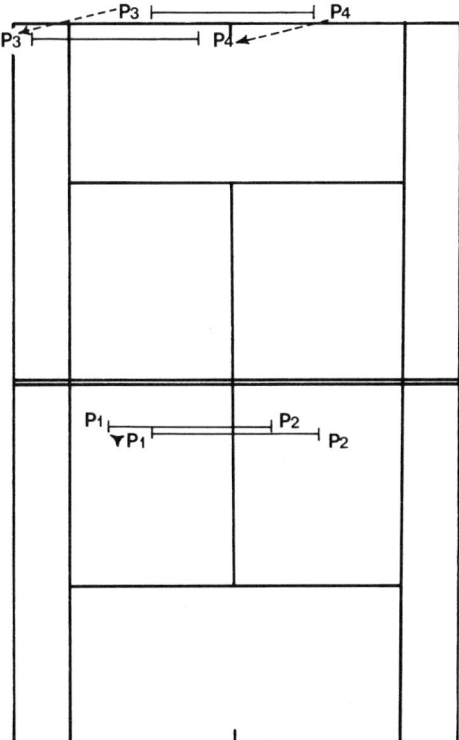

Figure 2.5 Coordinated doubles movement.

3. Recovery of a lob. Both players should run back when the ball is lobbed over a player's head. Although the concept of "recover the player's own lob" is favored by many doubles pairs, it is often best, when both players have moved back, to develop an understanding about who should "chase down" the lob under different match conditions.
4. The ball hit down the center of the court. This ball should usually be hit by the person who has the stronger volley (usually the forehand volley).

Both players in a doubles match position themselves at a relatively constant distance apart during a rally (Figure 2.5). If one player is moved out of position by a wide return, then the partner should move closer to the center of the court to ensure fullest court coverage. Doubles is a game in which both partners must keep moving. Players must be continually alert, ready to poach or to alter their positions with respect to their opponents and each other. The coordinated movement over the court and the sharing of areas of the court are the factors that, when mastered, help to ensure the success of a doubles combination.

General Doubles Tips

As stated previously, doubles is a team effort in which the team that controls the net, at all levels of play, generally *wins*.

1. The player with the more powerful or effective serve usually serves first. Always take the environmental conditions into account by assessing the direction of the wind and sun. Some players prefer to serve into the wind. Others may be able to use the breeze to advantage if serving from a particular end. In mixed doubles the man usually serves first.
2. Usually good doubles combinations are formed when two players complement each other's style, enjoy playing together, and *prefer* to return service from different sides. At beginner and intermediate levels, the player with the better forehand drive usually plays on the deuce court and the person with the stronger backhand, on the ad side. At advanced levels where the server can direct the ball with greater accuracy to the opponent's backhand, more factors must be taken into consideration. The player with the better backhand, particularly for a ball directed at the body, may be better on the deuce side. (This is essential if the ball is to be kept away from the net player.) The backhand hit along the line of the ball or across the ball from the ad court moves away from the net player and is generally an easier return.
3. If a left-handed player selects the ad side, preferring to return serve with an across-court forehand, then both partners must hit backhand volleys to the ball played down the center of the court. In advanced play the left-handed player may select the deuce side so that one player can always hit a forehand volley for the ball played down the center. Partners must therefore consider preference for a particular type of return, the ability to control the center of the court, and the preference of the left-hander's partner to poach from a particular side of the court.

References

1. Austin D. A.: "Developing a Winning Singles Strategy." *Scholastic Coach*, 49:96–97, 1980.
2. Hopman, H.: *Harry Hopman's Winning Tennis Strategy*. Bobbs-Merrill Co., Indianapolis, 1975.
3. Pucci, T: "Four Hitting Areas for the Advanced Player." *Scholastic Coach*, December 1977, pages 98–99.
4. Tilmanis, G. A.: *Advanced Tennis for Coaches, Teachers, and Players*. Australia and New Zealand Book Company, Sydney, Australia, 1975.

3

Sports Psychology and the Tennis Player

Introduction

How can a player improve his/her tennis and maximize the level of performance in tournaments? Should he/she rely on the advice, the motivation, and the strategy available from a coach? Should a player look further afield and seek the advice of leading players, or simply rely on the influence of parents, friends, and selected fellow players? These are typical examples of the questions that cross the minds of most tennis players at different stages in their tennis development.

Players, at times, question the value of their coaches' pep talks and instructions, both before and during matches. It is wise for players to enter a match with a basic strategy, but there is a limit to the amount of information that can be taken onto a court without running the risk of inhibiting performance.

Do the coach's suggestions really improve the player's performance level, and is a player more motivated to perform at a higher skill level following a coach/pupil discussion? In many cases, unfortunately, both the player and the coach are unaware of the major psychological factors that can affect performance. In recent years, however, players have developed a growing awareness that "something is missing" from their game, and more and more players are realizing that there is, in fact, a more formidable opponent inside their heads than across the net.

A player's ability to handle mental obstacles or stress often determines how successfully that player will perform. Stress, which is often self-imposed, creates mental obstacles that elicit weak second services or mis-hit volleys in pressure situations.

It is the aim of this chapter to provide players, coaches, and teachers with a brief overview of the important psychological factors that influence a player's performance. The reader is warned, however, that this chapter does not provide all the answers. Additionally, the reader is urged to review the recommended reading list to find a more detailed description of these factors.

Factors Influencing Performance

The improvements in player performance can occur only if both coach and player develop a joint understanding of the requirements for each particular situation. It is important to establish a clear course of action required to achieve the desired goals. In order for this to occur, the coach and the player need to be aware of the major factors that will influence on-court performance.

Simplistically, player improvement represents the successful integration of three major factors: (1) the body, (2) the mind, and (3) the environment (see Figure 3.1). Bjorn Borg is a classic example of a player whose body and mind appear to be working in harmony. Borg's ability to integrate the body and mind successfully in the competitive environment is facilitated through the development of certain coping strategies and an awareness that manifests itself in the form of emotional stability in stressful situations. It is not a short-term phenomenon, since Borg has competed successfully on the world tennis circuit for many years, under continual pressure.

This heightened state of "tennis awareness" represents the removal of inner obstacles, both physical and mental. The player develops a self-knowledge that enables the bodily actions and mind functions to flow into one "wholeness of action." Many of us, as players, can recall the disharmony and frustration that exist between what our mind wants and expects and what our bodies (and racket) actually do.

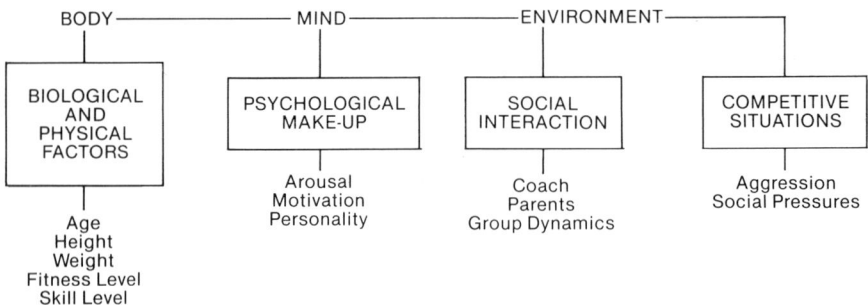

Figure 3.1

Figure 3.2 "My body hates me!"

This situation can be achieved within one's self, but it is dependent on the mind not demanding what the body is incapable of giving and on the body performing to the best of its ability. Players who have developed this "inner harmony" have, in fact, achieved an awareness of their own capabilities and limitations. A coach's ability to encourage new techniques in self-awareness can be a major contribution to a player's maximal performance levels.

A blending of the powers of the body and mind can carry the player to new plateaus of creative achievement. Shots that previously were affected by stress can be hit with fluency. Clearly, the focus of a player, with the guidance and facilitation of an understanding coach, should be toward the development of this "tennis awareness."

The Body

Effective coaching depends upon implementing sound principles in relation to the development of physical fitness and improved skill levels. Player fitness is a major factor in psychological preparation, because fatigue developed in a prolonged match results in skill deterioration and player frustration.

Coaches must ensure that both fitness and skill practices are varied and stimulating. This will contribute to the player's interest and enjoyment of the program. Training programs that provide little enjoyment or challenge tend to result in boredom, underpreparation, and lackluster performances.

As well as fitness and skill preparation, coaches need to focus on the attention players pay to feedback. Beginners rely on augmented feedback, which is basically the information contributed by the coach. It is essential that this type of feedback be immediate, specific, and positive if it is to benefit the performer.

The skilled performer, on the other hand, is more dependent on body feedback (biofeedback). This body feedback alerts the player to the position of the racket head in relation to the oncoming ball and is, in essence, a kinesthetic feedback. The racket head is too high to hit topspin; the legs are too straight to allow the body to be fully integrated into the shot; the ball is traveling too quickly to allow for a full backswing—all of these are good examples of feedback information that the body can use when preparing for a shot.

Feedback is available for use by all players, but unfortunately, in competitive situations, players are often so engrossed in making judgments about whether they are going to win the point that they tend to ignore this information. The mind takes over and tells the player, "What a terrible backhand; what a poor second service; gee whiz, that was weak!" Disharmony between the body and the mind creeps in; the body's detailed and accurate information, which could provide the solution to future mistakes, is lost. This situation is manifested as a loss in concentration as unproductive thoughts interfere with the feedback process.

The pressure of competitive situations tends to make players overtense their muscles, resulting in a distortion of body feedback. Players have to learn methods of relaxation; it is not sufficient for the coach simply to say, "Relax." Players need to develop an awareness of their internal responses, and this involves relaxing rather than tensing muscle groups prior to impact with the ball.

Coaches also need to be aware of the situations that their pupils find stressful and try to develop coping strategies that will enable their pupils to handle these situations better. By reducing the tension, coaches will enhance the continuation of the feedback process and, in turn, the overall performance.

Being aware of feedback also requires an awareness of the influence of reinforcement. Seeing a good shot go in (visual), listening to the ball hit the racket (auditory), and feeling the enjoyment (biofeedback) one can get when a ball is hit well are examples of reinforcement. They help a player develop a realization of the importance of body messages.

In too many instances players rely heavily on the mind telling them to "try and hit a hard return" or "try a hard second service." This results in the tensing of muscle groups, which in turn results in a distortion of skill and often a reduction in fluency. The body and mind are not functioning in unison, and a loss of stroke "rhythm" results. In situations like this, the experienced professional may tell the player to "slow down."

Repeated practices that develop an automation of the skill are important. Players must remember that skills should remain the same during a match. The variance in performance occurs when the mind takes over basic functions, resulting in poor skill reproduction and, consequently, poor performance. Players therefore must rely on their own internal biological information and must control the feelings that come from good and bad shots by feeding back productive information.

The Mind

One of the greatest obstacles to success lies within the mind. When referring to the "mind" it is important that we specifically isolate the major psychological components of motivation (arousal) and personality.

Classifying Motivated Behavior

Coaches must identify those behaviors that reflect a positive will and determination for success. Generally, the player who is highly motivated will demonstrate constructive actions (attending training and encouraging other players). Coaches need to encourage and reinforce desirable behaviors, in line with the behavioral norms of tennis, and should not condone negative actions. From the outset, players should be made aware of what the expected behavioral standards are for individuals and for groups or squads.

Establishing Behavioral Goals

Goals that are measurable and provide immediate reinforcement should be established. At training, players should be given clear objectives (e.g., hitting the ball to a particular area on the court during a specific pressure drill). Behavioral goals actively encourage involvement in what otherwise may be a dull activity.

Development of a "tennis awareness" is influenced by personal aspiration. Players are motivated toward tennis for a variety of reasons: health, fitness, pressure, fun, the desire to meet people and make friends, to learn a new activity, or to achieve success. Hence, the motivational drive of players governs the amount of effort they will expend.

It is important, therefore, for a coach to understand what attracts a particular individual toward tennis, for this is the basic area that determines whether a player wishes to play competitive or recreational tennis. Armed with this knowledge, the coach is better equipped to develop a program that will suit the individual needs of each player.

Motivation Toward Winning

How does one go about strengthening the determination to achieve success? What is the relationship between the "will to win" and "letting it happen," between the necessary effort and trying too hard? Gallwey[3] examines this complex relationship in his book *Inner Tennis: Playing the Game*.

To strengthen one's will, the solution lies first in clarifying goals. What does "winning" really mean? All other goals, less important and distracting from the player's purpose, must then be sacrificed. For example, a player can be distracted from winning if one goal is to look graceful while winning.

It is important also for the player to realize that in a competitive situation, a player must concentrate on winning *during* the game. This means being aware of each situation, that is, of the challenge and the demands of the moment (e.g., returning a difficult first service).

The player who focuses on the relationship between his/her effort and the outcome can remain in control. The main purpose of this type of player, in competing, is to perform at the best level possible, deriving benefit and experience from every situation.

Alternatively, a player may become anxious through an inability to achieve success. Here, once again, the barriers or inner obstacles become real (the opponent's better play or internal distractions—"looking good") and prevent the achievement of specific goals. Anxiety also becomes an obstacle that interferes with performance, resulting in a loss of control. Once a player becomes anxious and loses control, that player loses sight of the primary goal.

To avoid states of anxiety is to be aware of the barriers that prevent a player from achieving particular goals. A player needs to remain in control and focus on the quality and effort necessary to overcome the challenge and achieve a goal. Thus, trying too hard may cause loss of control.

Inner obstacles prevent a player from concentrating all effort and will toward the primary goal. Trying too hard and being anxious, which may result in poorer performance, represent an incongruence between body and mind. The best performances are often accomplished with less effort. Losers often make the statement that they "tried too hard," whereas winners invariably refer to "everything falling into place."

Overcoming obstacles or barriers, whether they are internal or external to the player, requires effort. No goal can be achieved without effort. Similarly, few games are ever won without the will to win. Effort and will to win are the nuclei on which motivated performance is based. Effort and will are observable behavioral characteristics. Effort is the amount of energy a player is prepared to expend at training or in a match. Will refers to the motivation behind performance and is influenced by the player's arousal (level of excitation) to achieve a desired goal. A final match may be sufficient motivation in itself, but the "will to win" in a first-round match may be low, because players are less aroused or motivated.

Success, both on and off the court, depends first on the goals the player establishes and second on the amount of energy an individual is willing to expend to achieve the goal, regardless of the obstacles that may be encountered. It is essential that coaches be able to assess players' motivations both on and off the court.

Gallwey identifies in *Inner Tennis*[3] the major strategies for strengthening the will to win:

1. Increased awareness of where the player is as a player.
2. Increased awareness of where the player wants to go as a player.
3. The need to overcome internal obstacles, self-doubt, fears, anxiety, and self-image as a player (letting go of the judging mind and the self-doubts that surround every action). For example, when a player attempts to play a shot, it will be less efficient if the player's mind says, "It may go out." It is best simply to play the appropriate shot with as much fluency as possible. Try not to make judgments about the possibilities of the shot being successful or not during the stroke.
4. The need to clarify objectives—directing energies toward a goal may mean limiting alternatives or reducing the "time" commitment to other activities.
5. The need to seek the support of people with similar objectives and desires.

Personality

The study of player personality represents a major area of sports psychology research, the net result of which remains confusing for most sports practitioners. For the coach, the importance of this concept lies in the realization that personality simply refers to "the sum total of an individual's characteristics which make him unique."[4] This implies that the behavior of individuals relates to (1) the social situations in which they find themselves, (2) the typical responses displayed by these individuals in all situations and events, and (3) the motivational state in which they find themselves. It is important, therefore, for coaches to assess each player, giving consideration to these three factors.

Coaches, in evaluating player performance, need to be aware of the player's typical response patterns in stressful situations, the player's motivational state, and the demands of the situation. This is crucial to understanding a player's consistency or inconsistency of performance across a number of matches or tournaments.

Understanding an opponent's personality is also essential for a player, particularly when he/she is formulating match strategy. If one player knows what situations cause anxiety to creep into the opponent's game, then this situation can be used to advantage. When a player is aware of an opponent's typical response patterns, the opportunity exists for anxiety to be introduced into the opponent's game.

The opponent may not like smashing or may not like being pressured. The list is practically endless.

For a detailed study of personality the reader is directed to the works of Adlerman[1] and Butt[2].

The Environment

The primary role of a tennis coach is to structure the learning environment so that stroke production can be developed and performance can be optimized. The successful integration and socialization of players into the competitive environment will facilitate the achievement of long-term goals.

The interrelationship between the environment and the player is discussed in Chapter 2. Players must overcome the stressful influence of environmental conditions (wind, sun, crowd) if optimal performance is to be achieved. Clear performance goals will also reduce the influence of social pressures, making the many hours of training bearable, even enjoyable.

References

1. Alderman, R. B.: *Psychological Behavior in Sport.* W. B. Saunders Co., Philadelphia, 1974.
2. Butt, D.: *The Psychology of Sport.* Van Nostrand Reinhold, New York, 1976.
3. Gallwey, W. T.: *Inner Tennis: Playing the Game.* Random House, New York, 1976.
4. Hollander, E. P.: *Principles and Methods of Social Psychology.* Oxford Press, New York, 1967.
5. Rushall, B. S.: "Psychological Factors in Sports Performance." In *Towards Better Coaching.* (ed. F. Pyke). Australian Government Publishing Service, Canberra, Australia, 1980.

4

The Coaching and Teaching of Tennis

The primary objective of the coach or teacher of tennis should be to develop an optimal level of stroke production related both to the player and the strategy of the game, while also promoting an interest in tennis by making all lessons enjoyable. To achieve this objective, coaching and teaching techniques must be assessed continually in an attempt to meet the needs of the pupils. This chapter outlines three areas of concern in coaching/teaching.

The Basis of Coaching/Teaching

The coach or teacher must understand the mechanics of stroke production and the theory behind coaching strategies so that the passing on of knowledge does not rely solely on past experiences, copying of current world trends, or leaving the performer to his/her own development, but integrates these three factors with sound stroke mechanics. The coach or teacher can then modify teaching techniques and stroke production requirements in a way that optimizes the chance of success for all pupils.

The Role of Past Experiences in Coaching/Teaching

All past experiences associated with the learning, playing, and teaching of tennis should be evaluated so that techniques and teaching methods that were found to be successful can be retained, while those that were unsuccessful can be discarded. These past experiences provide a foundation for coaching. In the teaching of the forehand drive, past experiences may provide the following information for integration into coaching:

1. A closed or semiclosed stance is beneficial to stroke production.
2. Greater racket head velocity and poorer control are the results of leading with the elbow or "slapping" with the wrist.
3. The weight should be on the front foot at impact with the ball.
4. The eastern forehand grip enables the ball to be hit opposite the front foot with power and control.
5. Keeping the head down with eyes on the ball is best during the stroke.
6. The best results are achieved when teaching for both speed and accuracy.
7. Selected drills have been found to be effective with young beginners, whereas others are preferred when teaching adults.

The Influence of World Trends in Coaching/Teaching

The coach or teacher should evaluate world trends in stroke production and teaching before changing coaching techniques. The current trend toward hitting groundstrokes with topspin should influence coaching technique as follows:

1. The position of the racket at the completion of the backswing should be lower than was previously taught, to allow the racket to move up through the ball.
2. The major emphasis is on what happens at "impact" rather than on stroke preparation or follow-through.

The Influence of the Pupil on Coaching/Teaching

The individual flair of each player for a particular technique should be considered in preference to molding all pupils with a common technique. Individual differences in movement patterns caused by body proportions, strength, or flair must be considered if optimal stroke production is to be achieved.

The Influence of Stroke Mechanics on Coaching/Teaching

Although there is no one correct technique for all players, skills must be developed within the limits of sound mechanical principles. Some of the factors that influence stroke production of the forehand drive are

1. The pathways of the ball and the racket at impact determine the spin and direction of the ball following impact. The ball is in contact with the strings during the stroke for such a brief period that

no purposeful movement of the racket can occur following impact that will influence the flight of the ball.
2. A closed or semiclosed hitting stance permits the player to "flatten the arc of the swing," thus enhancing the possibility of a successful return.
3. The ball will be returned with maximum power if hit at a right angle (90°) to its line of flight.
4. The wrist must be laid back at impact if the ball is to be played from in line with the front foot.

The coach or teacher is then influenced by these factors, so that any changes in stroke mechanics or teaching methods are made for a reason and not because another coach said or wrote that they were necessary. Teaching strategies will also play an important role in the formulation of an effective coaching program.

Teaching Strategies in a Coaching or Teaching Program

There is no single method that will produce a fluent stroke production. Each method attempted will be influenced by the personalities of the coach or teacher, the pupils to be taught, and the skill to be learned. The use of the whole-or-part and the speed-or-accuracy teaching strategies must be evaluated by all coaches interested in the development of their teaching methods.

Whole-Versus-Part Teaching Strategy

The best results in tennis seem to be obtained when a pupil's first attempts at a stroke are concerned with the total motor pattern to be learned. Attention should be directed to the total movement involved, not to minute details involved in the stroke.[1] The teaching of the separate parts and the integration of these parts into a fluent stroke is thus established in one sequence. When the "part" learning teaching method is used, extra effort is needed to connect the various parts of the skill together after they have been learned. The "whole" technique should therefore be emphasized in the teaching of most tennis strokes.

"Part" learning can, however, be used to improve a particular section of the stroke once fluency has been developed. Faults that the coach finds difficult to correct using the "whole" technique may be isolated for specific practice. If the wrist is not laid back at impact in a forehand drive (taught using the "whole" technique), a coach may use the following drill to emphasize this aspect of the stroke:

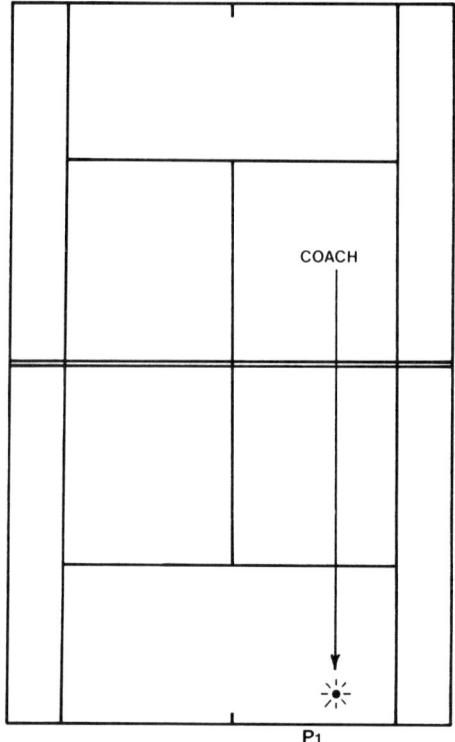

Figure 4.1 Half-volley drill from the baseline.

The coach hits the ball with power so that the player is forced to move into the stroke and play a half-volley or near half-volley from the baseline. This helps ensure that the ball is played from in line with, or in front of, the forward foot, which causes the wrist to be laid back at impact (Figure 4.1).

The coach then changes back to hitting forehands to the pupil, which can be played with a full backswing and follow-through.

The teaching of the serve, which is a complex stroke, should first be attempted using a combination of the "whole" and "part" teaching strategies (Table 4.1).

Speed and Accuracy Strategies in Teaching

In tennis, racket speed and control both play an integral role in the timing of a stroke. Overemphasis on accuracy in the early stages of learning will adversely affect fluency of stroke production. Equal emphasis on speed and accuracy during practice has been found to produce the most favorable results.[1] Both practice and learning situations should resemble the game,

TABLE 4.1 The Teaching of the Serve

"Whole" Technique	"Whole/Part" Technique	"Part" Technique
(a) Demonstration	(a) Demonstration	(a) Demonstration
(b) Teach the complete serve with ball and racket serving as one unit	(b) Develop a fluent swing (use key words as outlined in Chapter 1)	(b) Teach a correct ball toss
	(c) Fit the ball toss to the swing	(c) Develop the various sections of the service swing (use of half-serve and so on)
		(d) Develop a fluent swing by piecing the different sections together

with skills rehearsed as they would be performed in the game. For example, in teaching a backhand drive, both the speed of the racket and the path traced out by the racket head should be emphasized.

The coach who is conversant with all the current trends in stroke techniques and teaching strategies must still plan a program if all this information is to be presented effectively to pupils.

Planning the Coaching Program

There are a number of important facts that should be considered in the planning of an effective coaching program. They are as follows:

1. The objectives must be clearly stated. Any coaching plan should include general objectives related to a series of lessons together with specific objectives for each lesson.
2. A lesson plan can then be structured with due consideration of the specific objectives of each class. The majority of group lessons should comprise an introduction, skill development section, and culmination. Private lessons may follow a different format as dictated by the pupil in question. Here a coach may (a) diagnose the causes of weaknesses in the stroke being evaluated and (b) explain the cause of the problem in a manner that the pupil can understand. The coach then may supervise practice of the stroke using a recommended technique. Key phrases, mental images, and coaching hints should be used in an attempt to achieve the desired stroke mechanics. Finally, the coach may put the new stroke into an advanced drill situation to evaluate the student's technique under pressure.
3. The lesson plan should ensure maximum activity during the lesson. It is better to teach with four lines of three students rather

LESSON OBJECTIVES

Content	**Planned**	**Achieved**

Introduction
Physiological
  flexibility
  whole body
  agility
  speed
  strength

Psychological
  motivating
  fun
  variety
  social
  tone setting

Organizational
  related
  revised
  maximum participation
  control established

Skill Development
  logical/challenging
  progression
  individual differences

Culmination
Teaching
  reinforce
  games theme related
  strategies
  rules
  fun

Organization
  maximum participation
  concluding procedures

Figure 4.2 Lesson evaluation sheet.

than to have two lines of six students. Maximum participation following a competent demonstration affords pupils the greatest chance of success.

"To hear is to forget; to see is to remember; to do is to understand."

The plan also should ensure that pupils understand why a particular technique should be adopted. The more a student knows and understands about a particular technique, the easier that stroke will be to master. The explanation must, however, be related to the playing level and age of the group.

4. Each lesson plan should be evaluated so that improvements can be made in future coaching.

Figure 4.2 outlines a lesson evaluation sheet that a coach may find useful in assessing various stages of a lesson or series of lessons.

Reference

1. Singer, R. N.: *Motor Learning and Human Performance.* Macmillan Company; Collier-Macmillan Ltd., London, England, 1970.

5

Player Evaluation for Improved Performance

The primary components of tennis-playing success are efficient stroke mechanics, appropriate physiological capacities, and an apt psychological make-up.

It is important to evaluate stroke production, court movement, and functional fitness for tennis if a coach is to identify the factors that are limiting a player's performance. The coach must identify weaknesses in play and then prescribe specific training programs that will remedy these flaws in performance. This chapter concentrates on the means by which weaknesses in stroke production, court movement, and tennis fitness may be evaluated objectively by the coach. Clearly, any test that is used should be related to the aspiration level of the group or individual. For school or recreational play, the fundamentals of stroke production and court strategy should be of paramount importance. However, if advanced competitive play is the goal of any player, then more consideration must be given to the evaluation of fitness, stroke production under pressure, and court movement patterns. The identification and subsequent correction of faults is necessary at this advanced level because opponents have a greater ability to detect weaknesses in a player's game and will concentrate their attack on these areas.

The purposes of this chapter are threefold. First, it presents a procedural format for the assessment of stroke production. Second, it shows how weaknesses in stroke production and court movement can be identified by means of game analysis. Finally, it includes a test battery that may help coaches to identify areas of weakness in endurance fitness, speed, strength, and flexibility. Individual training programs can then be prescribed based on a diagnosis from test results.

Analysis of Stroke Production

A large proportion of any coach's time should be concerned with the analysis of stroke production. The first step in this analysis requires that the coach assess performance visually.

Analysis at this level is specific to each pupil and involves an evaluation of the three stages of movement: the preparatory, forward swing, and follow-through phases. Often, the coach is capable of analyzing movement patterns only of selected areas of the body at one time and so should observe the complete performance over repeated trials. In analyzing the service action, the coach should initially observe the complete stroke, looking for any flaws in the overall flow of the action. Attention then can be focused on different parts of the body, racket, and/or ball during the serve. Special emphasis should be given to (1) the relationship between the ball and the racket (the major fault to look for is the hands "splitting" too early in a marching action), (2) the transfer of body weight from the lower limbs up toward the ball, (3) the pathway traced by the racket, (4) the relationship between the racket and the upper limb, (5) the relationship between the wrist and the shoulder during the backswing phase, and (6) the speed and placement of the ball toss. The coach should always seek the "causes" of any fault in service technique.

Modern technology has now provided the coach with video systems that help in the analysis of stroke production. Any of these systems that have slow-motion playback and stop-frame facilities are of immense value to the coach. The video motion-analysis system (Sony SVM-1010[1]), with an exposure time of $1/500$ second and slow-motion playback facilities, is one system the authors have found to be extremely valuable in coaching because it permits the following:

1. The coach can view each stroke in slow motion, with the image "frozen," or played from frame to frame.
2. The coach and player can look at a repeated performance of each stroke so that any errors can be clearly delineated.
3. The player can evaluate his/her stroke production and thereby understand what the coach is trying to achieve in changing sections of a particular stroke.
4. The coach can show, frame by frame, a desirable trait that is being sought from all squad members.

Game Analysis

Game analysis techniques have been used very successfully in many sports to provide insight into what actually occurs during a match. A shot-by-shot analysis of a game can provide both objective and descriptive information on a player's strengths and weaknesses. Descriptive statements on play may include such comments as[2]

1. Down-the-line shots produced 1.5 times as many errors as cross-court shots, yet yielded an equivalent number of outright winners (consider the height of the net and the body position needed to play the down-the-line stroke).
2. Backhand down-the-line shots produced the most errors (consider the body position required for this stroke).
3. Two-thirds of all points won were a direct result of opponent's errors.
4. Match winners hit 1.3 times as many winning shots as did match losers while committing only 75 per cent as many stroking errors.[2]

Statistical analysis techniques that provide general information may also be used to indicate specific weaknesses that may be limiting a player's performance. The speed of the game, the many different strokes that can be played from a given position, and the outcome of the strokes are all factors that may complicate the sequential recording of the strokes played in a rally. One method of game analysis that has proved to be successful is shown in Figure 5.1.

Information from such a general analysis sheet can provide an insight into the effect of pressure on stroke production. Statistics must, however, be kept on both players (teams) so that the effectiveness of stroke production can be assessed accurately.

Statistics taken from the 1979 Wimbledon final between Bjorn Borg and Roscoe Tanner, which were collected from the first two sets (Tanner 7-6; Borg 6-1), demonstrate how changes in selected aspects of the match influenced the outcome of that set:

The percentage of service returns was similar in the first set (Tanner 66 per cent, Borg 70 per cent); both players hit 59 per cent of their first services into court.

In the second set Tanner reduced his first-service percentage to 35 per cent, while Borg increased his to 82 per cent. As Borg hit more first services into court, Tanner was forced into more errors on his service return (60 per cent). On the other hand, Tanner's second serve did not apply as much pressure to Borg's return, enabling Borg to hit 82 per cent of all services back into play.

Tanner's drop in first-service percentage also influenced the effectiveness of his serve-volley style of play. In the first set he played 39 volleys, of which 28 were effective, while only 12 of the 20 volleys played in the second set were effective.

Conversely, Borg increased his percentage of volleys in the second set, placing greater pressure on Tanner (first set, 7 volleys in 13 games; second set, 6 volleys in 7 games).

101 Game Analysis

Player: _____ Opponent: _____ Date: _____

Result: _____ Court surface: _____

	Right of Court	Mid-court	Left of Court	Out	Net
First Serve:					
Second Serve:					

	Crosscourt Shot					Straight Shot				
	Inef-fective*	Effec-tive†	Winner	Out**	Net‡	Inef-fective	Effec-tive	Winner	Out	Net
Forehand Svc Retn										
Backcourt										
Midcourt										
Net										
Backhand Svc Retn										
Backcourt										
Midcourt										
Net										
SMASH										
LOB										
VOLLEY										

Additional Comments:
List   (1) Turning points in a game or the match
          (2) Psychological factors that may have influenced the result of the match

*Ineffective —a return that enabled the opponent to play an aggressive shot (such as an approach shot)
†Effective —a return that placed pressure on the opponent
**Out —any ball that landed either wide or long with respect to the court area
‡Net —any ball hitting and then not clearing the net

Figure 5.1 General stroke analysis sheet.

Borg maintained a 77 per cent return average over both sets, whereas Tanner, who returned 81 per cent of balls in general play in the first set, dropped to 60 per cent in the second.

The general statistics sheet in Figure 5.1 is too complicated for one recorder to use, so either a number of recorders or only selected aspects of this sheet should be used during a match. Graphs of court movement patterns have also been used to evaluate the movement of players during a game.[3]

More specific statistics are required if a coach is to identify the reasons behind selected types of stroke production. A statistics sheet that provides some of this information is shown in Figure 5.2.

The experienced coach often is capable of identifying the reasons for a specific stroke pattern by concentrating on the aspect of the game that is causing concern.

If the coach can isolate a player's main fault, then correction of this error in stroke production or court tactics is often relatively straightforward. Players often respond more positively to a statistical uncovering of their weaknesses than to a subjective evaluation by their coach. Remember

Player:_____ Opponent:_____ Date:_____

Result:_____ Court surface:_____

Stroke: Forehand Drive

	Ineffective*	Effective*	Out*	Net*	Stance†	Racket Position**
BACKCOURT Crosscourt Drive						
Straight Drive						
MIDCOURT Crosscourt Drive						
Straight Drive						

* See key to Figure 5.1 for definition of terms
† Stance refers to position of the feet at impact (ie. semi-open)
** Position of the racket relative to the body at impact

Figure 5.2 Specific stroke analysis sheet.

that the identification of the cause of any deficiency in technique is paramount if long-term stroke efficiency is desired.

The use of tape recorders or video systems to further aid the collection of relevant statistics should also be considered by a coach. Video recording of a match is an ideal analysis tool because it permits both the coach and player to evaluate stroke production and court movement together. Tapes can be stopped, reversed, and replayed in an endeavor to gain further insights into a player's strengths and weaknesses.

Tennis Test Battery

Physical Characteristics

The three most important physical characteristics to be measured are height, weight, and body fat. Body fat is measured in addition to body weight because it plays no functional role in providing the internal force necessary for movement, and as such may be regarded as "dead weight," which is detrimental to both speed around the court and the ability to endure a long, hard match. Skinfold measurements should be taken, using calipers, from the following sites (Figures 5.3 to 5.6):

1. The back of the arm (triceps) is measured half-way between the elbow and shoulder joints.
2. The back (subscapular area) is measured at the lowest point of the scapula.
3. The hip (suprailiac area) is measured above the crest of the ilium and following the natural diagonal line.
4. The abdomen (mid-abdominal region) is measured immediately to the right of the navel and parallel to the long axis of the body.

For men, body fat levels at these four sites can then be used, either collectively or individually, to indicate the type of exercise program required for the player being tested. For women, these four sites can be tested as well, although usually only the triceps and suprailiac areas are measured. These measures can then be used to calculate the percentage of body fat.[4]

Energy Requirements

These tests help evaluate both the anaerobic and aerobic fitness levels of the players.

Anaerobic or Speed Tests

Both around-court speed and the need for repeated efforts should be tested, since they form the basis for court movement in tennis. A tennis speed test requiring a player to run a typical movement pattern

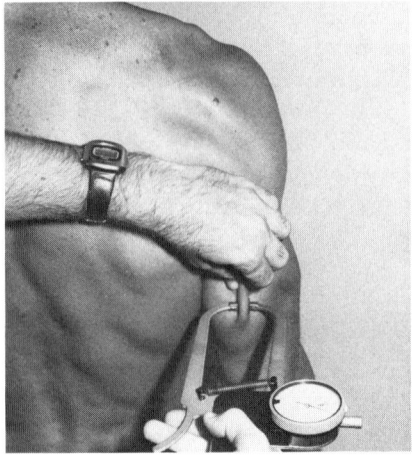

Figure 5.3 Triceps skinfold site.

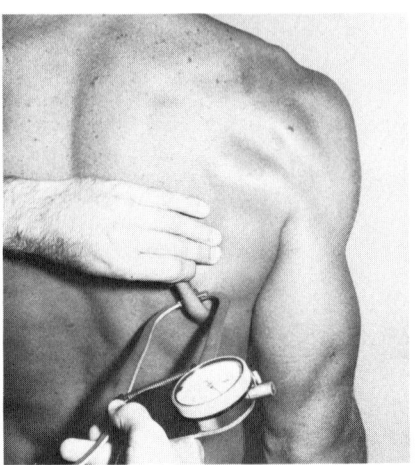

Figure 5.4 Subscapular skinfold site.

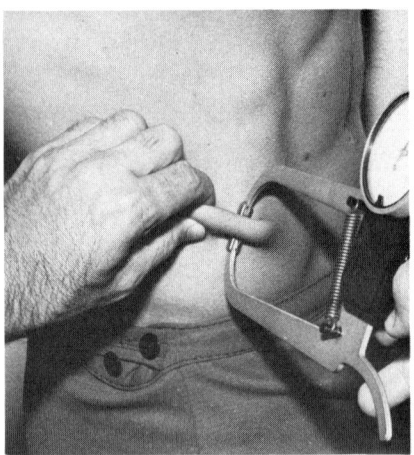

Figure 5.5 Suprailiac skinfold site.

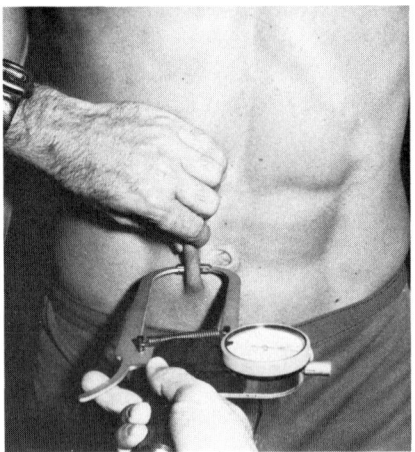

Figure 5.6 Mid-abdominal skinfold site.

while touching a racket at a series of positions on the court is shown in Figure 5.7. A single trial of this test, which takes approximately 7 seconds, can be used to indicate speed, while the time for repeated trials with a rest of 20 seconds between trials, realistically reproduces the game situation and provides another measure of the functional ability of the anaerobic energy system to respond to exercise. Results from this test (e.g., the time for the tenth trial) may then be expressed either as a percentage of the single trial time for individual player comparison or on a total basis for between-player comparisons. A

105 Tennis Test Battery

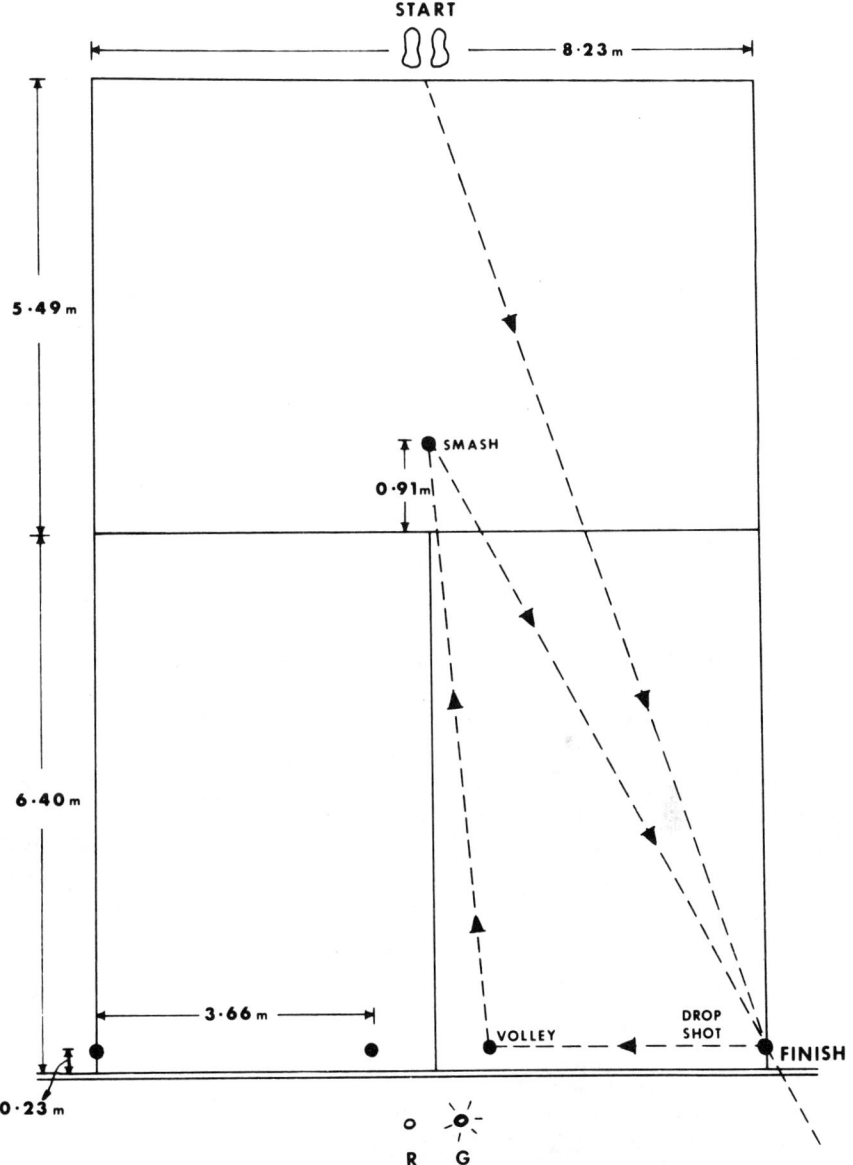

Figure 5.7 Tennis speed test. G = green light, indicating that a player should run the pattern shown here. R = red light, indicating that a player should run the same pattern on the right side of the court.

sprint of about 40 yards (40 meters) may also be used as a test of a player's speed.

Aerobic or Stamina Test

An aerobic fitness test should also be included in the test battery because it provides the base for both performance and the repayment of oxygen debt (the oxygen required to replenish anaerobic energy reserves). Because it is not often practical to assess the endurance capabilities of large groups of players on treadmills or bicycle ergometers, performance (distance covered) in a 15-minute run (for boys older than 16) or a 12-minute run (for girls older than 16) can be used as a guide to each player's aerobic fitness.

Flexibility Tests

Flexibility in tennis is important not only to allow more fluent stroking when forced to stretch, but also to prevent injuries to muscles and associated tissue. Two examples of practical tests of flexibility can be used by the tennis coach.

Sit, Reach and Hold Test (Figure 5.8)

This test determines functional flexibility of the hamstring muscle group and associated lumbar muscles and tissues. The player sits on the floor with legs extended and feet flat against a bench. The trunk is flexed and the fingers are placed along a scale. The player reaches equally with the fingers of both hands (keeping knees straight) and holds the position for 5 seconds.

Ankle Flexibility Test (Figure 5.9)

This test assesses the flexibility of the plantar flexors of the foot (muscles of the back of the leg). The player sits upright with the legs flat on the floor, feet relaxed and pointing toward the roof (Figure 5.9A). A

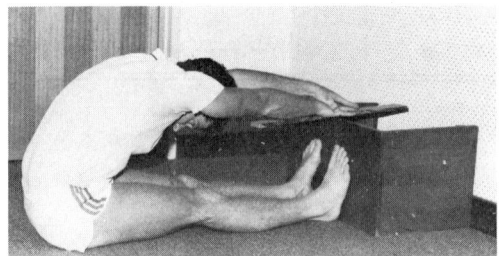

Figure 5.8 Sit, reach, and hold test of flexibility.

107 Tennis Test Battery

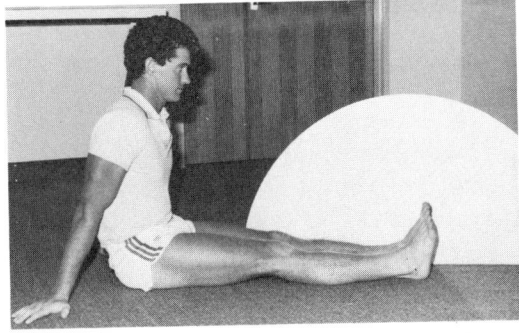

Figure 5.9 Ankle flexibility test.

board (marked in degrees) is placed vertically against the edge of the foot. The player, without moving the position of the ankle joint, dorsiflexes the foot toward the body (angle of maximum dorsiflexion marked) and then plantar flexes the foot (away from the body) as far as possible. The measure of ankle flexibility is the angle between maximum dorsiflexion and plantarflexion.

Figure 5.10 Grip strength test.

Miscellaneous Tests

There are two other tests that have proved successful.

Wrist Strength Test

This test determines the strength of the forearm and hand muscles, which are very important for a firm grip during stroke production (Figure 5.10).

Abdominal Strength Test

This test determines the functional strength of the abdominal muscles. The player lies on the floor with the lower limbs flexed to 90° at the knee joint and the arms crossed over the chest, as shown in Figure 5.11, with the hands grasping the opposite shoulder. The test involves performing as many bent-leg sit-ups as can be performed in 60 seconds. Each sit-up involves raising the trunk to a point at which the elbows can touch the knees.

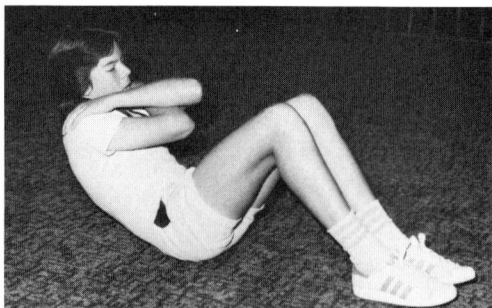

Figure 5.11 Abdominal strength test.

References

Analysis of Stroke Production
1. Sony Videostrobe System, Sony Australia Pty. Ltd., Australia.

Game Analysis
2. Hensley, L. D.: "Analysis of Stroking Errors Committed In Championship Tennis Competition." Proceedings of *A National Symposium on the Racquet Sports* (ed. J. L. Groppel). University of Illinois Press, Urbana-Champaign, 1979, pp. 225–235.
3. Tilmanis, G. A.: *Advanced Tennis for Coaches, Teachers and Players.* Australia and New Zealand Book Co., Sydney, Australia, 1975.

Tennis Test Battery
4. Pyke, F. S., Elliott, B. C., and Pyke, J. E.: "Performance Testing of Tennis and Squash Players." *British Journal of Sports Medicine, 8*(2):80–86, 1974.

6

Training for Tennis

Fitness is an integral part of the game of tennis, whether one is playing for enjoyment during leisure hours or competing in a tournament. This chapter, which provides the coach, teacher, or competitive player with an understanding of the theoretical basis of training, may also be of interest to the social player who desires a greater insight into the components of a tennis training program. The concept of "fitness for tennis" is examined here in five broad categories: (1) energy systems involved in the game, (2) tennis as a training program in itself, (3) squad preparation, (4) squad organization, and (5) tournament preparation.

Energy Systems Involved in the Game

Tennis is a game comprising repeated bursts of activity interspersed with short rest periods between shots and longer rest periods between rallies and when changing ends. Very little research has been reported on the energy requirements of the game, but heart rates and periods of play monitored throughout a game have indicated that tennis is an anaerobic activity (80 per cent) that requires a sound aerobic base (20 per cent). Therefore, an important determinant of a tennis player's success will revolve around the anaerobic systems. Anaerobic activity, which is the production of energy without oxygen, is of two types.

The first is the phosphate energy system, which lasts for 5 to 10 seconds and can be replenished very quickly. The second is the lactic acid system (glycogen), which provides energy for sustained efforts of 1 to 2

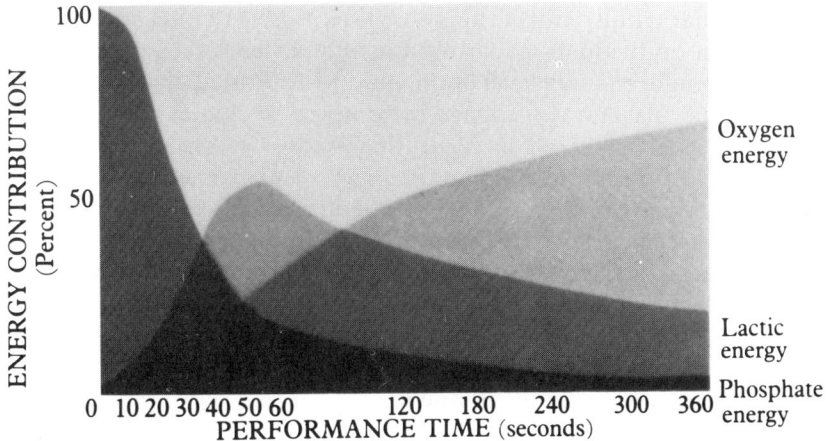

Figure 6.1 Contribution of the energy systems to tennis. (From Pyke: *Towards Better Coaching*, 1980.)

minutes. This results in the accumulation of lactic acid and accompanying muscular fatigue (Figure 6.1).

The energy requirements for each rally depend primarily on the length of the rally. If the rallies are short (5 to 10 seconds) a player would show few signs of fatigue, owing to rapid replacement of the phosphate system. However, if the rallies are extended, a player would rely on the lactic acid system for energy, which requires a longer replacement period. During recovery from each effort, oxygen is used to help replenish these anaerobic energy sources. Hence the aerobic (with oxygen) energy system is also important to the tennis player. The training methods employed to develop each of these energy sources should be specific to the game.

Tennis: A Training Program In Itself

Many tennis players believe that the intensity of playing singles at practice is sufficient effort to produce a training effect that will be of assistance during a grueling three-hour singles match. The general public is also looking to lifetime recreational activities, such as tennis, as a means of developing or maintaining a level of fitness needed for a healthy lifestyle. Tennis as a competitive sport or a recreational activity is therefore often selected in the expectation that it will provide sufficient intensity and duration of participation to elicit a training effect, especially in the cardiorespiratory (heart-lung) system.

Astrand[3] stated that optimal training effects are obtained when stress levels reach 75 to 85 per cent of the individual's maximum heart rate.

Recreational tennis on a competitive level raised the heart rate to 70 per cent of the individual's predicted maximum heart rate, a result that was independent of the skill level of the player.[4] Intermediate to advanced-level recreational players who engage in competitive singles competitions were found to exercise at an intensity that could be considered adequate to provide cardiorespiratory conditioning.[6,7] Tournament singles, however, caused the heart rate of the two competitors to be elevated to 85 per cent and 81 per cent, respectively, of their maximum value.[5]

Tennis, particularly singles play, can therefore contribute to improving and then maintaining the fitness levels of recreational players. Tournament players, however, require additional high-intensity on-court and off-court training to supplement their match play and practice, if a peak performance level is to be attained.

Squad Preparation: General Training Principles

There are a number of training principles that must be coordinated if an effective tennis training program is to be formulated. A brief review of these training principles follows.

Individual Needs

Each player has an individual requirement that must be determined by appropriate fitness tests. Results then can be compared with required levels of performance, and individual training programs can be adjusted accordingly.

Specificity

Specificity in training means that the best way to train is either by playing the game or by completing drill routines that simulate (and overload) the actions of the game. In other words, all training programs must be specific to developing the requirements of the game and to the needs of the individual. Specificity, with respect to on-court practices, dictates that drills be pressure-oriented, yet allow fluent stroke production by removing the "win using any technique" attitude often adopted during competitive play. Off-court training must also be specific, exercising the energy systems and particular muscle areas predominantly used during play.

Overload

For improvement to occur, the systems to be improved must be stressed to a level beyond which the individual is accustomed. In tennis, training over-

TABLE 6.1 Threshold Heart Rates for Moderate and Intense Training Effects

Age	Average Maximal Heart Rate (bpm)	Moderate Training Effect (Distance Training)			Intense Training Effect (Interval Training)		
		Resting Heart Rate (bpm)			Resting Heart Rate (bpm)		
		60	70	80	60	70	80
10	215	153*†	157	161	184**	186	188
15	205	147	151	155	176	178	180
20	200	144	148	152	172	174	176
30	190	138	142	146	164	166	168
40	180	132	136	140	156	158	160

Calculation of "Training Effect"

* Step 1	Take the resting heart rate	60 bpm
Step 2	Approximate maximal heart rate from table	215 bpm
Step 3	Calculate the difference	155 bpm
Step 4	Take 60% of this difference	93 bpm
Step 5	Add the answer from Step 4 to your resting level	153 bpm

† Since the heart rate begins to slow down as soon as exercise ceases, the post-exercise pulse count must be started within 5 seconds of stopping exercise. This pulse count should be taken for 15 seconds and then multiplied by four to give the rate per minute (see Figure 6.2).

** For interval training the 60% in Step 4 is replaced by 80% of the difference between resting heart rate and age-adjusted maximal heart rate.

load is linked with the concept of a "training effect." In training the anaerobic and aerobic energy systems, it is important to monitor players' heart rates (see Table 6.1 and Figure 6.2) to allow for individual differences and to check that work is of sufficient intensity to elicit a "training effect."

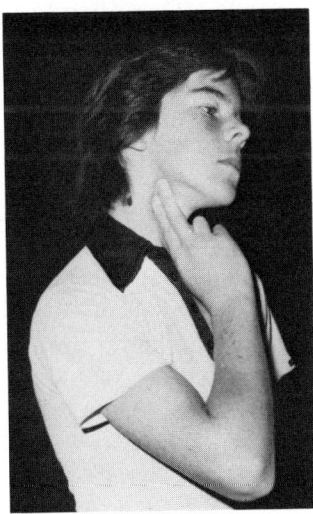

Figure 6.2 Carotid pulse (in neck) taken using the second and third fingers of the hand against the side of the neck.

Progression in Training

All training, whether on-court or off-court, must begin at a level the individual finds easy to maintain. Changes in the intensity of training should then be gradual to ensure that muscle soreness and injury do not occur.

Regularity and Frequency

Improvement does not happen without frequent training sessions, and any elevation in performance level is soon lost without continuation of this training. Physiological improvement will result from three running or weight sessions per week. Maintenance of this improvement requires one, but preferably two, sessions per week.

Motivation

To help obtain continued effort during training sessions, the coach should vary the routine to keep players motivated. Positive reinforcement and an explanation of the reason for the type of training being undertaken are required if players are expected to maintain a desirable attitude toward training. This concept is discussed further in the psychological development section of this book.

Evaluation

Each player must be evaluated continually to ensure progress, as a form of motivation, and to prevent overtraining, which may occur when the stress of training linked to possible social problems may be too severe for the player to handle.

Squad Organization: Physiological Development

Tennis, both as a form of recreation and as a competitive sport, is a year-round activity. Physical preparation for competitive tennis must therefore be integrated with the playing year, outlined in Figure 6.3. Professional circuit players cannot afford the luxury of foundation and preseason sections to their programs, since the tournament calendar dictates when they must "peak" and when they have time to rest. Young players who aspire to achieve state or national rankings should, however, integrate the training principles discussed in the previous section into a year-round training program. The following sections covering on-court and off-court fitness drills, on-court skill-fitness drills, and a typical training schedule are included to provide a base from which all coaches can formulate programs that are tailored to the needs of their players.

Figure 6.3 The tennis year.

Off-Court Training

Running

Before being exposed to the strenuous interval routines, which are more closely allied to the demands of the game, the player should "build a foundation" during the off and preseason. The concept of building a foundation relates to a player improving the capacity to consume oxygen and attaining levels of flexibility, muscular strength, and endurance necessary for competitive tennis. These training methods should be combined with skill practices aimed specifically at improving any weaknesses in stroke production.

In order to make the running component of this training specific to tennis, the duration of the run should gradually be increased to beyond an hour, with the intensity of effort being 70 to 80 per cent of maximum. That is, if a player can run about 7.5 miles (12 kilometers) in an hour, then training runs should be aimed at achieving about 6 miles (10 kilometers) in that time. This longer, continuous running can then be blended with Fartlek training,[8] in which the runner engages in short sprints approximately 65 to 85 yards (60 to 80 meters) throughout the continuous training effort.

As stated earlier, tennis is an anaerobic game that is made up of short, intense work bouts followed by periods of recovery. The longer, slower interval running should also play a role in preseason training as well as in the early stages of training during the season. A running program follows.

1. 4 × 100 meters in 13 seconds, departing every 1 minute
2. 3 × 200 meters in 32 seconds, departing every 2 minutes
3. 2 × 400 meters in 68 seconds, departing every 4 minutes
4. 3 × 200 meters in 32 seconds, departing every 2 minutes
5. 4 × 100 meters in 13 seconds, departing every 1 minute

When an interval training program is being constructed, a number of variables can be manipulated to make it specific to the game. These include the duration and intensity of the work period and the number of repetitions of the work-to-recovery sequence to be completed. Research has indicated that a work-to-recovery ratio of 1:2 is the most appropriate to tennis,[4] since too short a recovery period would tend to exhaust the player too quickly. If a smaller ratio is used (1:1), then longer rest periods must follow the interval drills to ensure that lactic acid does not accumulate in large quantities. Lactic acid buildup can occur if the work period either is too long or involves too great an effort, and if the recovery period is too short.

As the season progresses the interval training should be supplementary to on-court work, since a player should be playing five to six times per week. The shorter, faster interval running that closely approximates the energy demands of the game should then be completed once, preferably twice, per week.

1. 8 × 25 meters in 4 seconds, departing every 15 seconds
2. 6 × 50 meters in 7 seconds, departing every 30 seconds
3. 4 × 75 meters in 10 seconds, departing every 45 seconds
4. 6 × 50 meters in 7 seconds departing every 30 seconds
5. 8 × 25 meters in 4 seconds, departing every 15 seconds

The interval training court sprint routine can also be used during the playing season. This routine can be completed at the end of each racket training session, as follows: (1) Start at the baseline, (2) run and touch the left net post, (3) run and touch the back corner, (4) run and touch the right net post, (5) run and touch the back corner, and (6) return to (1).

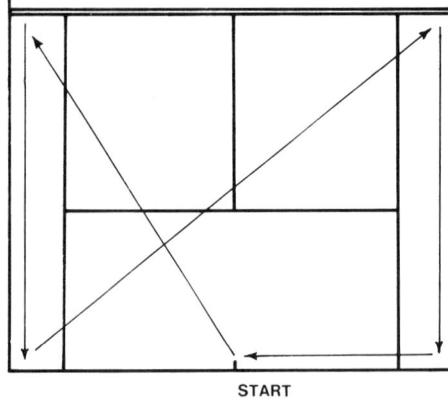

Figure 6.4 On-court interval sprints (with racket).

Muscle Strength and Endurance Training

Strength training should not be thought of as a replacement for on-court racket work or as something that can be used to keep a player occupied when the weather prohibits skill practice. Muscle force, which is required to control fluent stroke production and provide a stable hitting position for impact, is a prerequisite for all players aspiring to national or international rankings. To ensure that weight training is specific to tennis, it is necessary to exercise the muscle groups that are used in the game.

If muscle strength and endurance conditioning are considered to be important, then the focus should be on three major areas.

Training Time

Muscular strength and endurance work should be integrated into a year-round program. A six-week period during the Active Rest and Foundation sections of the program should be devoted to three sessions per week of weight training.[11] This number can be reduced to two sessions per week during preseason training and can be reduced further to one session per week during the playing season.

Type of Training

The decision on the type of training is governed by the availability of equipment. An isokinetic training regimen should be followed if the equipment is available.

An *isokinetic contraction* occurs when the muscle shortens as tension is developed through a full range of motion performed at a constant speed. Isokinetic machines permit the player to exercise at a constant speed against a resistance that changes to meet alterations in

A *B*

Figure 6.5 The weight lifted is determined by how much can be lifted from *A* to *B* while the muscles are in their weakest pulling position.

A. Bench press.

B. Half squat.

C. Forearm curl.

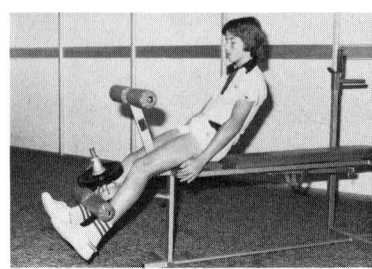

D. Quadricep extension.

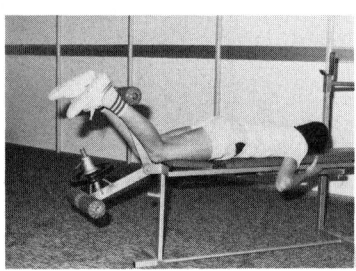

E. Hamstring flexion.

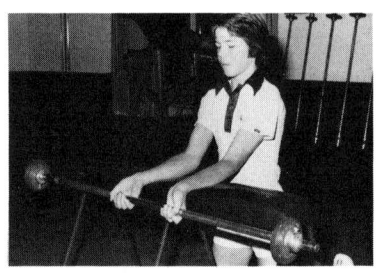

F. Wrist curl.

G. Sit-ups.

H. Behind-neck press.

I. Forehand drive.

J. Backhand drive.

Figure 6.8 Strength training for tennis using the isotonic lifting principle. (Spotters should be stationed at each end of the bar, particularly for exercises *A* and *B*.)

3. The partner who provides the opposition for the isometric contraction should *not* force the person into a new position of improved stretch.
4. The exercises should be performed at less than maximum effort until both participants are accustomed to the activity.

Individual stretching exercises, adopting the concept of static stretch, can also be useful for improving flexibility. The following individual "stretch and hold" flexibility activities are an alternative to the Holt 3S partner exercises. They should be performed slowly, with an emphasis on holding the fully flexed position statically. Bouncing should *not* be used to attain a greater reach for any of the exercises (Figure 6.10A to H).

Hamstring Stretch
The player lies with hands behind the head, then raises the right leg as far as possible, keeping it straight, and holds for 15 seconds. This procedure is then repeated for the left leg. Rest and repeat.

Trunk Rotation
The player, with arms extended, twists to the left, holds for 15 seconds, then twists to the right. Rest and repeat.

Calf Stretch
The player stands on the balls of the feet, lowers slowly, holds for 15 seconds, then extends to a position on the toes that is also held for 15 seconds. Rest and repeat.

Groin Stretch (*The Butterfly*)
While sitting on the ground, the player grasps the feet and leans forward, holding for 20 seconds. Rest and repeat.

Side Trunk Stretch
The player stands straight with both feet flat on the floor, extends one arm along the side of the leg as far as possible, and holds for 10 seconds. Repeat with other arm.

Back Stretch
The player reclines on the back, brings the lower limbs over the head, then holds for 10 seconds. The lower limbs must be kept straight. Rest and repeat.

Arm Stretch
The player tries to hold hands with himself behind his/her back. Rest and repeat.

Trunk Stretch
With fingers interlaced and arms straight over the head, the player forces the arms backward, holding for 10 seconds. Rest and repeat.

A. Hamstring stretch.

B. Trunk rotation.

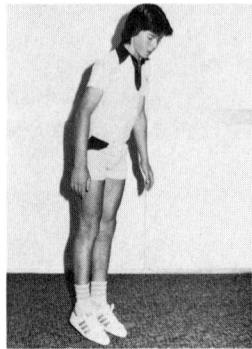
C. Calf stretch.

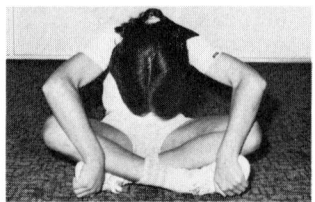
D. Groin stretch.

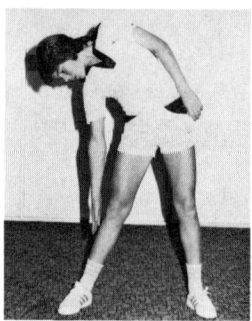
E. Side trunk stretch.

F. Back stretch.

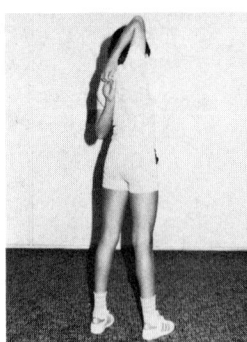
G. Arm stretch.

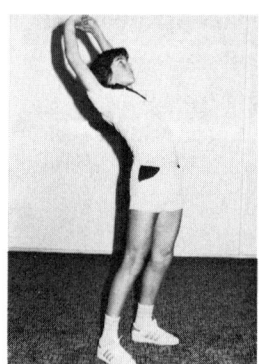
H. Trunk stretch.

Figure 6.10 Stretch and hold flexibility exercises.

125 Squad Organization: Physiological Development

Figure 6.11 Pre- and post-match mobility-stretching exercises.

A. Ankle mobility.

B. Knee mobility.

C. Hamstring stretch.

D. Hamstring stretch.

E. Groin and side stretch.

F. Side stretch.

G. Back stretch.

H. Neck mobility.

I. Shoulder mobility.

J. Shoulder mobility.

K. Hand mobility.

These flexibility exercises are only some of the many activities that can be used to increase the flexibility of the body areas predominantly used in tennis.

In performing these exercises the following precautions should be strictly adhered to:

1. The exercises must be performed slowly.
2. Each activity must be stopped when the position adopted begins to hurt.
3. Bouncing into a new position (ballistic stretching) must be avoided.

A series of pre-match and post-match mobility-stretching exercises that have proved successful is shown in Figure 6.11A to K.

On-Court Training: Skill-Fitness Drills

These drills can be used throughout the training year because they can enhance stroke production and are specific to fitness development. The following drills are oriented to skill or fitness or a combination of both.

Scatter Drill (Figure 6.12)

A feeder hits consecutive balls to different court locations for a player to return using the appropriate shot. This drill ideally can be run for 1 minute with a 2- or 3-minute rest before being repeated (Figure 6.12).

Combination Drill

This drill requires each player to return a sequence of shots from the positions shown in Figure 6.13. Two typical sequences controlled by a coach or feeder are described:

1. Forehand, backhand, forehand approach shot, volley 2, and a smash.
2. Service, volley 1, volley 2, recover lob with a forehand, backhand, and a backhand off a short ball for a winner.

The player then runs to pick up the same number of balls as were hit in the drill before returning to the center of the baseline ready for the same or a changed sequence of strokes.

Two-on-one Drills

In these drills one player is opposed to two players who have a ready supply of balls. The drill may be played first to 11 points and then rotated, or it may be played for a set period. Two typical examples of this drill type are described:

1. Two players are at the net, and the third player is at the center of the baseline. Either net player hits a relatively easy forehand to the baseline player, who must try to win the rally (Figure 6.14).

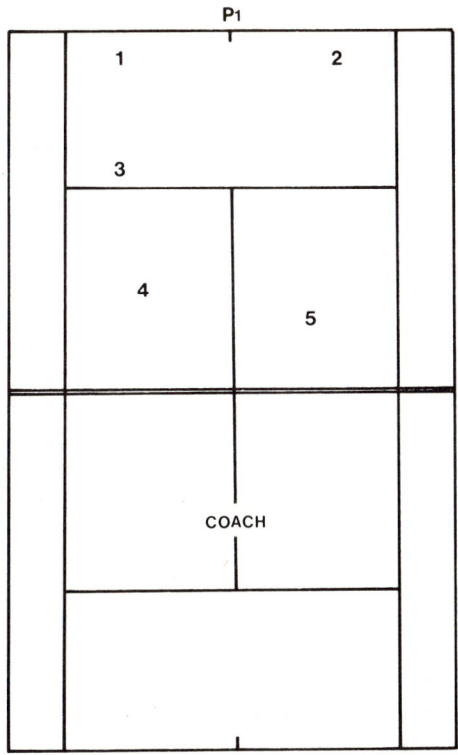

Figure 6.12 Scatter drill.

S	SERVE
F/B	FOREHAND OR BACKHAND DRIVE
AS	APPROACH SHOT
V_1	FIRST VOLLEY
V_2	SECOND VOLLEY
PDS	PICK UP A DROP SHOT
RL	RECOVER A LOB
SM	SMASH

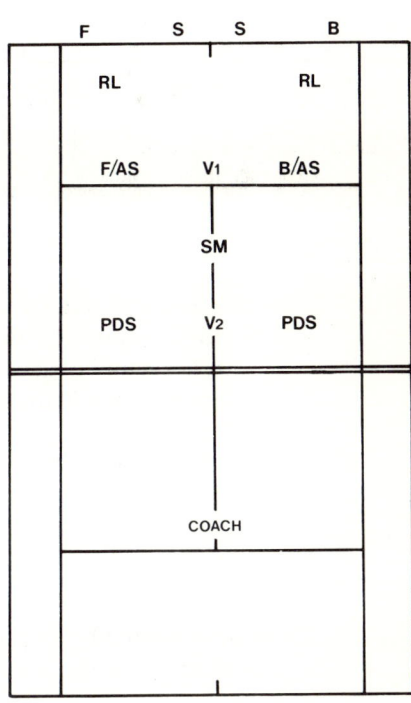

Figure 6.13 Combination drill.

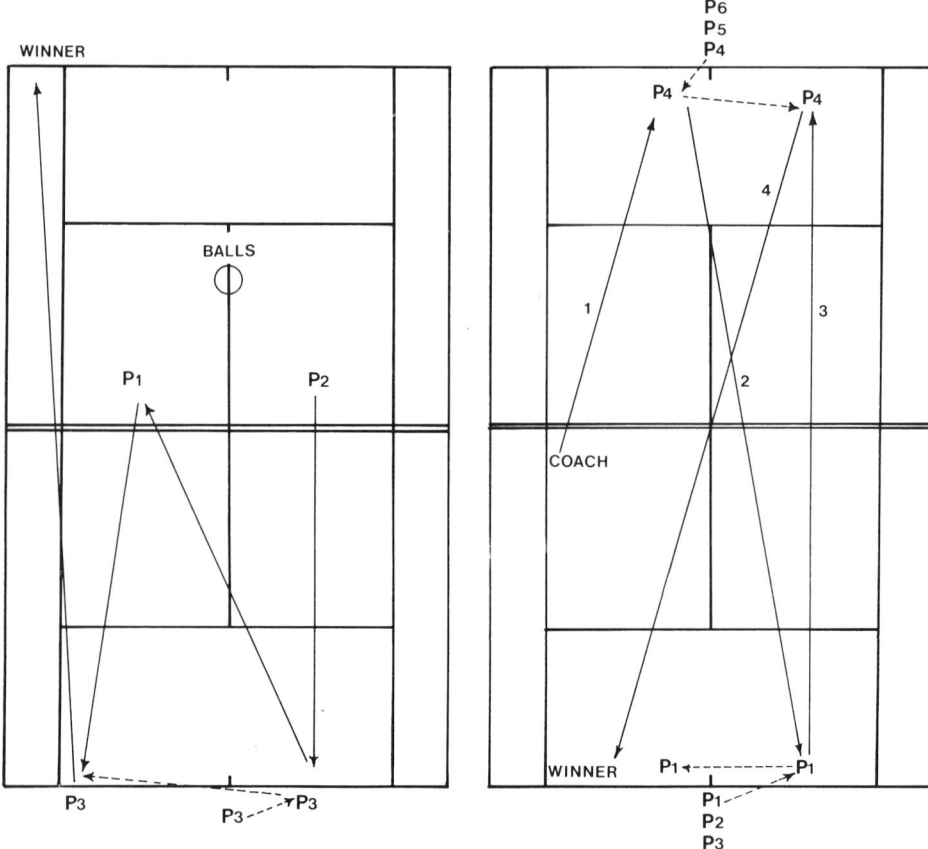

Figure 6.14 Two-on-one drill practicing groundstrokes and volleys.

Figure 6.15 One-on-one drill practicing groundstrokes.

2. The players may be in the reverse positions, with the two players on the baseline and the third player on the net. The rally is started with a groundstroke from the baseline to the net player, and the following rally is then played to a conclusion.

One-on-one Drills

Using the court positions shown in Figure 6.15, any combination of one-on-one drills may be operated having two, four, or six players to a court. Two such sequences are suggested:

1. The coach or feeder hits the ball to player 4 on the baseline, who rallies with player 1 until the point is completed. Players then change ends, the winner of each rally scoring one point.

2. The coach hits a short ball to player 5, who plays an approach shot and takes up a volley position at the net. A rally with player 2 follows, with scoring and movement as in 1.

The introduction of scoring provides for competition within the drill situation; however, as long as "formalized sets" are not played, it appears that fluent stroke production does not suffer.

Stretch Volley Drill

The coach hits as many volleys to a net player as is possible in one minute. The player must return all these with a volley (Figure 6.16).

The number of drills a coach may use to improve both fitness and stroke production is limited only by the coach's imagination.

Weekly Tennis Training Schedule

The in-season schedule shown in Table 6.2 should be used as a guide for those players (14 to 18 years of age) aspiring to state ranking or selection. A number of sessions should be deleted for those players who do not seek such

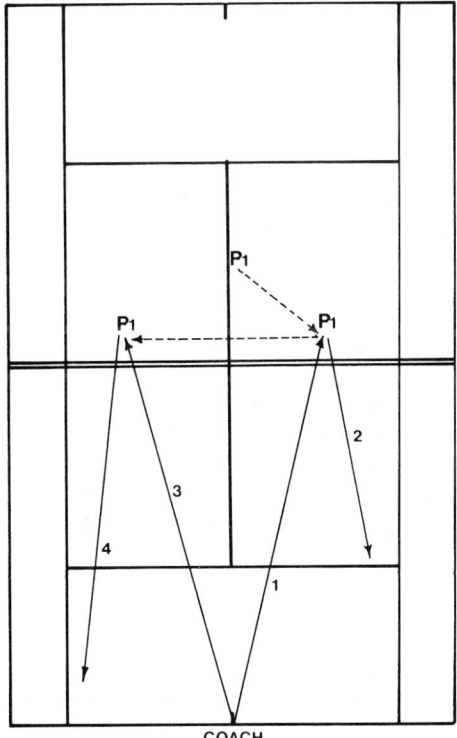

Figure 6.16 Stretch volley drill.

TABLE 6.2 Weekly Training Schedule

Monday	**Medium Training Day**
	Flexibility exercises Half-hour specific pressure drills (with coach) Half-hour service practice
Tuesday	**Heavy Training Day**
	Two-hours stroke production as directed by the coach Match practice Off-court interval training routines
Wednesday	**Medium Training Day**
	Flexibility exercises One-hour specific pressure drills Half-hour stroke production (remedial work) Off-court strength work
Thursday	**Heavy Training Day**
	One-hour specific drill routines One three-set match Off-court interval training routines
Friday	**Light Training Day**
	Flexibility exercises Half-hour stroke production (with coach) Half-hour match (coach present)
Saturday	**Competitive Tennis**
	Flexibility exercises Competition match
Sunday	**Heavy Training Day**
	Two-hour specific drill or stroke routines One three-set match against a partner of similar ability Off-court interval training routines

a high level of achievement; however, players whose goal is national selection will have to train even harder than indicated in this program.

All sessions must be preceded by a thorough warm-up. Ideally, players will work in squads so that coaches can both supervise the drill routines and continually monitor stroke production. A typical squad training format should be as follows:

1. Warm-up (5 minutes)
2. Flexibility exercises (5 minutes)
3. "11-up" all court drill (10 minutes). In this drill the rally is started by a bounce-hit backhand. Scoring: first player to 11 points wins, with the service (a backhand) rotating from players 1 through 4.

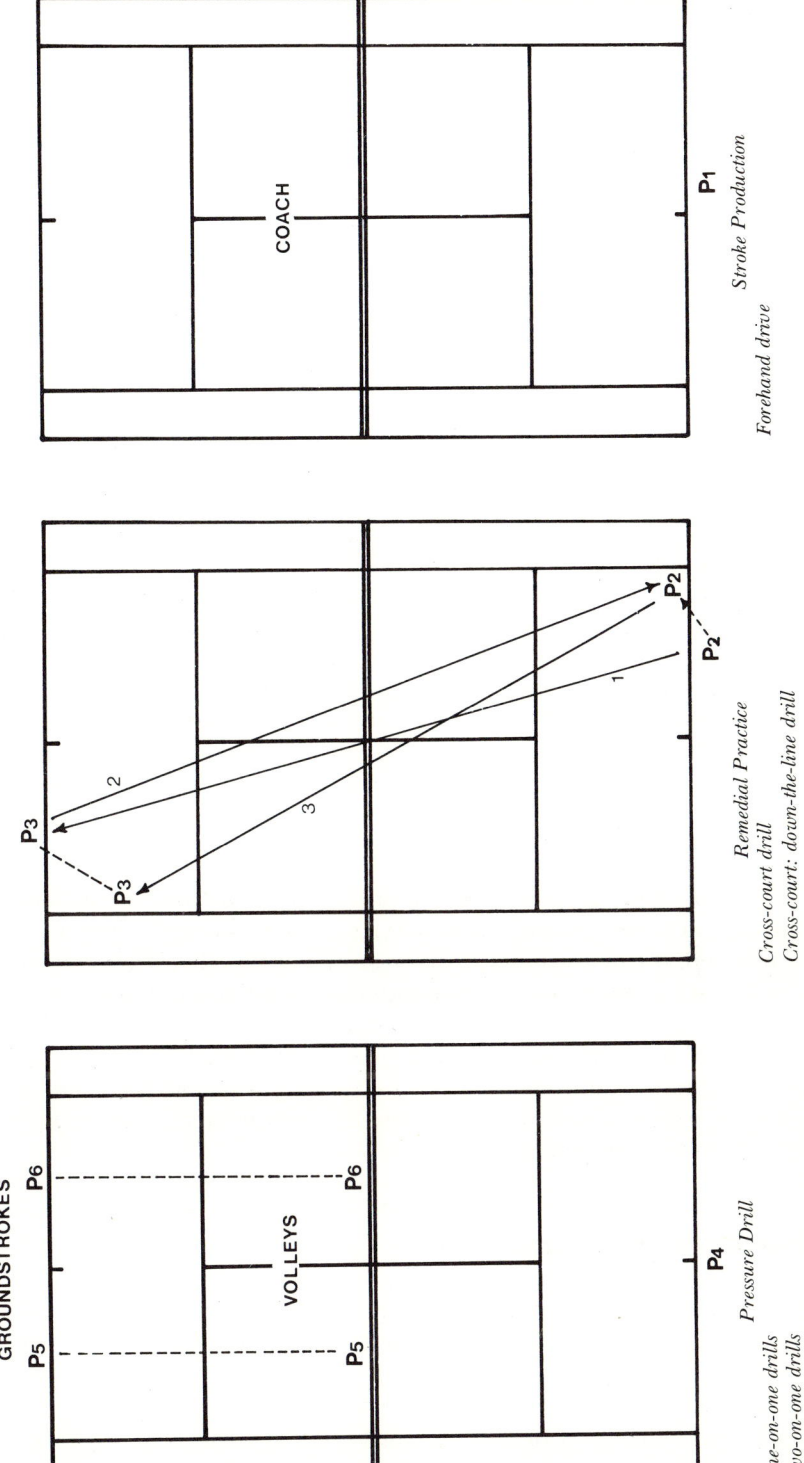

Figure 6.17 Squad organization.

4. Drills: Stroke production (60 minutes). The coach, having explained what stroke will be highlighted in the session, divides the squad into three groups (Figure 6.17).
5. Games (60 minutes)

   1 vs. 2 court 1
   3 vs. 4 court 2
   5 vs. 6 court 3

   Each match will be based on the total number of points won in 20 minutes using a table tennis serving format; that is, the service changes every five serves and ends are changed at the end of every ten points. At the end of 20 minutes,

   winner of 1 vs. 2 plays winner of 3 vs. 4
   loser of 1 vs. 2 plays winner of 5 vs. 6
   loser of 5 vs. 6 plays loser of 3 vs. 4

   The same format for change is used at the end of the following 20 minutes. Both players will complete six court sprints at the end of each service sequence. In a court sprint, the player starts at the center of the baseline, sprints to the front of the court and touches the net, then returns to the center of the baseline.
6. Cool-down (10 minutes' slow run). During the slow run the coach should briefly discuss the training session or coming events. This run should be used to cement group cohesiveness and encourage better training performances.

A year-round tennis program can now be structured so that anaerobic capacity, aerobic capacity, flexibility, muscular strength, and endurance supplement the many hours spent on stroke production. Players who do not aspire to the epitome of performance should still use the principles set out in this chapter to provide the physiological basis for their training. In conclusion, it can be said that any tennis match is likely to tire both players, and the fitter of the two will not necessarily win. On the other hand, a superior stroke-maker will often lose to an opponent possessing greater fitness and determination.

Tournament Preparation

The successful tennis player, having developed sound stroke mechanics and having reached a high level of fitness, must also prepare systematically for each tournament. Adequate sleep, mental preparation, food and fluid intake, and a thorough warm-up prior to each match complement the stroke mechanics and fitness, enhancing a player's chances of success.

Final Stages of Preparation

The player should follow a normal training program until the Thursday before a tournament starting on Saturday. Thursday and Friday should be light workdays with emphasis on fluent stroke production and mental preparation. Strenuous training sessions should be avoided in the two days before a tournament begins.

With such a long competitive season, the coach has a problem in deciding on when to "peak" the individual members of the squad. Tournaments may be a month apart, so some players striving for state selection or ranking need to "peak" for specific trials or tournaments. The optimal number of times a player can be expected to "peak" in one year is about four or five. Individual player characteristics should, however, direct the coach in determining how many "peaks in performance" a player can effectively produce over one season.

Food Intake

The tennis player should follow a well-balanced diet containing the daily essential nutrients (carbohydrates, fats, proteins), vitamins, and minerals necessary for participation in tennis. These can be obtained from the four food groups.

Protein, including meat, fish, poultry, peas, and beans
Dairy foods, including milk, cheese, yogurt, and ice cream
Cereals and grains, including bread, cereal, rice, and spaghetti
Fruits and vegetables, including apples, oranges, and salads

By virtue of the high energy expenditures of the game and training programs, a tennis player requires a greater caloric intake than a sedentary person. A diet high in carbohydrates (spaghetti, bread, potatoes, rice, and so on) should be followed for three days before a tournament.

A pregame meal high in carbohydrates should be eaten approximately three hours before a match. If a liquid carbohydrate meal (chilled) is preferred, this may be ingested approximately two hours before a match. Meat, other proteins, and fats should be avoided in the pregame meal. No glucose or concentrated forms of carbohydrate (such as chocolate) should be taken in the hour before a match because this can induce a low blood sugar level, which reduces both energy capacity and skill performance.

Fluid Intake and Replacement

Adequate fluid replacement during both training and competition is essential if optimal performance is to be maintained. Fluid replacement is important because it helps reduce dehydration, which can result from heavy sweating, and reduces the possibility of overheating. Although the level of fluid intake is an individual characteristic, the following guidelines should be followed:

1. A player should be well hydrated before competition. Approximately 10 to 16 oz (300 to 500 milliliters) of fluid should be taken 30 minutes before training or competition.
2. Approximately 4 oz (120 milliliters) of fluid should be taken at each change of end.
3. A player can drink more than thirst would dictate at the end of a match or training session.

Water is the most important ingredient of fluid replacement. If commercial electrolyte and glucose solutions are used, they should be diluted[12] to achieve ideal concentration levels (use approximately twice the amount of water suggested for a particular amount of mix).

A close check should be kept on changes in body weight during play, particularly in hot or humid conditions. A procedure that can be used to monitor body weight is as follows:

1. The player should be weighed before a match (dressed in minimal clothing).
2. The amount of fluid taken onto the court and the amount remaining immediately following the game should be noted. One quart (about 1 liter) of water weighs 2 pounds (about 1 kilogram).
3. The player should be weighed again at the end of the match (dressed as in the initial weighing) before the ingestion of any more fluid.

When fluid replacement is insufficient to maintain body weight within 3 per cent of the pre-match level, excessive demands are placed on the cardiovascular and thermoregulatory systems of the player, and decrements in performance are certain to occur.[13] Fluid replacement during competition is therefore essential if optimal performance is to be maintained throughout a tournament.

References

Energy Systems Involved in the Game
1. Fox, E. L.: *Sports Physiology*. W.B. Saunders Co., Philadelphia, 1979.
2. Pyke, F. S.: "Strategy of Training." Proceedings of Sports Coaching Seminar, Melbourne, 1975. In *Sports Coaching*. Australian Government Printer, Canberra, Australia, 1976.

Tennis: A Training Program in Itself
3. Astrand, P. O. and Rodahl, K.: *Textbook of Work Physiology*. McGraw-Hill Book Co., Sydney, Australia, 1970.

4. Docherty, D.: "A Comparison of Heart Rate Responses of Players During Participation in Tennis, Badminton, and Squash Relative to Their Age and Skill Level." (unpublished paper)
5. Kilderry, R.: "What A Match Takes Out of You." *Sunday Times*, Perth, Australia, 12 November 1978.
6. Misner, J. E., Boileau, R. A., Courvoisier, D., Slaughter, M. H., and Bloomfield, D. K.: "Cardiovascular Stress Associated With the Recreational Tennis Play of Middle-Aged Males." *American Corrective Therapy Journal, 34*(1):4–8, 1980.
7. Wilmore, J. H., Davis, J. A., O'Brien, R. S., Vodak, P. A., Walder, G. R., and Amsterdam, E. A.: "Physiological Alterations Consequent to 20-Week Conditioning Programs of Bicycling, Tennis, and Jogging." *Medicine and Science in Sports and Exercise, 12*(1):1–8, 1980.

Squad Preparation: Physiological Development
8. Fox, E. L.: *Sports Physiology.* W.B. Saunders Co., Philadelphia, 1979.
9. Holt, L. E.: *Scientific Stretching for Sport.* Dalhousie University Press, Halifax, Nova Scotia, 1974.
10. Pucci, T. and Stucky, J.: "Strength Program for Tennis Players." *Scholastic Coach, 48*(6):6)–61, 1979.
11. Pyke, F. S.: "Physiology of Training." *Towards Better Coaching* (ed. F. S. Pyke). Australian Government Publishing Service, Canberra, Australia, 1980, pp. 111–144.

Tournament Preparation
12. Fitch, K. and Pyke, F.: "Factors Influencing Sports Performance." *Towards Better Coaching* (ed. F. S. Pyke). Australian Government Publishing Service, Canberra, Australia, 1980, pp. 177–213.
13. Wyndham, C. H.: "Heat Stroke and Hyperthermia in Marathon Runners in the Marathon: Physiological, Medical, Epidemiological, and Psychological Studies." In *Annals of the New York Academy of Sciences* (ed. P. Milvy), *301:*128–138, 1977.

Controversy in Tennis

This chapter attempts to answer some of the controversial questions that have caused disagreement among coaches and players.

Controversy 1

It is possible to alter substantially the period that a ball is in contact with the racket strings by altering stroke production.

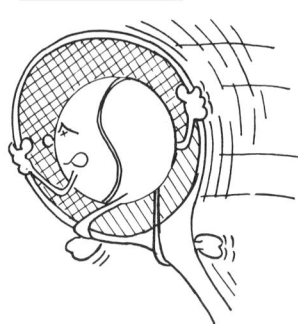

Fact

The time of contact between the ball and the strings varies minimally from approximately 3 to 5 milliseconds.[11] It is therefore impossible to alter substantially the time of contact by altering stroke mechanics.

Application

The ball is in contact with the strings only for a very brief period. This dictates that the racket should be in the desired position before impact so that the relative paths of the racket and ball decide the type of spin imparted, rather than any sudden movement that is attempted while the ball is in contact with the strings.

Controversy 2

There is no benefit, other than length of reach, in using a closed or semiclosed hitting stance.

Fact

A closed or semiclosed stance enables correct body rotation and transfer of weight onto the front foot for impact. These factors then enable the racket to follow a flattened arc before contact, increasing the momentum (mass times velocity) of the racket in the desired direction of the hit.[16]

Application

Flattening the arc of the swing makes it easier to hit a ball along an intended direction, since the contact point that will produce this effect is elongated. A closed or semiclosed stance is therefore important for both the accuracy of the return and the amount of force that can be imparted to the ball.

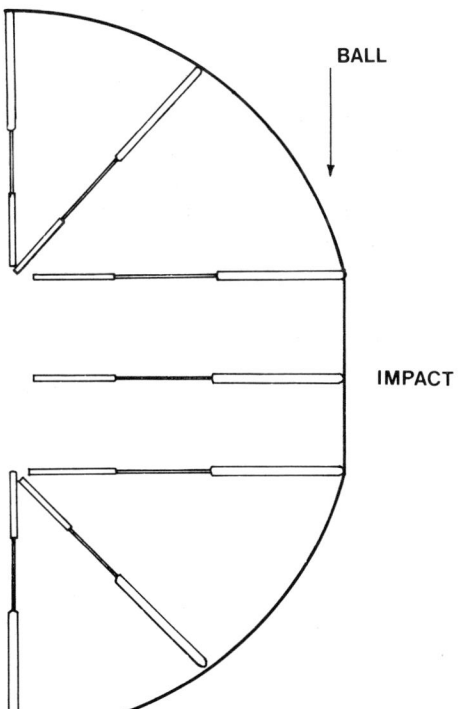

Controversy 3

Firmness of grip is a major contributing factor in obtaining a controlled return.

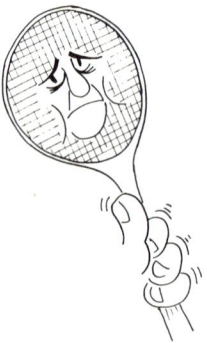

Fact

The role played by grip firmness is still somewhat controversial. One line of thought is that, for a given ball velocity before impact, the ball velocity after impact with the center of the strings is independent of the firmness of the grip. Some research, more allied to the requirements of the game, found that a firm grip is a prerequisite for optimal performance, particularly when off-center impacts occur.[11]

Application

The racket must be gripped firmly on impact to ensure an effective return, particularly for balls impacted off center. The racket should be gripped firmly before the impact of a ball hit with great speed. Grip firmness before impact can, however, have a harmful effect on the service action. The fluent movement of the racket in the serve requires a supple wrist and, since the ball is under the control of the server, any firming of the grip should be timed precisely with the impact.[11] Tactics, however, may dictate that a loosened grip be used for some touch and angled strokes.

Controversy 4

Players have enough time to change grips during a rally.

Fact

Tennis players must initiate a response before the ball arrives, to allow enough time to complete a controlled stroke. The time taken for the ball to travel the distances *XA, XB* and *XC* are as follows:[6]

   XA: Service return
           Velocity of ball: 85 mph (38 m/s) average speed
           Time of ball travel: 0.658 second
   XB: Groundstroke from a groundstroke
           Velocity of ball: 40 mph (17.9 m/s) average speed
           Time of ball travel: 1.341 seconds
   XC: Volley from a groundstroke
           Velocity of ball: 50 mph (22.4 m/s) average speed
           Time of ball travel: 0.625 second

The movement time (time to prepare for the stroke to be played) would be approximately 0.4 second for a ball hit to the player. This then gives the player time to react to the ball.

Application

There is then sufficient time for a player to change the grip for a service return, a groundstroke played from a groundstroke, or a volley played from a groundstroke. In rapid volley exchanges the player may have to maintain the same grip for both forehand and backhand volleys.

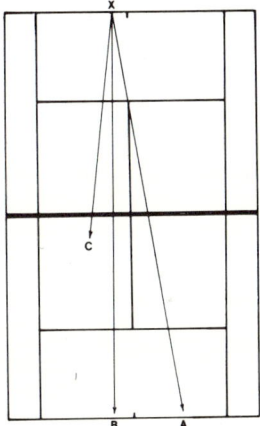

Controversy 5

Can the size of a child's tennis racket hinder the learning of a sound stroke production?

Fact

The size of any tennis racket should be tailored to the physical stature of the player. With children, the weight of the racket, although important, is not the

most critical factor to be considered. The key factor is where the weight is distributed relative to the player's hand. A child should use a racket that is light and that has the weight concentrated relatively close to the pivot point between the hand and the racquet.[4] Such a racket also improves the spatial orientation between the young player and the ball.

Application

A child's racket should be appropriate in size and length for the child's body build. Very young children most certainly should use the new sub-junior rackets.

Controversy 6

Should a beginner be taught the one-handed or two-handed backhand drive?

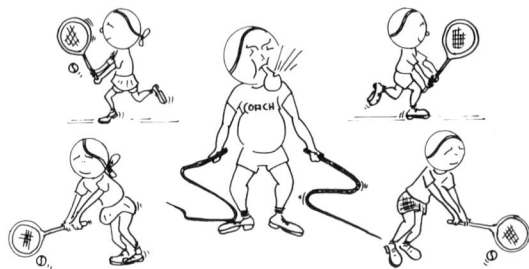

Fact

There is no evidence to suggest that one technique is superior to the other; each has favorable attributes.

The one-handed backhand provides a longer reach, a more natural movement with one arm, and the basis for the hitting position that will be used when the backhand volley is taught. With this stroke it is possible to hit the ball flat, with underspin, or with topspin when using one hand. In addition, it can be used on all court surfaces with only minor technique modifications.

With the two-handed backhand the player has greater strength to control both the racket and the force imparted to the ball. This stroke is deceptive, since either hand may be used to change the direction of the shot. Also inherent in this technique is the ability to hit the ball with topspin because of the low position of the racket at the start of the forward-swing phase of the stroke. It is easier to hit the backhand when the upper limbs act as a single unit, thereby reducing the tendency to lead with the elbow. This stroke removes the need to change the grip from forehand to backhand (some coaches, however, teach that the lower hand should change grip so that the player is capable of playing a one-handed backhand if forced to stretch).

Application

It appears that both techniques possess almost unique advantages. The coach should therefore allow variations in stroke production in accordance with the flair, strength, or desire of the player. Young players who appear to have inadequate strength to perform a one-handed backhand can often accomplish the stroke if they are told to "hit carefully along a line and not across the flight of the ball."

Controversy 7

In the action of serving, the ball is struck at its highest point after the ball toss.

Fact

The height of the ball toss and the drop of the ball before impact varies considerably among top players. The great majority, however, hit the ball after it has reached its height and is on the way down.[10]

Application

Each player should hit the ball at an optimal height, which is usually just below the peak of the toss. This allows time for an unhurried backswing and racket adjustment in accordance with minor deviations of the ball toss. Always be aware, however, of individual variations in technique. Roscoe

Tanner, for example, hits the ball before it reaches its peak. Many faults in the service action are the result of the variation in ball toss.

Controversy 8

What is the role of the follow-through phase of a tennis stroke?

Fact

In tennis the follow-through permits an optimal velocity to occur at impact and then allows the body segments to "slow down" after contact. This gradual slowing down of body segments also helps to protect muscles, tendons, and ligaments from sudden changes in direction.[4]

Application

A fluent follow-through that follows the intended flight path of the ball should be encouraged. Any stroke production that is highlighted by a sudden start-stop action in the forward swing and follow-through phases should not be used.

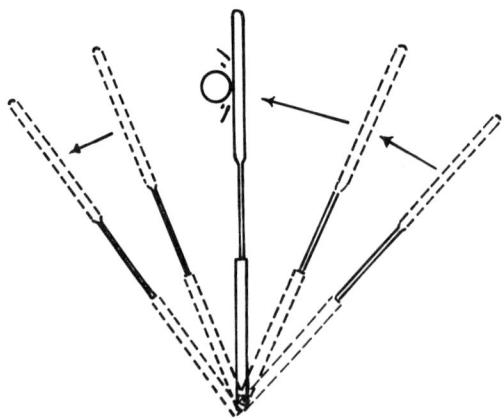

Controversy 9

Tennis is a game won by hitting winners.

Fact

More points are won from opponent errors than by hitting winning placements.[8,16] Seventy-five per cent of all points scored in tennis are due to player errors, three quarters of which are the result of balls hitting the net.[16] Bjorn Borg has effectively eliminated the net by hitting the ball with extreme topspin.

Application

The concept of playing "percentage tennis" is important to all competitors. When the shot is there to be hit, it should be played for a winner, but consistency of stroking is also extremely important. By overlearning the skill (automation of stroke production), consistency develops, but speed need not be reduced to gain accuracy.

Controversy 10

Speed is a genetic gift handed down from a player's parents and, as such, cannot be increased with training.

Fact

While the type of muscle fiber a player possesses will influence the absolute speed that is attainable, effective increases in speed can be achieved with appropriate training.[14]

Application

Speed training should be implemented in the off-season or preseason and should emphasize (1) running with knees high, (2) correct technique, (3)

acceleration runs, (4) down-hill runs, and (5) hopping for about 55 yards (50 meters). To increase speed it is often necessary to improve sprint technique by altering body position, stride length, and stride rate. Incorporating improved joint mobility into the correct sprint action has also been found to help increase running speed. A complete list of the activities needed to increase running speed can be found in the Sandstrom article listed in the references.[14]

Controversy 11

Girls and boys should never train together.

Fact

Although there are physiological and anatomical differences between men and women that may influence performance, today there is sufficient evidence to show that women respond to exercise in the same way as men and gain the same benefits from it.[3] It is important for the coach to understand physiological, sociocultural, and psychological similarities and differences between the sexes in order to achieve maximum development of each student's talent.[15]

Application

Individual characteristics of the members of the team (male and female) should dictate the training procedures adopted.

Controversy 12

Weight training will masculinize women by causing the development of bulky muscles.

Fact

Women can benefit from weight training, and since they still live in a society that often finds muscular development incompatible with feminity, they should be reassured that their increase in strength will not be accompanied by large increases in muscle bulk.[2] The woman tennis player who is interested in improving her strength to enhance performance and safeguard against injury can achieve a 30 per cent increase in strength after six months of weight training with less than a 5 per cent increase in muscle size.[2] Weight training, when performed in conjunction with swimming, increases strength and improves swimming speed without any significant change in muscle bulk.[1]

Application

Women tennis players who aspire to achieve optimal performance should follow a program of weight training, as described in Chapter 6.

Controversy 13

It is necessary to take salt tablets during a long match to replace the salt content of the body lost through sweating.

Fact

Sweat is lower in electrolyte concentration than blood. Even with heavy sweat loss, the actual electrolyte losses are minimal. However, the concentration of the remaining electrolytes in the blood is increased because of the fluid loss. The effects of such an increase in concentration can be alleviated only by fluid replacement and not by the ingestion of salt tablets.[13]

Application

The most important fluid consideration when playing in hot or humid conditions is the replacement of water. A detailed account of pregame and during-game fluid replacement levels is given in Chapter 6.

Controversy 14

"Tennis elbow" is caused primarily by poor stroke mechanics.

Fact

Tennis elbow is an injury that has led to a fair amount of disagreement among doctors, paramedical people, and coaches. Generally it is considered to be an injury, near the elbow (usually the outside), of the extensor muscles controlling the wrist.[9] It is caused by *overstrain* mainly following repeated minor traumas. It may be caused by any exercise that involves repeated and

forcible extension movements of the wrist. Although poor technique often accentuates this overstrain, other factors such as the number of years the game has been played, the frequency of games per week, and the type of racket used all influence the likelihood of developing some of the symptoms of tennis elbow.[5,11,12]

Application

Some suggestions that may help prevent tennis elbow or at least help protect the elbow during play are

1. The player should develop muscular strength and endurance in the forearm.
2. A gradual warm-up, starting off the court with some forearm exercises of low intensity and then hitting some slow ground strokes, is a good idea. The player should *never* try to serve at match-pace before having practiced at a much slower rate.
3. The player should develop a sound technique for all his/her strokes.

Remember that off-center impacts, which produce much larger forces at impact than center impacts, must be absorbed by the forearm.[11] Some common technique errors that may result in forearm injuries are listed here.

1. The player leads with the elbow in the backhand or hits flicking-type shots with the wrist.
2. The player's racket has too small a grip, causing greater tension in the muscles of the forearm during general play.
3. The player suddenly stops the follow-through so that the force cannot be dissipated gradually during the smooth deceleration of a full follow-through.

References

1. Blanksby, B. A. and Gregor, J.: "Selected Anthropometric Strength and Physiological Changes in Male and Female Age Group Swimmers With Normal Training and a Programme of Progressive Resistance Exercises." *Australian Journal of Sports Science,* *1*(1):3–6, 1982.
2. Brown, C. and Wilmore, J.: "The Effects of Maximal Resistance Training on the Strength and Body Composition of Women Athletes." *Medicine and Science in Sports,* *6:*174–177, 1974.
3. Drinkwater, B.: "Myths and Realities of Women's Performance in Sport." Paper presented at the *Fit To Play Conference,* Sydney, Australia, 1980.
4. Elliott, B. C.: "Biomechanics of Sport." In *Towards Better Coaching* (ed. F. S. Pyke). Australian Government Publishing Service, Canberra, Australia, 1980, pp. 93–110.
5. Elliott, B. C., Blanksby, B. A., and Ellis, R.: "Vibration and Rebound Velocity Characteristics of Conventional and Over-Sized Tennis Rackets." *Research Quarterly,* *51*(4):608–615, 1980.
6. Glencross, D. J. and Cibich, B. J.: "A Decision Analysis of Games Skills." *Australian Journal of Sports Medicine,* *9*(3):72–75, 1977.
7. Groppel, J. L. and Ward, T.: "Coaching Implications of the Tennis One-Handed and Two-Handed Backhand Drives." *Science in Racquet Sports* (ed. T. Terauds). Academic Publishers, Del Mar, California, 1979, pp. 81–88.
8. Hensley, L. D.: "Analysis of Stroking Errors Committed in Championship Tennis Competition." Proceedings of *A National Symposium on the Racquet Sports* (ed. J. L. Groppel). University of Illinois Press, Urbana-Champaign, 1979, pp. 224–235.
9. La Freniere, J.: "Tennis Elbow: Evaluation, Treatment, and Prevention." *Physical Therapy,* *59*(6):742–746, 1979.
10. Plagenhoef, S.: *Fundamentals of Tennis.* Prentice-Hall, Englewood Cliffs, N.J., 1970.
11. Plagenhoef, S.: "Tennis Racket Testing Related to Tennis Elbow." Proceedings of *A National Symposium on the Racquet Sports* (ed. J. L. Groppel). University of Illinois Press, Urbana-Champaign, 1979, pp. 291–310.
12. Priest, J., Braden, V., and Gerberich, S.: "An Analysis of Players With and Without Pain." *The Physician and Sportsmedicine,* *8*(4):81–91, 1980.
13. Rate, R. and Pyke, F. S.: "Replacing Fluids." *Sports Coach,* *3*(4):21–22, 1979.
14. Sandstrom, R.: "Speed of Movement—The Improvement of Rapid Acceleration." *Sports Coach,* *2*(4):14–18, 1978.
15. Shapiro, R. L.: "Coaching Male and Female Racquet Teams: Are Different Approaches Necessary?" Proceedings of *A National Symposium on the Racquet Sports* (ed. J. L. Groppel). University of Illinois Press, Urbana-Champaign, 1979, pp. 75–85.
16. Tilmanis, G. A.: *Advanced Tennis for Coaches, Teachers, and Players.* Australia and New Zealand Book Co., Sydney, Australia, 1975.

8

Junior Development in Tennis

The development of effective programs that will produce champion players while also providing all children with a sound grounding in the fundamentals of tennis is the major concern of all coaches, teachers, and parents. This chapter considers the principles on which the development of a children's tennis program can be based. The physical and psychological effects of tennis training and a system that looks at talent identification in young players are also included.

Principles for the Design of a Children's Tennis Program

The great majority of young children learn to play tennis with no immediate ambition other than to hit a ball over the net. The desire to compete, which develops later, is usually caused by the inward drive of the player, parental pressure, or the desire to emulate a tennis hero (John McEnroe, Chris Evert Lloyd, and so on). Coaches, teachers, administrators, and parents should all be aware of the factors that control children's attitudes toward tennis. The successful integration of the following principles* into the coaching program will ensure an improved performance level and better coach-child and parent-child relationships.[2]

*The principles listed are taken from "Principles for the Design of a Children's Sport Environment." *Sports Coach*, 1(2):15–21, 1977, with the permission of the author, G. G. Watson.

Social Interaction

Activities presented, if modeled on children's needs and not on adult expectations, should be of interest to those being taught. The desire to develop a sound stroke production, to compete in drills, or to enter a tournament should be intrinsically motivated. That is, the activity should be an attraction in itself and should not require an external reward (money, gifts) to motivate interest.

In a group lesson the very young child (four to five years old) has difficulty, not so much in acquiring the physical skill being taught, but in understanding why such a stroke must be learned for the enjoyment of the game. Learning to cooperate with other group members in sharing the coach's time also proves difficult for children in this age bracket. By the end of the first year of school (six to seven years old), children are more familiar with learning in a group situation, and their desire to play tennis should be the guiding factor in determining when they are introduced to the formal tennis lesson. Children should be introduced to hand-eye coordination skills before they are enrolled in a group lesson. Coaching in the form of private lessons and learning by imitation of parents, friends, or skilled performers are possible before the somewhat arbitrary age of six to seven years. In this environment the coach can continually model the lesson to the child's needs.

The Activity Principle

The skills of the game must be learned through participation during tennis lessons. A varied program, based on maximum participation, should be molded to the requirements of the game so that each child will be stimulated by the activities presented. Increased time for imitation and practice of an activity will both stimulate learning and produce an optimal skill level.

The Developmental Principle

Children under eight years old require a period of unstructured "free practice" in each lesson that is centered on them. The children should be given a period in which they can bounce-hit forehand drives into a fence or across the net in a relatively informal setting.

For 8 to 11-year-old children, time should be provided for cooperative practice in the development of stroke production. Emphasis should be placed on skill learning through enjoyment in this age bracket. This group may prefer to participate in cooperative forehand practices in which the aim of the drill is the total number of consecutive hits across the net.

For children older than 12, learning is best stimulated by presenting meaningful challenges in competitive situations. This group may prefer drills in which one player wins a rally (one-on-one drills).

The Motivation Principle

Allowance should be made for mastery of skills that are meaningful challenges to the group. Within this setting each child should be given the maximum opportunity to succeed. The training squad or coaching group should be encouraged to develop a sense of identity so that both individual excellence and a cooperative effort are the desires of all the players.

The Performance Principle

The younger the child, the greater should be the emphasis on skill learning. Expectations should be based on the mastery of progressive skill levels, not on the importance of winning. The older the child, the greater should be the emphasis on performance under pressure and within competitive situations.

The Competitive Principle

Rather than expecting one general standard for all children, the coach should encourage development of each child's ability and competition between players. The competitive setting will then provide a realistic situation related to a child's individual talents. That is, a skill test that demands thirty consecutive backhands to be hit over the net would be a totally unrealistic expectation for a group of beginners. During competition, it is best to praise continually any skill learning that has been accomplished.

It is difficult to arrive at a definitive age at which children should begin competitive tennis. Are all children over 12 ready for competitive tennis? Physical activities such as tennis provide children with a domain in which they can express their competitive drive. Competitive tennis will introduce children to the thrill of winning, as well as to the harsh reality of losing. Children should be prepared for the consequences of a competitive match by using many varied competitive drills in the coaching program. The best age for each child to begin tournament or competitive tennis must be determined on an individual basis. The performance principle should be used as a guide, but the primary concern of coaches of young children (under 12 years old) should undoubtedly be directed toward stroke production.

The Personality Principle

A coach should distinguish between the child who is highly anxious and one who is relaxed under pressure. These two types of players must be motivated and encouraged in different ways. The more anxious child needs to be reassured by being given constant support to minimize the effects of stress, whereas the relaxed player may have to be highly motivated before the beginning of an important match. If each child on a team is treated as an individual, improved performance will almost inevitably result.

The Sex-Role Principle

While recognizing the fact that physical, physiological, and psychological differences do exist between boys and girls in a squad,[1] coaches can still integrate the sexes in an effective training program. Outlets for the expression of achievement, aggression, affiliation (friendliness), and the learning of basic skills should be available to both boys and girls. It is necessary for the coach to be conscious of stereotyped expectations that discriminate against either sex, particularly the expectation of lowered achievement from girls.[2]

Physical Effects of Tennis Training

There is little reason to believe that the demands of competitive tennis, with its associated training, in any way adversely affect the physical growth of young tennis players.[4,6] In fact, physical activity, which is necessary to support normal growth of bone and muscle tissue, also serves as a stimulant to the development of the cardiovascular and respiratory systems. Only when physical activity is sufficiently strenuous and repetitious to bring about chronic fatigue, or sufficiently stressful to induce trauma to a body part, is there danger of adverse effects on normal growth.[5,6]

A predominance of shoulder and elbow injuries has been reported in preadolescent tennis players.[3] Coaches should therefore ensure that specific training is directed toward strengthening these areas of the body.

Coaches are often warned by doctors and educators of impending joint and bone injuries in young players from overtraining. The epiphyses (area of bone growth) have almost all fused by the skeletal age of 18 years in boys and 16 years in girls.[5] Injuries to the growth plate are extremely rare in tennis players, and a sensible attitude to training will ensure that they do not occur. Children may be subject to stress fractures if required to run long distances on hard surfaces while wearing inappropriate shoes. Again, an informed approach to training will reduce, if not remove, this injury problem.

Psychological Effects of Tennis Training

Based on the evidence to date, it would be difficult to conclude that competitive tennis constitutes an emotional danger to young players.[7] It is important for coaches and parents to assess the potential of young players realistically and to formulate programs and goals that are within the children's physical and mental capacity. A spirit of striving to achieve optimal personal performance, however, is an important aspect of any tennis program.

Coaches must be able to recognize the mental as well as physical qualities of their young players and be capable of utilizing, not exploiting, their sense of loyalty, enthusiasm, and idealism.[7] Both coaches and parents should remember not to force young players to succeed for the adult's gratification. This will often lead to drop-outs who are either burned out or soured on tennis or to children who lack development in other aspects of life.[7] The key to producing well-adjusted, competitive players rests with coaches who are capable of administering appropriate programs that enable young talent to be both identified and developed.

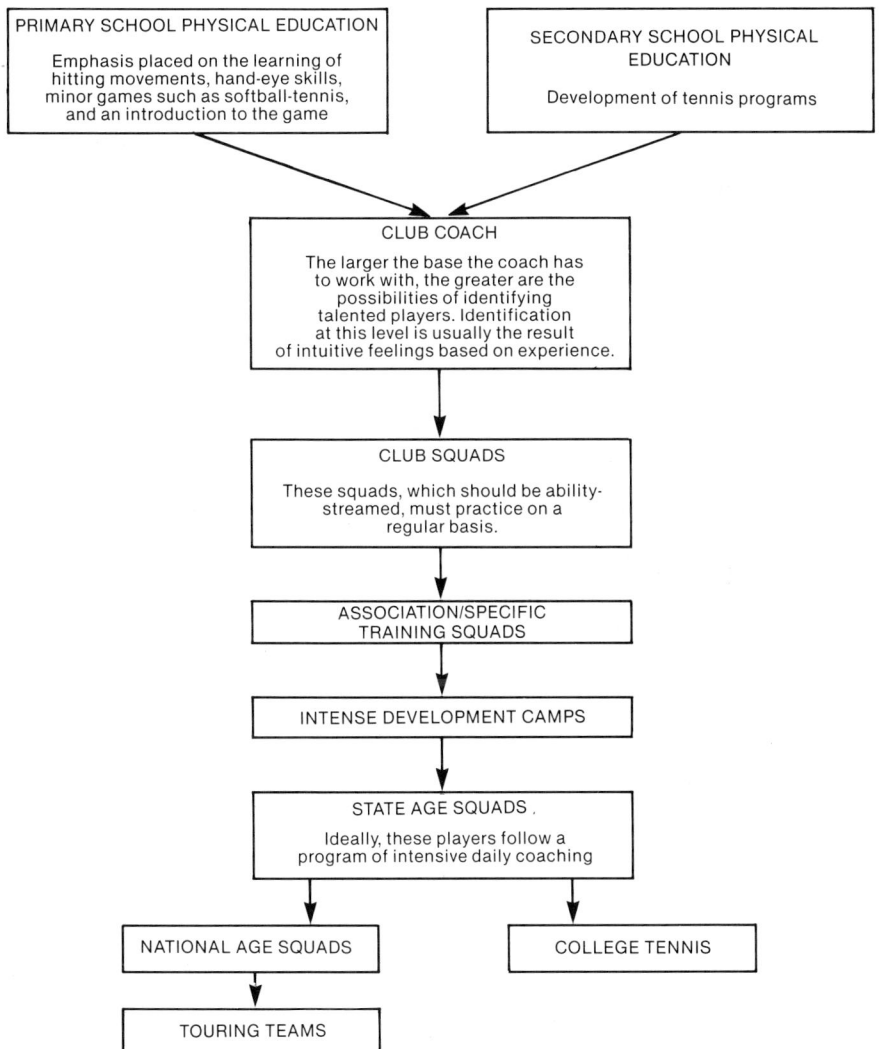

Figure 8.1 Flow diagram for tennis talent identification and development.

Talent Identification and Development

Talent identification and development should be an integral part of the philosophy of all tennis coaches and associations. The attainment of excellence in performance will be achieved only if talented young tennis players (12 to 13 years old) are identified and then trained to an optimal level of achievement. This training takes the form of a counseling process in which individual excellence in performance is nurtured.

What type of program enables tennis talent to be identified and then developed? A flow chart shows the general directions that tennis development can follow (Figure 8.1).

Developmental Assessment

It is often advantageous for the coach to know the skeletal ages of his training squad in preference to their chronological ages. In many sports the performance of a late developer often is superior to that of the early maturer.

References

Principles for the Design of a Children's Tennis Program
1. Docherty, D.: "Structural and Functional Differences Between Boys and Girls from 7 to 17 Years of Age." *Co-Educational Physical Education.* Australian Council for Health, Physical Education, and Recreation, Perth, Australia, 1980.
2. Watson, G. G.: "Principles for the Design of a Children's Sport Environment." *Sports Coach,* 1(2):15–21, 1977.

Physical Effects of Tennis Training
3. Barnes, L.: "Preadolescent Training—How Young is Too Young?" *The Physician and Sports Medicine,* 7(10):114–119, 1979.
4. Larson, R. L.: "Physical Activity and the Growth and Development of Bone and Joint Structure." *Physical Activity, Human Growth, and Development* (ed. G. L. Rarick). Academic Press, New York, 1973, pp. 33–59.
5. Menelaus, M. B.: "Sports Injuries in Children and Adolescents." Conference Report of *XXth World Congress in Sports Medicine,* Melbourne, Australia, 1974, pp. 485–487.
6. Rarick, G. L.: "Competitive Sports in Childhood and Early Adolescence." *Physical Activity, Human Growth, and Development* (ed. G. L. Rarick). Academic Press, New York, 1973, pp. 364–386.

Psychological Effects of Tennis Training
7. Seal, R. E.: "Sport and the Child: Psychological Considerations." Conference Report of *XXth World Congress in Sports Medicine,* Melbourne, Australia, 1974, pp. 479–481.

9

Tennis Administration

This chapter deals with the administration of tennis at a club, school, or community level. Emphasis has been placed on the organization of social and competitive club play and on tournament organization.

Social and Competitive Club Play

Organization of the players who attend social tennis at a club, school, or community center has always been a problem. A system developed by Ray Neuling has proved to be a highly efficient method of organizing matches for either social or competitive club play.

Players, upon arriving, write their names on cards, the men using blue felt pens and the women using red felt pens (Figure 9.1). The set organizer then uses a code to "set the board," as shown in Figures 9.2 and 9.3: Using this method, one person can organize up to 16 courts while a match of 25 minutes is being played. The code can be used as follows:

Blue color: men's doubles
Red color: women's doubles
Green color: mixed doubles
—: a player arrived late
X: a player is resting
Number: the court where the match is to be played
Name(s): both player(s) and opponent(s)
bar (1): a bar or no bar under the court number indicates doubles partners

156 Tennis Administration

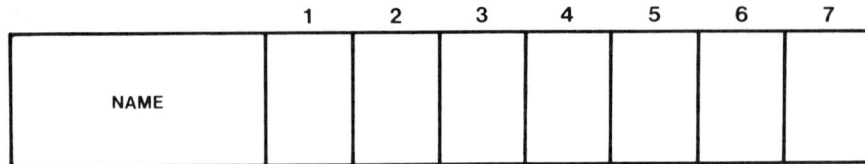

Figure 9.1 Individual player card.

Using this code, the supervisor can tell (1) with whom each player has been drawn to play by looking down each column to check if the same court number appears; and (2) the type of matches played by looking at the color code along each individual's card.

The court numbers, in the appropriate color code, are marked on the cards *after* all courts have been checked. Once the players have seen on which court they are scheduled to play and with whom they are playing, the organizer can begin to arrange the next group of matches. This is done by moving the individual cards to another board. Figure 9.3 shows the board set for the sixth match of an afternoon's play. The arrows on this figure highlight some of the points that allow this system to operate efficiently.

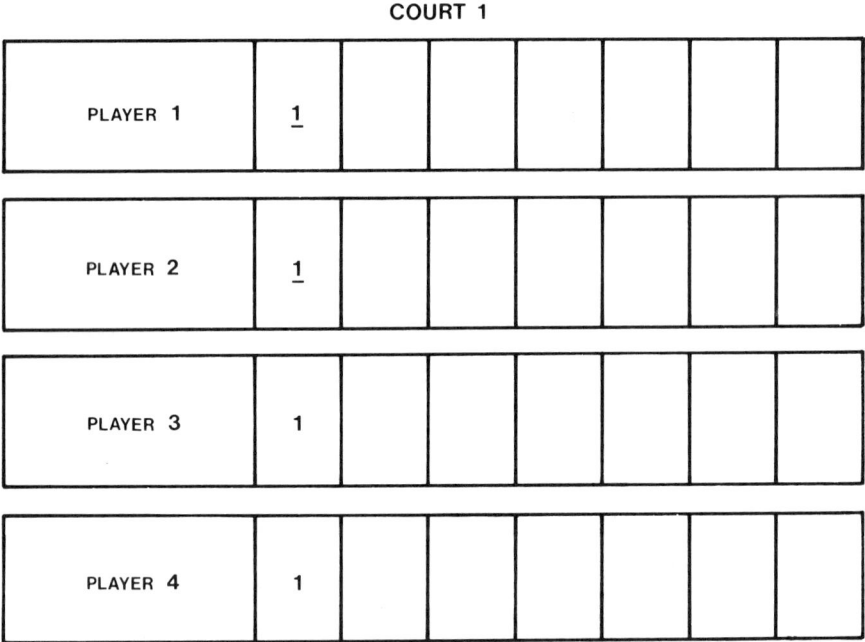

Figure 9.2 Player cards for one match: Players 1 and 2 vs. players 3 and 4 on court 1.

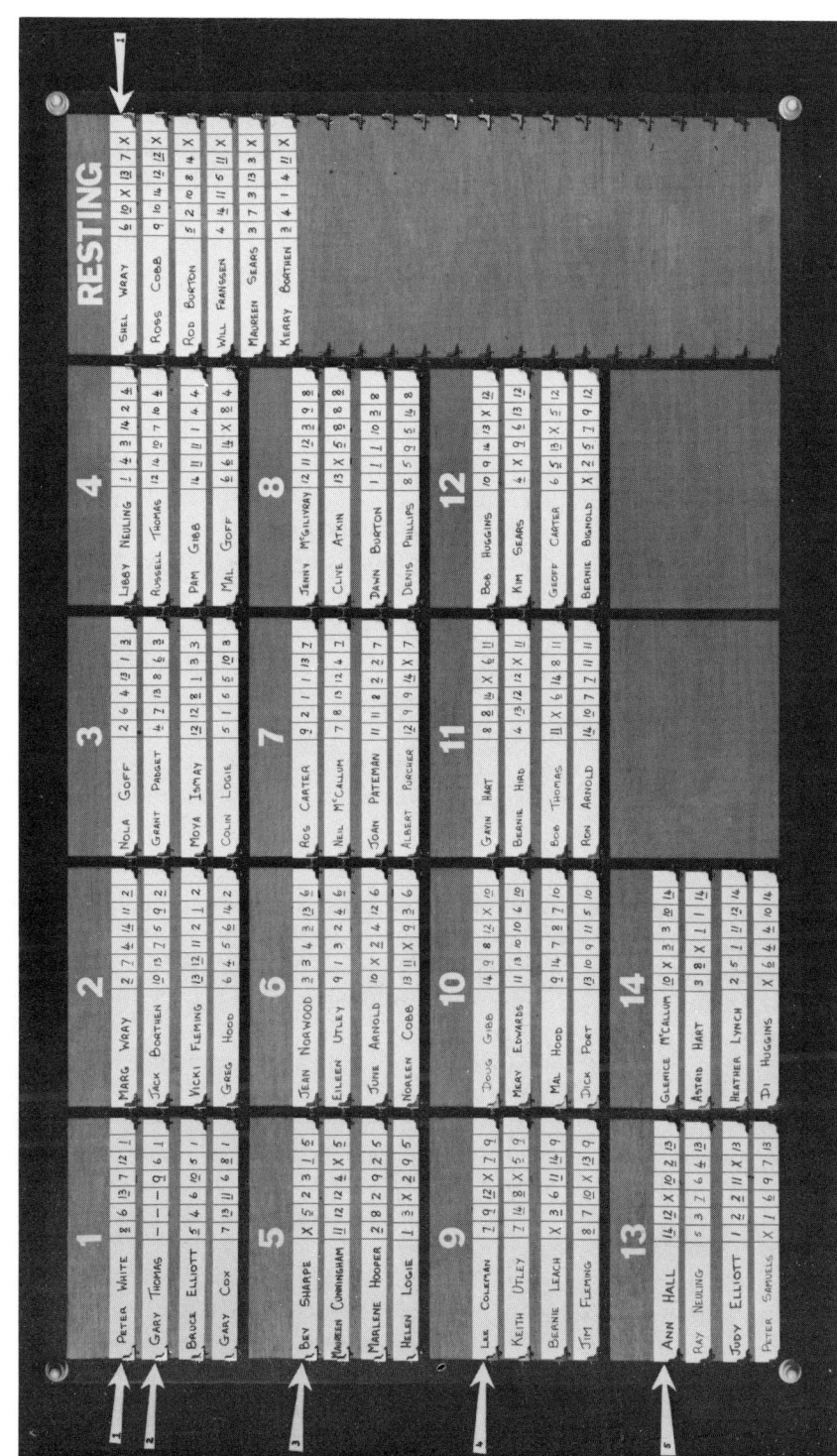

Figure 9.3

Arrow 1
Peter White has played six matches. If Figure 9.3 were color-coded, then all the blue numbers would represent men's doubles, and all the green numbers would represent mixed doubles. Shel Wray, who has missed two matches, should have been exchanged with Peter White on court 1 since Peter has not rested for any matches while Shel has missed two matches.

Arrow 2
Gary Thomas arrived late and missed the first three matches.

Arrow 3
The set on court 5 shows that Bev Sharpe and Marlene Hooper played together in the third match. (This can be checked by looking down each of the columns.) These two players are drawn to play against each other in this match. (In the third column the number 2 appears for both players without a bar, indicating that these players were partners in the third match.)

Arrow 4
The match on court 9 has been poorly organized since Keith Utley and Lee Coleman, who played together in the first match, are partners again in this sixth match. (In the first column the number 7 appears with a bar for both players, indicating that they were partners in that match.) They should switch partners in the same way as the women on court 5.

Arrow 5
Many clubs have a combination of court surfaces, some of which may be more pleasant to play on than others. The court numbers permit a record to be kept of where each person played his or her match. At the club where this board was photographed, courts 13 and 14 are hard courts, while 1 to 12 are grass. Ann Hall was therefore scheduled to play on the hard courts twice during the afternoon.

This system can be used to aid the organization of the many "fun tournaments" run at a club or community level. There are many ways in which these tournaments can be run.

Round Robin

In this tournament each pair is drawn to play every other pair. Matches may be one set, the best of eight games, or decided on a time basis. If there is a great diversity of standards, handicapping may prove desirable (Figure 9.4).

Many clubs form teams that compete in an intraclub round robin series similar in format to the interclub shield or pennant competition. A typical draw for such a series follows.

	SCORE								Grand
Pair	1	2	3	4	5	6	Total	Handicap	Total
1	X								
2		X							
3			X						
4				X					
5					X				
6						X			

Figure 9.4 Round robin scoresheet.

5 or 6 Teams (for 5 teams, no. 6 becomes the bye)

Round 1	Round 2	Round 3	Round 4	Round 5
1 vs. 6	2 vs. 3	1 vs. 2	2 vs. 4	1 vs. 3
3 vs. 4	4 vs. 1	3 vs. 5	3 vs. 6	4 vs. 5
5 vs. 2	6 vs. 5	6 vs. 4	5 vs. 1	6 vs. 2

7 or 8 Teams (for 7 teams, no. 8 becomes the bye)

Round 1	Round 2	Round 3	Round 4	Round 5	Round 6	Round 7
1 vs. 8	2 vs. 5	1 vs. 4	2 vs. 1	1 vs. 7	2 vs. 4	1 vs. 3
3 vs. 6	4 vs. 3	3 vs. 2	5 vs. 8	3 vs. 5	3 vs. 8	4 vs. 7
5 vs. 4	6 vs. 1	5 vs. 7	4 vs. 6	6 vs. 2	5 vs. 1	6 vs. 5
7 vs. 2	8 vs. 7	8 vs. 6	7 vs. 3	8 vs. 4	7 vs. 6	8 vs. 2

In this draw the first-named team is the home team. If the competition is to have two complete rounds this draw can be used, but all the numbers must be reversed.

Self-handicapping

Although matches are usually organized in a doubles format, each player's scores are recorded individually. Each match is played for a given time limit, in preference to playing to the conclusion of a set, so that all matches can be easily controlled. In this system of handicapping, a pair starts from minus one point (-15) for each one-game difference in set scores, to a maximum of minus three points (−40) for a difference of three or more games.

Team A	Team B
1 game (−15)	0 games
2 games (−30)	0 games
3 games (−40)	0 games
4 games (−40)	0 games
4 games (−40)	1 game
4 games (−30)	2 games
4 games (−15)	3 games

Scores recorded at the end of 25 minutes of play were: members of team A each scored four games, while the members of team B each scored three games.

Switch-Partner Doubles

In this tournament each match consists of eight games. At the end of the fourth game, two of the players change partners. This system is ideal for mixed doubles, although it is equally effective in men's or women's doubles where the players that are to change must be nominated by the match coordinator. Scores are kept on an individual basis.

Team A/B	Team C/D
3	1

Team A/C	Team B/D
2	2

Scores at the end of an eight-game match were: player A, five games; player B, five games; player C, three games; player D, three games.

Handicap

A modified version of the handicapping system common to association handbooks has been found to be both efficient and easy to administer. Each player or pair is allocated a handicap with either a negative value (owed points) or a positive value (received points), as shown in Figure 9.5. The handicapping range for this system is from "−18" for the best possible entrant in the tournament to "+18" for the poorest possible entrant. In such a tournament, the organizer should (1) rank all the entrants in the tournament, (2) decide on the handicapping range that will provide all players with an equal chance of success, (3) assign a handicap to each player of pair, and (4) draw the tournament.

Social and Competitive Club Play

	TABLE 1*						TABLE 2*					
ADJUSTED HANDICAP	OWED ODDS (−)						RECEIVED ODDS (+)					
	Games						Games					
	1	2	3	4	5	6	1	2	3	4	5	6
1	–	–	–	–	15	–	–	15	–	–	–	–
2	–	–	15	–	15	–	–	15	–	15	–	–
3	15	–	15	–	15	–	–	15	–	15	–	15
4	15	–	15	–	15	15	15	15	–	15	–	15
5	15	–	15	15	15	15	15	15	15	15	–	15
6	15	15	15	15	15	15	15	15	15	15	15	15
7	15	15	15	15	30	15	15	30	15	15	15	15
8	15	15	30	15	30	15	15	30	15	30	15	15
9	30	15	30	15	30	15	15	30	15	30	15	30
10	30	15	30	15	30	30	30	30	15	30	15	30
11	30	15	30	30	30	30	30	30	30	30	15	30
12	30	30	30	30	30	30	30	30	30	30	30	30
13	30	30	30	30	40	30	30	40	30	30	30	30
14	30	30	40	30	40	30	30	40	30	40	30	30
15	40	30	40	30	40	30	30	40	30	40	30	40
16	40	30	40	30	40	40	40	40	30	40	30	40
17	40	30	40	40	40	40	40	40	40	40	30	40
18	40	40	40	40	40	40	40	40	40	40	40	40

*This Table is not carried beyond the sixth game, since the odds recur in the same position for the next and every succeeding six games.

Figure 9.5 Format for handicap points.

When players who are both on owed points play one another, the handicap of the lower-ranked player is deducted from that of the higher.

Player A: "−12"
Player B: "−8"

The difference in handicap is "−4," so player A starts at "−15 points" in the first, third, fifth, and sixth games (Table 1 in Fig. 9.5). Player A, therefore, needs to win five points to win these four games, provided the score does not reach deuce.

When players who are both receiving points play one another, the smaller number is again deducted from the larger.

> Player C: "+14"
> Player D: "+9"

The difference in handicap is "+5," so player C starts at "+15 points" in the first, second, third, fourth, and sixth games (Table 2 in Fig. 9.5). This player requires only three points to win the game, provided the score does not reach deuce.

When a player on owed points meets a player on received points, both tables in Figure 9.5 must be used. The player on owed points uses Table 1 to ascertain where points must be given, while the player on received points uses Table 2 to determine where points are received.

> Player A: "−12"
> Player C: "+14"

Player A starts every game at "−30 points," while player C starts the first, third, fifth, and sixth games at "+30 points" and the second and fourth games at "+40 points."

The singles handicap can then be used to organize both the doubles and mixed doubles handicapping. Before drawing pairs, the organizer places the better half of players in one pool and the other half in another pool. A player is then drawn from each pool to create a men's or women's doubles pair. Players who nominate for the mixed doubles event are placed in four pools of players: (1) top-half men, (2) top-half women, (3) lower-half men, and (4) lower-half women. The pairs are then cross-drawn so that, for example, a top-half man is paired with a lower-half woman. Alternatively, two separate events can be organized, with the top-half men and women being drawn as partners in one division and the lower-half men and women in the other division.

For men's or women's doubles, the two singles handicaps are added together and divided by two. All final handicaps are rounded off to the lower number for negative totals and to the higher number are positive totals.

> Player A: "−12"   Player B: "−8"
> Player E: "+1"   Player D: "+9"
> Handicap for pair: A/E, "−5"; B/D, "+1"

For the mixed doubles competition, the men's handicap is multiplied by two and added to the women's handicap. This total is then divided by three and rounded to the lower number to achieve the handicap for the pair.

> Player A: "−12"
> Player F: "+2"
> Handicap for pair A/F: (A "−24," F "+2") "−7"

163 Tournament Organization

Tournament Organization

The procedures to follow in organizing a major tournament and the individual duties of the tournament officials are well documented in tennis association handbooks. The organization of a seeded tournament and a tournament planning sheet for use at a club or community level are shown in Figures 9.6 and 9.7. For this type of draw, the number of players to be

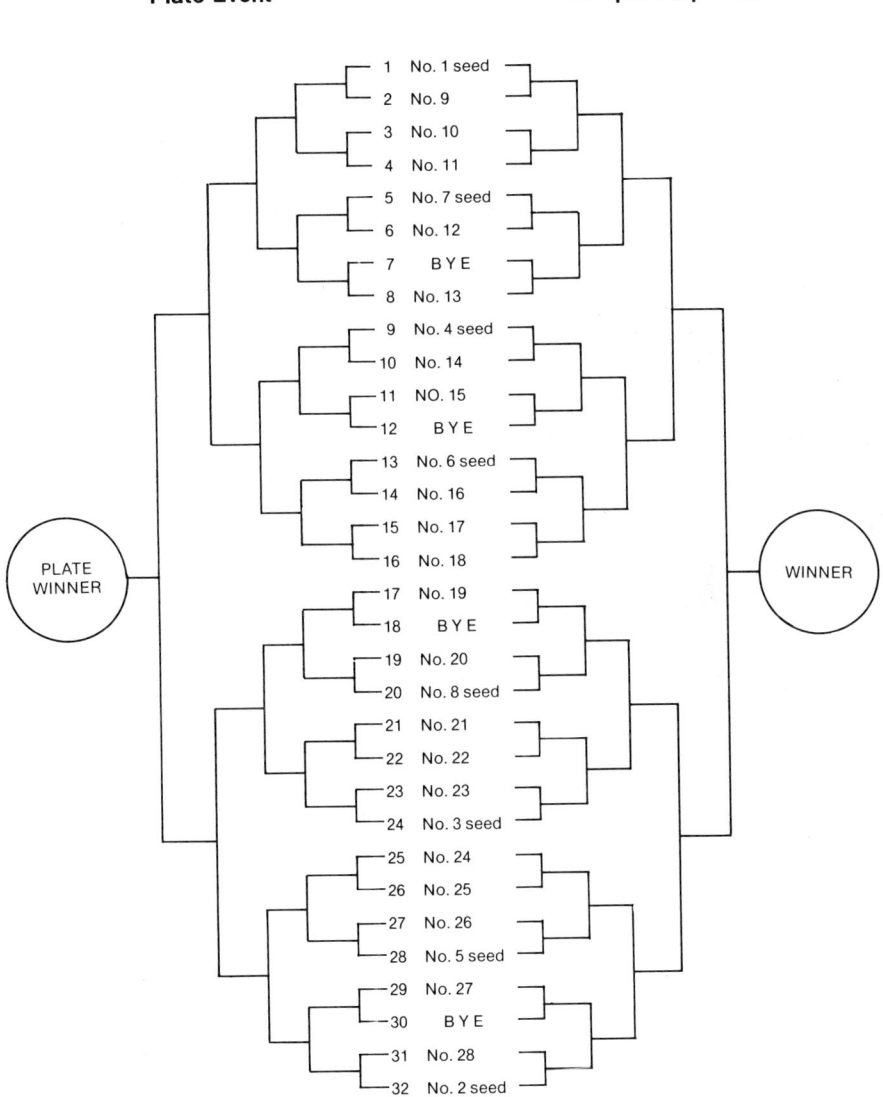

Figure 9.6 Draw sheet for 28 competitors.

Name	Events			Time								Time								Paid
	S	D	M	9	10	11	12	1	2	3	4	9	10	11	12	1	2	3	4	

S = Singles
D = Doubles
M = Mixed Doubles

Figure 9.7 Tournament planning sheet.

seeded is as follows:

    32 competitors: 8 seeds
    48 competitors: 8 seeds
    64 competitors: 16 seeds

The seeds for a tournament with 28 competitors are as follows (Figure 9.6):

    No. 1   Top of the upper half
    No. 2   Bottom of the lower half
    No. 3 and 4   Drawn by lot. The first drawn is placed at the bottom of the third quarter and the second drawn is placed at the top of the second quarter.
    No. 5, 6, 7 and 8   Drawn by lot. The first drawn is placed at the top of the fourth eighth, the second at the bottom of the fifth eighth, the third at the bottom of the seventh eighth, and the fourth at the top of the second eighth.

The structure of the plate event is shown in Figure 9.6. Figure 9.7 can be used as a guide for the structure of a tournament planning sheet that is used as a master plan for tournament play.

10

Unit Structure

The teaching and coaching units included in this chapter should be used as guides in the formulation of programs that are specific to the needs of the children or adults being taught. Each lesson is structured to include an introduction, skill development period, and a culmination. Some of the most important teaching points are reviewed here. A complete list of teaching points, with an outline of the drills and games used in these programs, can be found in Chapter 1. Many teaching points and drills have been repeated in different lessons in an endeavor to specifically aid teachers who need a quick reminder of the salient points of each lesson.

School Program for Children Eight to Nine Years Old

Lesson 1 (1 hour)

Introduction

Agility running: The children are required to change direction and leap into the air.

Hand-eye coordination drills: Racketball or subjunior tennis rackets should be used, along with "energy-absorbing" balls.

One-handed catching: The children step forward, working in pairs for a preferred-hand catch, using a tennis or "energy-absorbing" ball.

Skill Development: Forehand Volley

1. The coach demonstrates the forehand volley. (Demonstration will always include both the stroke being taught and the drill to be used.)
2. The players adopt the correct grip.
3. The teacher gives all players two or three hits each.
4. In pairs, the children throw and volley.
5. The players follow the action of the teacher/coach in a shadow drill.
6. The children repeat throwing and hitting in pairs.

Teaching Points

1. Grip: eastern forehand.
2. Ready position.
3. Watching the ball.
4. Stepping into the volley.

Culmination

The children work in pairs, competing to see (1) which group has the best technique, (2) which group feeds the ball the best, and (3) which group can score the most catches or the greatest number of consecutive catches in a given period. The lesson ends with a fun game in which all the children are involved.

The forehand volley is taught in the first lesson so that each child may have a feeling of achievement. By working in pairs, children have the opportunity to relate to someone of similar ability. In this format the children are not continually being evaluated by the group when performing a skill, and therefore they often respond more positively.

Lesson 2

Introduction

Jog around the court: The players jog and call the appropriate name of the lines with the teacher.
Hand-eye coordination: The children catch and throw individually and in pairs.
Hand tennis: In pairs the children play, using "energy-absorbing" balls.
Hand-eye coordination: The players integrate simple ball and racket drills.
Revision volleys: In pairs the players engage in revision volleys.

Skill Development: Forehand Drive

1. The teacher demonstrates the stroke.
2. The players follow a bounce, step, and hit sequence (into fence).

3. The players engage in shadow work, following the teacher/coach.
4. In pairs the children throw (underarm) and hit approximately 6.5 to 11 yards (6 to 10 meters) apart.
5. In pairs the hitters attempt to play a catch to feeders.

Teaching Points

1. Bounce, step, and hit technique: side-on, racket back, ball in the palm of the hand (stress ball tossing technique).
2. Firm wrist.
3. Lifting action with the racket.

Culmination

The lesson ends with a game of baseball-tennis. The batter at this stage of tennis should hit the ball with a bounce-hit forehand.

Lesson 3

Introduction

Agility running: The players run within a specific area of the court.
Hand-eye coordination: The children practice ball and racket skills.
Free practice on forehand drive: The players hit either to a partner or into a fence.
Overarm throwing: The children aim at different targets.

Skill Development: Service (emphasis on the swing)

1. The teacher demonstrates the technique.
2. The players assume the proper grip.
3. The children follow the coach, who emphasizes the full swing using the following key phrases:

   "Point the rifle"
   "Past the toes"
   "Win the fight"
   "Hit the backside—wrist and shoulder close together"
   "Turn and hit—up to the ball."

4. The players serve at a fence (full swing).

Teaching Points

1. Grip: eastern forehand.
2. Reinforcement of the concept of a fluent swing.
3. Fitting the ball into the swing. (The actual mechanics of the ball toss will be emphasized later in the unit structure.)
4. Arms going down together and coming up together.
5. Hitting up and out toward the ball.

Pupils should be given time to practice the swing before the teacher places emphasis on hitting the ball. The teacher/coach should finish this lesson with a brief doubles demonstration so that the children can see the game they are learning.

Culmination
The children serve at a range of court areas: (1) over the net, (2) into the correct half of the court, and (3) into the correct service area. The lesson ends with an award for the "swing of the day."

Lesson 4

Introduction

Follow the coach: The coach and students engage in stretching exercises and an agility run.
Hand-eye coordination: The coach introduces skills that require the use of the nonpreferred hand. The players perform racket and ball drills.
Serving practice: The students practice serving in pairs.

Skill Development: Backhand Drive

1. The coach demonstrates the stroke.
2. The players learn the grip.
3. The players follow the coach in a shadow backhand.
4. In pairs, one player drops the ball on a predetermined spot so that the other player can step and hit a backhand from the full backswing position after the bounce (into a fence).
5. In pairs, the children throw and hit catches approximately 6.5 yards (6 meters) apart.

Teaching Points

1. Grip: eastern backhand.
2. Knuckles lead the shot.
3. Exaggeration of the side-on position.
4. Arm close to the body during the forward swing.
5. "Lifting" the ball over the net.
6. Firm wrist at impact.

Culmination: Skills Tabloid
The players should be able to tabulate (1) their hand-eye skills, (2) the number of consecutive volleys, (3) the number of forehands at selected target areas (from a bounce-hit), (4) the number of serves over the net into the service area, (5) the number of throws into a bucket using the nonpreferred hand, and (6) the amount of points out of ten for a service swing.

Lesson 5

Introduction

Relays: The players engage in relays, carrying their rackets.
Hand-eye coordination: The children perform racket and ball drills.
Skill drills: The players use the nonpreferred hand.
Free stroke practice: In pairs, the players practice forehands, backhands, and service.

Skill Development

1. The coach demonstrates the service, with emphasis on the integration of the ball toss with the swing.
2. The players throw the ball up into the air so that it fits into the path of the "perfect swing."
3. The players practice throwing the ball into the air so that it lands in an area marked in front of and to the right of the forward foot.
4. The players serve in pairs.
5. The players serve at target areas on the court.

Teaching Points

1. "Fitting the ball into the swing."
2. Holding the ball with the end of the thumb and the first two fingers.
3. Not holding the ball too tightly
4. Not rushing the ball toss or the racket-arm.
5. Both arms going down together and then moving up together.
6. Height and position of the ball toss.

Culmination

The lesson ends with a game of baseball-tennis. The batter at this stage of the course should be capable of hitting a ball cooperatively fed by a member of the opposing team.

Lesson 6

Introduction

Hand-eye coordination drills: The players practice running with the ball on the racket, bouncing the ball while running, and trying for a number of consecutive bounces on the racket.

Skill Development/Culmination

The coach demonstrates "11-up," using a bounce-hit forehand to begin the rally. The children play "11-up" using the "king of the mountain" format.

The children play the preceding game, starting the rally with a service. The rules could be: three chances to get the ball over the net (the teacher/coach may wish to introduce a 1–2–3–4 scoring system for this second game).

School Program for Children 13 to 14 Years Old

Lesson 1 (1½ hours)

Introduction

Agility running: The children run, changing directions.
One-handed catching: The children step forward, working in pairs, for a preferred-hand catch.
Hand-eye coordination drills: The players use an eastern forehand grip.

Skill Development: Forehand Volley

1. The coach demonstrates the stroke. (Demonstration will always include both the stroke being taught and the drill to be used.)
2. The children adopt the correct grip.
3. In pairs, the players throw and volley.
4. The children follow the action of the teacher/coach in a shadow drill.
5. In pairs, the players try to achieve the highest number of volley catches in two minutes and the highest number of consecutive volleys in two minutes.

Teaching Points

1. Grip: eastern forehand.
2. Ready position.
3. Stepping into the volley (pushing with the back leg).
4. Racket head position at impact.
5. Watching the ball onto the strings.

Many coaches and teachers may prefer to teach the forehand volley following the groundstrokes and service. The authors have found that the success experienced with the forehand volley has been a motivating factor for subsequent stroke development.

Skill Development: Forehand Drive

1. The coach demonstrates the forehand drive.
2. The players bounce, step, and hit (into the fence).
3. The players bounce, step, and hit to a partner over the net.
4. The players follow the teacher/coach in a shadow drill.

5. In pairs, the children throw (underarm) and hit approximately 6.5 yards (6 meters) apart.
6. In pairs, the hitters attempt to play a catch to the feeders.

Teaching Points

1. Grip: eastern forehand.
2. Ready position.
3. Swing.
4. Bounce, step, and hit progression.
5. Laid-back wrist at impact, in line with the front foot.

Culmination

The lesson ends with a game of baseball-tennis.

Lesson 2

Introduction

Jog around the court: The players jog and call the appropriate name of lines with the teacher.
Hand-eye coordination: The children practice ball and racket skills.
"11-up": The coach introduces the game, starting each rally with a bounce, step, hit forehand.

Skill Development

1. The coach reinforces the learning of the forehand drive with a demonstration.
2. The players bounce hit to opponents from the service line and then from the baseline.
3. The players engage in a half-court drill of forehand drive to forehand drive.

Teaching Points

1. Reemphasis of the points in Lesson 1.
2. Watching the ball coming off the opponent's racket.
3. Reinforcement of the sequence of bounce, step, and hit.

Culmination

1. The children play matches of "11-up" using the "king of the mountain" format to change teams.
2. The lesson ends with a demonstration of next week's skill, the serve.

The teacher/coach should evaluate the group at this stage so that the drills and culmination drills or games are aimed at the general ability level of the pupils.

Lesson 3

Introduction

Follow-the-leader: The players follow the coach in stretching exercises and an agility run.

Hand-eye coordination: The children practice ball and racket skills.

Revision of strokes covered: The players work on the forehand drill and the forehand volley drill.

Skill Development: Service (emphasis on the swing)

1. The coach demonstrates the serve.
2. The players adopt the eastern forehand grip (players who are being coached may wish to use a continental grip).
3. The children practice in pairs. This enables students both to experiment with the action and to experience the problems in the service action.
4. The players follow the coach, who emphasizes the full swing using the following key phrases:

    "Point the rifle"
    "Past the toes"
    "Win the fight"
    "Hit your backside"
    "Turn and hit up to the ball"
    "Follow-through out and then down"

5. The players practice the serve, emphasizing the swing (into a fence).
6. The players practice the serve in pairs, aiming for the correct service court.
7. The children play matches of "11-up," beginning each rally with a serve that must go over the net and into the other end of the court (three service attempts may be used).

Teaching Points

1. Ready position.
2. The swing is the thing.
3. Both arms going down together and coming up together.
4. Body weight moving up and forward at impact.
5. Hitting up and out toward the ball.

Culmination: Tabloid

The players incorporate the following:

volleys
forehand drive

service over the net
hand-eye coordination drills

Lesson 4

Introduction

Follow-the-leader: The children follow the coach in stretching exercises and an agility run.
Free practice: The players practice the forehand drive, the forehand volley, and the service.

Skill Development: Service

1. The coach demonstrates integration of the ball toss with the "perfect swing."
2. The players practice the swing and ball toss without hitting the ball (with the eyes closed initially and then with the eyes opened).
3. The students practice the serve, emphasizing the ball toss (marking an area on the court into which the ball must fall).
4. The children practice serving in pairs.

Teaching Points

1. Holding the ball with the end of the thumb and the first two fingers.
2. Not rushing the action.
3. Both arms going down together and then moving up together.
4. Height and position of the ball toss.

Culmination

The coach conducts the following games:

Consecutive forehand drive competitions (four on a court at a time, working cooperatively as a team).
Consecutive volley competitions (four on a court at a time).
Target serving competitions (with individual or team totals).

The lesson ends with a game of baseball-tennis.

Lesson 5

Introduction

Follow-the-leader: The coach leads the children in stretching exercises and an agility run.
Half-court drill: This drill emphasizes the forehand drive and forehand volley.

Hand-eye coordination drills: The players use the eastern backhand grip.

Skill Development: Backhand Drive

1. The coach demonstrates the backhand drive and the grip to be used.
2. In pairs, one player drops the ball on a predetermined spot so that the partner can step and hit a backhand from the full backswing position after the bounce (into a fence).
3. The children play a backhand drive from an underarm throw.

Teaching Points

1. Grip: eastern backhand.
2. Knuckles lead the shot.
3. Exaggeration of the side-on position.
4. Arm close to the body during the forward swing.
5. "Lifting" the ball over the net.
6. Weight moving forward at impact.
7. Firm wrist at impact.

Skill Development: Backhand Volley

1. The coach demonstrates the backhand volley.
2. The children adopt the correct grip.
3. In pairs, the players throw and volley.
4. In pairs, the students try to achieve the highest number of volley catches in two minutes and the highest number of consecutive volleys in two minutes.

Teaching Points

1. Grip: eastern backhand.
2. Ready position.
3. Stepping forward into the volley.
4. Racket head position at impact.
5. Watching the ball onto the strings.

Culmination

The children play "11-up," serving with a bounce, step, hit backhand. (If some players find this too difficult, switch back to a bounce-hit forehand.)

Lesson 6: Tournament Day

This day should be structured to meet both the needs and the abilities of the pupils. Some of the competitions that can be used are

Consecutive forehand, backhand, or volley contests
Accuracy contests
"11-up" matches from a serve or a bounce-hit groundstroke

Although playing standards may not allow pupils to enjoy a game of tennis doubles, it is probably beneficial for all children to be introduced to the game. This will require a quick explanation of court positions and basic scoring before a doubles tournament is organized. Pupils may be motivated to compete in a doubles tournament.

Adult Tennis Program: Preparation for Intermediate Club Play

Lesson 1 (1 to 1½ hours)

Introduction
The pupils engage in stretching exercises, a slow jog around the court, and hand-eye coordination drills, using an eastern forehand grip.

Skill Development: Forehand Volley

1. The coach demonstrates the stroke, including a demonstration of the full stroke and the drill to be performed.
2. The players adopt an appropriate grip.
3. In pairs, the students throw and volley.
4. In pairs, the players conduct volley-to-volley drills.

Teaching Points

1. Grip: eastern forehand or continental.
2. Ready position.
3. Stepping into volley.
4. Racket head position at impact.
5. Watching the ball onto the strings.

Skill Development: Forehand Drive

1. The coach demonstrates the forehand drive and the bounce, step, and hit progression.
2. In pairs, the players throw (underarm) and hit.
3. The coach supervises ability streaming, with the better players performing hit-to-hit rallies, and those having trouble practicing strokes from a ball fed by a partner.

Teaching Points

1. Grip: eastern forehand.
2. Ready position: modifications may be necessary (racket already back).

3. Backswing: straight back or loop (discussion of advantages and disadvantages of each).
4. Stepping into the ball.
5. Laid back wrist at impact.
6. Hitting "through" the ball.

Culmination

The students play "11-up," using a bounce-hit forehand, in ability groups. Culmination games should be enjoyable, specifically related to the skill developed in the lesson, and organized so that all participants have a good chance of success. The lesson ends with forehand tip for the week.

Lesson 2

Introduction

The coach shows the players how to record their heart rate. The pupils then engage in a slow jog around the court, stretching exercises, and then revise the forehand drive and forehand volley (a half-court drill can often be used for this purpose).

Skill Development: Service

This is considered a priority for adult recreational players.

1. The coach demonstrates the serve, highlighting these critical aspects of the swing:

   "both arms go down together and move up together"
   "back-scratch position"
   "hit up and out toward the ball"

2. In pairs, one partner serves while the other assists him/her by coaching (reciprocal coaching).
3. The group discusses common problems associated with the group's service action and then participates in the following:

   further demonstration
   swinging in time with the coach
   swinging with the eyes closed
   fitting the ball to the swing

4. The coach supervises ability streaming. Players who can fit the ball into a fluent swing work in pairs serving, and players who modify their swings in an attempt to strike the ball work with the coach on the "service swing."

Teaching Points

1. Grip: continental or eastern forehand.
2. Swing.

Culmination

The students play "11-up," using the serve to get the ball into play. The "king of the mountain" format may be used if the coach feels the ability levels of the various players are not too diverse.

    To end the lesson, the coach briefly explains the role that tennis can play in developing a healthy lifestyle. He or she also explains the heart rate that is required for a training effect to occur.

Lesson 3

Introduction

The players engage in (1) stretching exercises, (2) a slow jog combined with an agility run, and (3) the revision of the forehand drive and the serve, hitting at targets.

Skill Development: Backhand Drive

1. The coach demonstrates the backhand drive.
2. In pairs, the students throw (underarm) and hit.
3. The players follow the coach in a shadow drill.
4. The coach supervises ability streaming with a backhand-to-backhand rally. (This may best be organized as a groundstroke to a groundstroke, with an emphasis on the backhand drive.) Ability streaming continues with backhands off a ball fed by the coach.

Teaching Points

1. Grip: eastern backhand.
2. Side-on approach.
3. Firm wrist.
4. Keeping the arm "tucked in" to the body for as long as possible.
5. Using the legs to help "lift the ball" over the net.

Culmination

The students play "11-up," first using the bounce, step, hit backhand, to begin the rally and then using the service to begin the rally.

    The lesson ends with a backhand tip for the week and a fitness tip for the week.

Lesson 4

Introduction

The players warm-up by jogging, stretching, and agility running. Then the players run for one minute and check their heart rate. The students practice serving against an opponent in a half-court format and then practice groundstrokes using a one-on-one format.

Skill Development: Backhand Volley

1. In pairs, the players throw and volley.
2. The students hit a backhand volley from a ball fed by the coach.
3. In pairs, the players volley from a drive.

Teaching Points

1. Grip: eastern backhand or continental.
2. Racket head up.
3. Hitting the ball in front of the body.
4. Minimal backswing and shortened follow-through.
5. Firm wrist at impact.

Culmination

The teacher explains the correct court positions and player rotations for a game of doubles. Players, grouped on ability, then compete in a game of doubles (using correct tennis scoring). The coach should use this period to evaluate stroke production and tactics of the players in the group. The coach finishes the lesson with a brief discussion on doubles tactics and a tactics tip for the week.

Lesson 5

Introduction

The players perform stretching exercises and a slow jog around court. Then they engage in hand-eye coordination drills and target hitting, using the service action, the forehand (from a bounce, step, hit), and the backhand (from a bounce, step, hit).

Skill Development: Return of Service/Revision of Service Action

1. The coach demonstrates the service return.
2. In pairs, one partner throws balls from the service line alternately to the backhand and forehand sides of the player returning serve.
3. The players practice returning a ball hit by the coach, serving from the service line.
4. The players practice return of service from a serve from the baseline.
5. Using the "11-up" scoring system, the students play a game with alternate serving (this may not be possible if a sufficient number of courts are not available).

Teaching Points

1. Watching the ball come from the opponent's racket.
2. Watching the ball bounce.
3. Stepping into the ball after it has bounced.

4. Anticipating the service direction and standing in a position that affords the best possible chance of an effective return.
5. Playing the appropriate shot after the ball has been served, not before.

Culmination

The students play sets of doubles (service rules may be modified in accordance with the level of each pupil). The coach finishes with a service return tip for the week.

Lesson 6

Introduction

The students engage in stretching exercises and a slow jog, followed by low-intensity interval drills. A combination drill incorporating a forehand, backhand, forehand approach shot, a forehand volley, and a backhand volley is an ideal way of combining skill revision with a low-intensity interval drill. (Players' heart rates should be taken to give an idea of exercise intensity.)

Skill Development: Revision Session—Introduction of the Approach Shot

Forehand/Backhand Drive

1. In pairs, one partner throws to the forehand side and then to the backhand side of the other (this player should change grips for efficient stroke production).
2. The players practice groundstrokes using a one-on-one drill.
3. In fours, the students play "11-up," using a bounce, step, hit forehand to begin each rally.

Service

The students practice target serving and, in pairs, service and return of service.

Volley

1. In pairs, one partner throws to the forehand volley and then to the backhand volley of the other (this player should change grips or use the continental grip).
2. In pairs, one partner bounce-hits a forehand from the baseline for the other player to volley at the net.

Approach Shot

1. The coach conducts a demonstration, followed by a discussion of the modification of forehand or backhand drive technique needed for an approach shot.

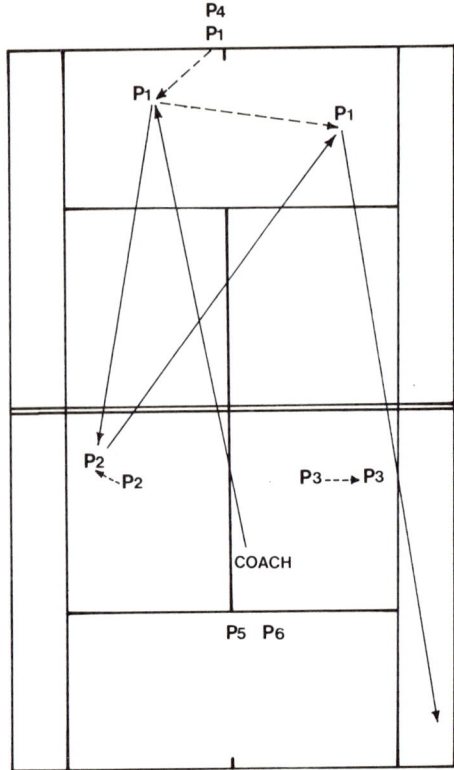

Figure 10.1 Two-on-one drill emphasizing groundstrokes and volleys.

2. The coach and players discuss when and where to hit the approach shot.
3. The players perform an approach shot drill.

Culmination
The players engage in a two-on-one drill with two volleyers against a player on the baseline hitting groundstrokes (Figure 10.1).

Lesson 7

Introduction
The players perform stretching exercises and agility running, carrying their rackets. Then they engage in a combination drill, using the service, the forehand drive, the backhand drive, the backhand approach shot, and the forehand volley.

Skill Development: Lob (Offensive and Defensive)

1. The coach demonstrates the lob.
2. In pairs, the ball is fed to one partner, who attempts a lob over the outstretched racket of the feeder.

3. The players engage in a one-on-one drill, integrating the lob into this drill.

Teaching Points

1. Difference between offensive and defensive lobs.
2. Hitting up through the ball.

Culmination

The students engage in handicapped doubles play (the coach explains any rules that need to be understood so that players can enjoy a game of doubles).

Lesson 8

Introduction

The students perform stretching exercises and agility running, carrying their rackets. Then they perform a combination drill, utilizing the serve, the forehand drive, the backhand drive, the backhand approach shot, the forehand volley, and the recovery of a lob with a lob.

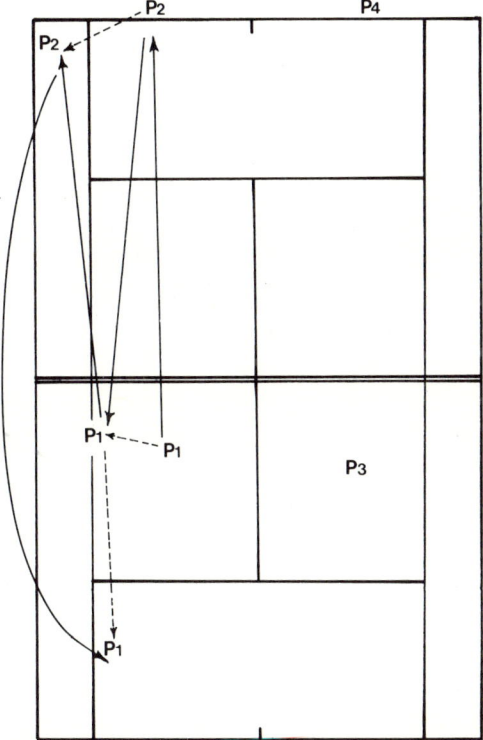

Figure 10.2 Half-court drill emphasizing the smash.

Skill Development: Smash

1. The coach demonstrates the smash.
2. In pairs, a feeder throws the ball into the air so that his/her partner can move under the ball and catch it with the nonracket hand.
3. In a half-court drill, player 1 begins the rally with an easy-feed to player 2; player 2 may then attempt to pass player 1 with either a groundstroke or a lob (Figure 10.2).

Teaching Points

1. Pointing at the ball.
2. Moving under the line of flight quickly.
3. Racket back with elbow at the same height as the shoulder.
4. Eyes on the ball.
5. Transferring the weight into the hit.

Culmination

The players perform a two-on-one drill, as in Lesson 6, but the baseline player may now use the lob. The coach finishes with a tip for the week.

Lesson 9

Introduction

The players do stretching exercises and a slow jog. Then, they engage in a combination drill, utilizing the forehand drive, the backhand drive, the forehand approach shot, the backhand volley, and the smash.

Skill Development: Basic Singles Tactics

The players engage in best-of-three games and then change.

Teaching Points

1. Returning to the center of the court.
2. Percentage tennis.
3. Keeping the ball deep.
4. Moving the feet quickly.
5. Early preparation.
6. Trying not to serve too hard.

Culmination

The lesson ends with target serving and a consecutive-hits competition.

Lesson 10

Introduction
The players do stretching exercises and a slow jog.

Skill Development/Culmination
The coach emphasizes basic doubles tactics, and the lesson ends with a doubles tournament.

Finish of Course

The coach provides evaluation, tips for improvement, and encouragement of players to join a club and continue playing this lifetime recreational activity.

Adult Tennis Program: Preparation for Advanced Club Play

Tennis is a game that can be enjoyed by all ages provided the basic skills inherent to the game have been mastered. This unit, which could be run as a tennis camp for adults or as a series of lessons, is aimed at improving both stroke technique and game strategy so that the general standard of play is improved.

There should be a minimum of two courts, and 16 contact hours should make up one lesson series. Each class should be of two hours' duration, the first hour devoted to stroke production and the second spent on integrating the skills of tennis into the game environment. A prerequisite for such a course is a series of lessons in basic stroke production.

Teaching Progressions

Teaching progressions for singles and doubles play are shown in the following tables:

Tennis Singles

Lesson	Stroke Preparation	Tactics
1–2	Grips and groundstrokes	Basic Singles Tactics 1. Keep the ball deep 2. Always place the ball 3. Play the opponent's weaknesses 4. Hit consistently 5. Move quickly back to a central court position

Tennis Singles (*cont.*)

Lesson	Stroke Preparation	Tactics

3	Serve and service return	Service Tactics
		  1. Placement
		  2. Spin
		Tactics for the Return of Service
		  1. Placement
		  2. Variation

4	Approach shot and volley	Tactics Involving Approach Shots and Volleys (Including Passing Shots)
		  1. When to play each shot
		  2. Where to hit each shot
		  3. Percentage play

5	Lob and smash	Tactics Involving the Lob and Smash
		  1. Types of lobs
		  2. When and where to lob
		  3. Where to smash

6	Drop shot	The Role of the Drop Shot
		  1. When to play this stroke
		  2. Where to direct it

Tennis Doubles

Lesson	Stroke Preparation	Tactics
7	Stroke revision (particularly the service action)	Court Positions Court Responsibility Coordinated Movement

8	Stroke revision	Advanced Doubles Tactics
		  1. Men's or women's doubles
		  2. Mixed doubles

Tennis Camp for Children 10 to 16 Years of Age

Organizational Structure

Arrival: Sunday, 4:00 PM
  1. Enrollment
  2. Camp rules
  3. Administrative arrangements
  4. Purpose of the camp
Tennis Groups
  Group 1: Advanced players
  Group 2: Intermediate players
  Group 3: Beginners

185 Tennis Camp for Children 10 to 16 Years of Age

Approximately twenty pupils should be allocated to each group. Although tennis ability is the guiding factor for group allocation, consideration must also be given to the ages of the children.

Facilities
- Five indoor courts
- Eight outdoor courts
- Gymnasium

Additional Activities
- Swimming
- Roller skating
- Tenpin bowling
- Grass skiing
- Gymnastic activities (emphasis on body awareness)

Recreational Activities
- Tennis
- Table tennis
- Pool
- Volleyball

Meal Times

Breakfast	7:15–7:45 AM
Mid-morning snack	10:30–10:45 AM
Lunch	12:30–1:00 PM
Afternoon snack	3:00–3:30 PM
Dinner	6:00–6:30 PM
Late snack	9:30 PM

Schedule

Monday

Group 1

8:30–10:30 AM	Stroke production—indoor courts
10:45–12 NOON	Practice drills—indoor courts
1:30–3:00 PM	Stroke production—outdoor courts
3:30–5:00 PM	Match play—outdoor courts
6:30–7:30 PM	Free time

Group 2

8:30–10:30 AM	Stroke production—outdoor courts
10:45–12 NOON	Practice drills—outdoor courts
1:30–3:00 PM	Stroke production—indoor courts
3:30–5:00 PM	Match play—indoor courts
6:30–7:30 PM	Free time

Group 3

8:30–10:30 AM	Stroke production—outdoor courts
10:45–12 NOON	Stroke production—outdoor courts
1:30–5:00 PM	Additional activity session
6:30–8:00 PM	Optional tennis—indoor courts

Evening Program

8:00–10:30 PM	Disco

Tuesday

Group 1
- 8:30–9:30 AM — Free time
- 9:30–12 NOON — Additional activity session
- 1:30–5:00 PM — Video analysis of strokes/practice drills—indoor courts
- 6:30–7:30 PM — Free time
- 7:30–10:00 PM — Organized match play (discussion of match strategies)—indoor courts

Group 2
- 8:30–12 NOON — Stroke production—outdoor courts
- 1:30–5:00 PM — Additional activity session

Group 3
- 8:30–12 NOON — Video analysis of strokes/practice drills—indoor courts
- 1:30–5:00 PM — Mini-tournament/tabloids—outdoor courts

Evening Program
- 8:00 PM — Guest speaker

Wednesday

Group 1
- 8:30–10:30 AM — Stroke production—outdoor courts
- 10:45–12 NOON — Practice drills—outdoor courts
- 1:30–3:00 PM — Stroke production—indoor courts
- 3:30–5:00 PM — Mini-tournament—indoor courts

Group 2
- 8:30–12 NOON — Video analysis of strokes/practice drills—indoor courts
- 1:30–5:00 PM — Mini-tournament/tabloids—outdoor courts

Group 3
- 8:30–9:30 AM — Free time
- 9:30–12 NOON — Additional activity session
- 1:30–5:00 PM — Stroke production/practice drills—outdoor courts

Evening program
- 6:30–7:30 PM — Free time
- 7:30–9:30 PM — Tennis and other organized recreational activities

Thursday

Group 1
- 9:00–10:30 AM — Fitness tests for tennis (see Figure 10.3)
- 10:45–12 NOON — Individual stroke appraisal (see Figure 10.3)
- 1:30–3:00 PM — Match play (emphasizing match tactics)
- 3:30–5:00 PM — Tournament—outdoor courts

Group 2
- 8:30–10:30 AM — Individual stroke appraisal—indoor courts
- 10:45–12 NOON — Fitness tests for tennis
- 1:30–5:00 PM — Intermediate singles and doubles play—indoor/outdoor courts

Tennis Appraisal

Service _____

Forehand _____

Backhand _____

Volleys _____

Smash _____

Footwork _____

General Comments _____

_____

_____

Signed: _____

Fitness Appraisal

Speed _____

Endurance _____

Agility _____

Flexibility _____

Strength _____

Weight _____

General Comments _____

_____

_____

Signed: _____

Figure 10.3 Fitness and tennis appraisal form.

    Group 3
        8:30–10:30 AM   Individual stroke appraisal—outdoor courts
        10:45–12 NOON   Fitness tests for tennis
        1:30–3:00 PM   Basic doubles play—indoor courts
        3:30–5:00 PM   Introductory singles tactics—indoor courts
    Evening Program
        8:00–10:30 PM   Roller skating

Friday

    All Groups
        8:30–10:30 AM   Stroke production reinforcement—indoor and outdoor courts
        10:45–12 NOON   Tennis games—indoor and outdoor courts
        12:00–5:00 PM   Barbeque picnic (with organized activities)
        7:30–9:00 PM   Evening concert
                              Presentation of awards

Saturday

        9:00–9:30 AM   Camp clean-up
        9:30–10:30 AM   Issuing of reports—discussions with parents

11

Equipment Design

There was a time in tennis when the weight and the grip size were the only factors considered in the purchase of a new racket. The tennis boom, however, has brought with it a corresponding increase in the influence of technology on the equipment developed for the game. The focal point of this technological thrust has been aimed primarily at the ultimate weapon of the game, the racket. Many more questions now must be considered in the purchase of a racket.

1. What type of racket does the player prefer: wooden, aluminum, steel, graphite, or Fiberglas?
2. Does the player prefer a conventional racket or the oversized style?
3. What weight is best?
4. Does the player prefer a heavy or light racket head?
5. What grip size is needed?
6. Does the player prefer a stiff or flexible shaft?
7. Does the player prefer gut or synthetic strings?
8. What tension is needed in the strings?

This chapter is aimed at aiding the player in selecting the correct racket to suit individual needs. Technology, in developing new designs, has moved so fast that the sports scientist has been unable to substantiate many manufacturers' claims about their products. We hope this chapter will increase the range of questions that the player can ask his or her local tennis professional before purchasing a racket. It is imperative that the racket "feels good" when the player swings it.

Racket Weight, Balance, and Grip Size

Every tennis player at some stage has been faced with deciding which racket to purchase. Such a decision should be based on the player's size, strength, and style of play.

When selecting a racket the player must recognize that it is the distribution of weight, with respect to the pivot point (the base of the index finger), that influences the ease with which the racket may be swung, not the absolute weight of the racket. The distribution of weight (moment of inertia) or "swing weight," in influencing the ease with which the racket may be swung, has a direct effect on stroke production (Figure 11.1). A light racket with a heavy head may be more difficult to swing than a heavier racket with a light head.

Racket Selection for Children

A small racket with the weight relatively close to the pivot point should be used by young children. If asked to play with an adult-size racket, a child will naturally grip the racket midway up the shaft, thus reducing the "swing weight" and making the implement easier to manipulate. If the only racket available is a junior or an old lightweight senior racket, then the shaft

Figure 11.1 Tennis racket selection. *From left:* children's design, junior design, and two adult designs.

should be reduced in length and the grip refitted so that the weight is moved closer to the pivot point. Young children who were taught with a racket related to their own body size have been found to (1) achieve a greater horizontal velocity of the racket at impact, (2) hit the ball with greater accuracy, and (3) use less wrist action during the stroke.[2]

The spatial relationship between the eye and the center of the strings also dictates that young children use a racket related to their body size. A racket related to the child's strength, arm length, and general body size will facilitate learning and thus aid the development of stroke production. As a general rule, children from 7 to 10 years old should use a subjunior racket, whereas those older than 10 should use a junior design.

Racket Selection for Adults

It is equally important that adults select a racket that is related to their needs. The first decision to be made is about racket construction. There is such a variety of frame types available, each with differing characteristics, that personal preference at present plays an integral role in selecting the racket type. Wood is still the favorite material, compared with metal or composite alternatives. Wooden rackets, with their combination of dissimilar materials (cellulose and resin), tend to dampen vibrations effectively.[3] Graphite rackets and many of the metal rackets available today also dampen the vibrations of impact.[1] Until much more research on racket construction is completed, the selection of racket type must be left to the individual.

The oversized (jumbo) and the midsized rackets offer further alternatives to the standard implement. A more effective reduction in the vibration levels from center and off-center impacts, with correspondingly higher rebound velocities from the oversized rackets, may help recreational players by increasing the surface area for more effective rallying.[1] If players are hampered by "tennis elbow," then using a racket with a larger head appears to be beneficial.[4]

The choice of racket weight should be related to body size and strength. Racket balance should be determined with regard to both the player's style of play and the general subjective feel of the racket in the hand. A player who prefers to rally from the baseline may prefer a heavy racket head to assist with groundstrokes, whereas an attacking player may prefer a light racket head to enhance faster court movement and reflex volleys. The all-court player may prefer an evenly balanced racket that is adaptable to both groundstrokes and volleys.

The size of the grip should be related directly to the size of the player's hand. The three most common methods of determining grip size are

1. measuring the distance from the middle lifeline in the palm of the hand to the distal part of the middle finger

2. checking that the thumb fits against the first knuckle (distal joint) of the third digit of the racket hand
3. the subjective feel of the racket[2]

If the grip is too small the player's arm will tire more quickly than it would if the correct grip was selected, because the player will generally grip the handle too tightly, placing strain on the arm. A slightly larger grip is better than a small one because the radius from the grip center to the surface is increased, which decreases the need for hand squeeze.[4] Also, to counter-twist, a high-friction grip is better than a smooth one.[4] The size of the hand should dictate grip size in the same way as the weight of the racket depends upon the physical build and muscular strength of the player.

String Type, Tension, and Racket Flexibility

String type, tension, and racket flexibility are three other factors that must be considered when purchasing a new racket. Gut strings have a slight edge over synthetic strings in their ability to store energy from the incoming ball and then to return energy to the ball.[6,7] Gut and synthetic gut have nearly identical coefficients of elasticity and elongation under strain, but there is a difference in the surface of the two string types. The rougher texture of gut reduces string movement when compared with synthetic material, and thus less energy is dissipated through friction.[8] The lifespan of gut is usually shorter than that of synthetic strings, and gut loses its tension more rapidly in damp climates or when wet.

Most rackets should be strung to a tension of between 55 to 65 lb (25 to 30 kg) unless they have a large or small head. Most players should probably use a tension of approximately 56 to 58 lb (25.5 to 26 kg). It has been demonstrated with clamped rackets that higher string tension does not necessarily result in increased rebound velocity.

The flexibility of the frame (when strung) must also be considered by the tennis enthusiast. The attacking player should probably choose a more rigid frame to take advantage of the superior control of the ball on the serve and when volleying. The baseline player who relies on groundstrokes may select a more flexible frame to help in the generation of power and speed.[6] In these cases the frame is working for and not against the player. As a general rule, higher tensions of about 60 to 65 lb (27 to 30 kg) are associated with greater control, whereas lower tensions of about 52 to 58 lb (23.5 to 26 kg) are associated with power. For this reason, rackets with a flexible shaft should be strung at lower tensions and rackets with a stiff shaft should generally be strung at higher tensions. However, if the player prefers a flexible racket and is having trouble with control, a higher tension may be of assistance.

References

Racket Weight, Balance, and Grip Size
1. Elliott, B. C., Blanksby, B. A., and Ellis, R.: "Vibration and Rebound Velocity Characteristics of Conventional and Oversized Tennis Racquets." *Research Quarterly for Exercise and Sport, 51*(4):608–615, 1981.
2. Groppel, J. L.: "Tennis Racquet Selection Based Upon Selected Anthropometric Indicators." Paper presented at the National American Association for Health, Physical Education, and Recreation Convention, Seattle, Washington, 1977.
3. Nelson, R.: "Can an Exotic New Racket Improve Your Game?" *Scholastic Coach, 46:*46–50, 1976.
4. Plagenhoef, S.: "Tennis Racket Testing Related to 'Tennis Elbow.'" Proceedings of a National Symposium on the Racket Sports (ed. J. L. Groppel). University of Illinois Press, Urbana-Champaign, 1979, pp. 291–394.

String Type, Tension, and Racket Flexibility
5. Baker, J. and Wilson, B.: "Tennis: The Effect of Racket Stiffness and String Tension on Ball Velocity After Impact." *Research Quarterly, 49*(3):255–259, 1978.
6. Bosworth, W.: "How Your String Job Can Help You Win Matches." *World Tennis,* July 1979, pp. 33–34.
7. Ellis, R., Elliott, B., and Blanksby, B.: "The Effect of String Type and Tension in Jumbo and Regular-Sized Tennis Racquets." *Sports Coach, 2*(4):32–34, 1978.
8. Nelson, R.: "Can an Exotic New Racket Improve Your Game?" *Scholastic Coach, 46:*46–50, 1976.

APPENDIX A

Rules of Tennis

The rules of tennis (approved in 1980) are outlined here to enable the reader to become fully conversant with the regulations that govern the game. Information on how to mark out a court, requirements for artificial lighting, and the duties of tournament officials can be found in tennis association handbooks.

The Singles Game

1. The court shall be a rectangle 78 ft (23.77 m) long and 27 ft (8.23 m) wide. It shall be divided across the middle by a net suspended from a cord or metal cable with a maximum diameter of 0.33 in. (0.8 cm), the ends of which shall be attached to, or pass over, the tops of two evenly painted posts, 3.5 ft (1.07 m) high and not more than 6 in. (15 cm) square or 6 in. (15 cm) in diameter, the center of which shall be 3 ft (0.91 m) outside the court on each side. The net shall be extended fully so that it fills completely the space between the two posts and shall be of sufficiently small mesh to prevent the ball passing through. The height of the net shall be 3 ft (0.91 m) at the center, where it shall be held down taut by a strap not more than 2 in. (5 cm) wide and completely white in color. There shall be a band covering the cord or metal cable and the top of the net for not less than 2 in. (5 cm) nor more than 2.5 in. (6.3 cm) in depth on each side and completely white in color. There shall be no advertisement on the net, strap band, or singles sticks. The lines bounding the ends and sides of the court shall

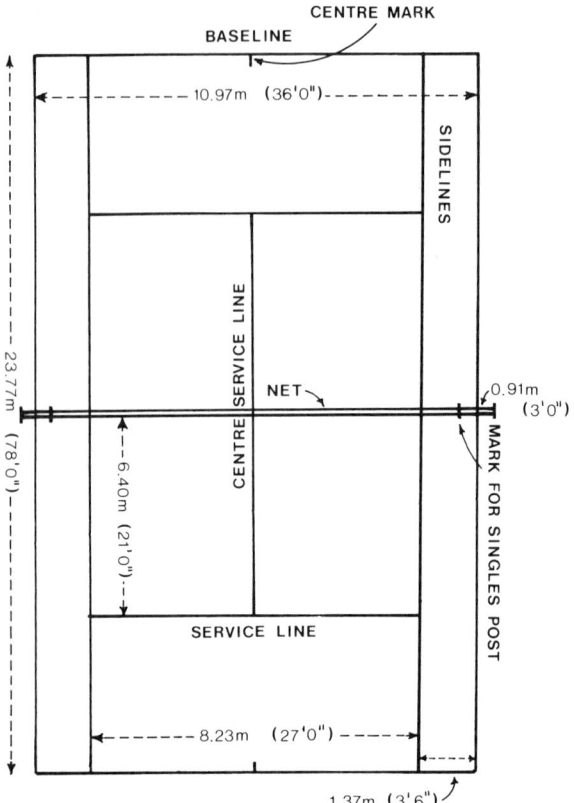

Figure A.1 The tennis court.

respectively be called the baselines and the sidelines. On each side of the net, at a distance of 21 ft (6.40 m) from it and parallel with it, shall be drawn the service lines. The space on each side of the net between the service line and the sidelines shall be divided into two equal parts, called the service courts, by the center service line, which must be 2 in. (5 cm) in width, drawn halfway between and parallel with the sidelines. Each baseline shall be bisected by an imaginary continuation of the center service line to a line 4 in. (10 cm) in length and 2 in. (5 cm) in width called the center mark, drawn inside the court, at right angles to and in contact with such baselines. All other lines shall be not less than 1 in. (2.5 cm) nor more than 2 in. (5 cm) in width, except the baseline, which may be 4 in. (10 cm) in width, and all measurements shall be made to the outside of the lines.

Note: In the case of the International Lawn Tennis Championship (Davis Cup) or other official championships of the International

Federation, there shall be a space behind each baseline of not less than 21 ft (6.4 m) and at the sides of not less than 12 ft (3.66 m).

2. The permanent fixtures of the court shall include not only the net, posts, singles sticks, cord or metal cable, strap and band, but also where there are any such, the back and side stops, the stands, fixed or movable seats and chairs around the court, and their occupants, all other fixtures around and above the court, and the umpire, netcord judge, foot fault judge, linesmen, and ball boys or girls, when in their respective places.

   Note: For the purpose of this rule, the word "umpire" includes the umpire, the persons entitled to a seat on the court, and all those persons designated to assist the umpire in the conduct of a match.

3. The ball shall have a uniform outer surface and shall be white or yellow in color. If there are any seams they shall be stitchless. The ball shall be more than 2.5 in. (6.35 cm) and less than 2.63 in. (6.67 cm) in diameter, and more than 2 oz (56.7 g) and less than 2.17 oz (58.5 g) in weight. The ball shall have a bound of more than 53 in. (135 cm) and less than 58 in. (147 cm) when dropped 100 in. (54 cm) upon a concrete base. The ball shall have a forward deformation of more than 0.22 in. (0.56 cm) and less than 0.29 in. (0.74 cm) and a return deformation of more than 0.35 in. (0.89 cm) and less than 0.425 in. (1.08 cm) at 18 lb (8.165 kg) load. The two deformation figures shall be the averages of three individual readings along three axes of the ball, and no two individual readings shall differ by more than 0.03 in. (0.08 cm) in each case. All tests for bound, size, and deformation shall be made in accordance with the official regulations.

4. The racket shall consist of a frame and a stringing. The frame may be of any material, weight, size, or shape. The strings must be alternatively interlaced or bonded where they cross, and each string must be connected to the frame. If there are attachments, they must be used only to prevent wear and tear and must not alter the flight of the ball. The density in the center must be at least equal to the average density of the stringing.

5. The players shall stand on opposite sides of the net; the player who first delivers the ball shall be called the Server, and the other, the Receiver.

6. The choice of ends and the right to be Server or Receiver in the first game shall be decided by toss. The player winning the toss may choose or require his opponent to choose
   (a) the right to be Server or Receiver, in which case the other player shall choose the end; or
   (b) the end, in which case the other player shall choose the right to be Server or Receiver.

7. The service shall be delivered in the following manner. Immediately before commencing to serve, the Server shall stand with both feet at rest behind (i.e., further from the net than) the baseline and within the imaginary continuations of the center mark and sideline. The Server shall then project the ball by hand into the air in any direction and before it hits the ground strike it with his racket, and the delivery shall be deemed to have been completed at the moment of impact of the racket and the ball. A player with the use of only one arm may utilize his racket for the project.
8. The server shall throughout the delivery of the service
   (a) not change his position by walking or running;
   (b) not touch, with either foot, any area other than that behind the baseline within the imaginary extension of the center mark and sideline.

   Note: The following interpretation of Rule 8 was approved by the International Federation on 9th July, 1958:
   (a) The server shall not, by slight movements of the feet which do not materially affect the location originally taken up by him, be deemed "to change his position by walking or running."

9. (a) In delivering the service, the Server shall stand alternately behind the right and left courts beginning from the right in every game. If service from a wrong half of the court occurs and is undetected, all play resulting from such wrong service or services shall stand, but the inaccuracy of station shall be corrected immediately it is discovered.
   (b) The ball served shall pass over the net and hit the ground within the Service Court which is diagonally opposite, or

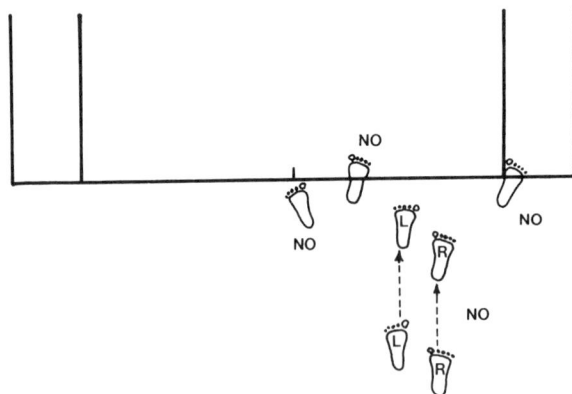

Figure A.2 Common foot fault errors.

upon any line bounding such court, before the Receiver returns it.
10. The service is a fault:
   (a) if the Server commits any breach of Rules 6, 7 or 8;
   (b) if he misses the ball in attempting to strike it;
   (c) if the ball served touches a permanent fixture (other than the net, strap, or band) before it hits the ground.
11. After a fault (if it be the first fault) the Server shall serve again from behind the same half of the court from which he served that fault, unless the service was from the wrong half, when, in accordance with Rule 8, the Server shall be entitled to one service only from behind the other half. A fault may not be claimed after the next service has been delivered.
12. The Server shall not serve until the Receiver is ready. If the latter attempts to return the service, he shall be deemed ready. If, however, the Receiver signifies that he is not ready, he may not claim a fault because the ball does not hit the ground within the limits fixed for the service.
13. In all cases where a let has to be called under the rules, or to provide for an interruption to play, it shall have the following interpretations:
   (a) when called solely in respect of a service that one service only shall be replayed.
   (b) when called under any other circumstance, the point shall be replayed.
14. The service is a let:
   (a) if the ball served touches the net, strap, or band and is otherwise good, or after touching the net, strap, or band touches

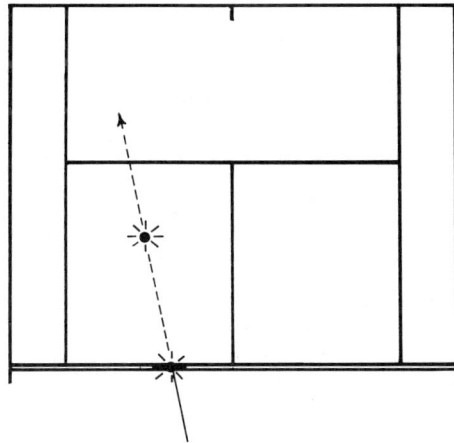

Figure A.3 Service let.

the Receiver or anything which he wears or carries before hitting the ground.
  (b) if a service or a fault be delivered when the Receiver is not ready (see Rule 12).

  In case of a let, that particular service shall not count, and the Server shall serve again, but a service let does not annul a previous fault.

15. At the end of the first game the Receiver shall become Server, and the Server Receiver, and so on alternately in the subsequent games of a match. If a player serves out of turn, the player who ought to have served shall serve as soon as the mistake is discovered, but all points scored before such discovery shall be reckoned. If a game shall have been completed before such discovery, the order of the service remains as altered. A fault served before such discovery shall not be reckoned.

16. The players shall change ends at the end of the first, third, and every subsequent alternate game of each set, and at the end of each set, unless the total number of games in such set be even, in which case the change is not made until the end of the first game of the next set.

    If a mistake is made and the correct sequence is not followed, the players must take up their correct station as soon as the discovery is made and follow their original sequence.

17. A ball is in play from the moment at which it is delivered in service. Unless a fault or a let be called it remains in play until the point is decided.

18. The Server wins the point
    (a) if the ball served, not being a let under Rule 14, touches the Receiver or anything which he wears or carries, before it hits the ground.
    (b) if the Receiver otherwise loses the point as provided by Rule 20.

19. The Receiver wins the point
    (a) if the Server serves two consecutive faults.
    (b) if the Server otherwise loses the point as provided by Rule 20.

20. A player loses the point if
    (a) he fails, before the ball in play has hit the ground twice consecutively, to return it directly over the net (except as provided in Rule 24(a) or (c)).
    (b) he returns the ball in play so that it hits the ground, a permanent fixture, or other object, outside any of the lines which bound his opponent's court [except as provided in Rule 24(a) and (c)].
    (c) he volleys the ball and fails to make a good return even when standing outside the court.

199 The Singles Game

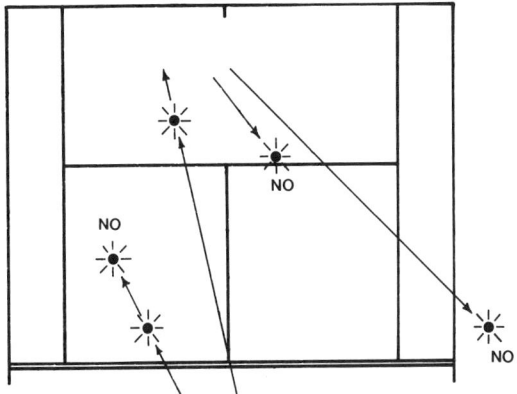

Figure A.4 Common return errors.

    (d) in playing the ball he deliberately carries or catches it on his racket or deliberately touches it with his racket more than once.
    (e) he or his racket (in his hand or otherwise) or anything which he wears or carries touches the net, posts, singles sticks, cord or metal cable, strap or band, or the ground within his opponent's court at any time while the ball is in play.
    (f) he volleys the ball before it has passed the net.
    (g) the ball in play touches him or anything that he wears or carries, except his racket in his hand or hands.
    (h) he throws his racket at and hits the ball.
    (i) he deliberately and materially changes the shape of his racket during the playing of the point.
21. If a player commits any act which hinders his opponent in making a stroke, then, if this is deliberate, he shall lose the point, or if involuntary, the point shall be replayed.
22. A ball falling on a line is regarded as falling in the court bounded by that line.
23. If the ball in play touches a permanent fixture (other than the net, posts, singles sticks, cord or metal cable, strap or band) after it has hit the ground, the player who struck it wins the point; if before it hits the ground, his opponent wins the point.
24. It is a good return
    (a) if the ball touches the net, posts, singles sticks, cord or metal cable, strap or band, provided that it passes over any of them and hits the ground within the court.
    (b) if the ball, served or returned, hits the ground within the proper court and rebounds or is blown back over the net, and the player whose turn it is to strike reaches over and plays the

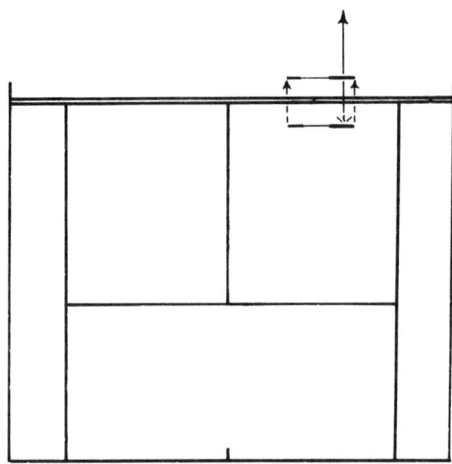

Figure A.5 The racket may pass over but not touch the net after impact.

ball, provided that neither he nor any part of his clothes or racket touches the net, posts, singles sticks, cord or metal cable, strap or band, or the ground within his opponent's court, and that the stroke be otherwise good.

(c) if the ball be returned outside the post or singles stick either above or below the level of the top of the net, even though it touches the post or singles stick, provided that it hits the ground within the proper court.

(d) if a player's racket passes over the net after he has returned the ball, provided the ball passes the net before being played and be properly returned.

(e) if a player succeeds in returning the ball, served or in play, which strikes a ball lying in the court.

Note to Rule 24: In a singles match, if for the sake of convenience, a doubles court be equipped with singles sticks for the purpose of a singles game, then the doubles posts and those portions of the net, cord or metal cable, and the band outside such singles sticks shall at all times be permanent fixtures and are not regarded as posts or parts of the net of a singles game.

A return that passes under the net cord between the singles stick and adjacent doubles post without touching either net cord, net, or doubles post and falls within the area of play, is a good return.

25. In case a player is hindered in making a stroke by anything not within his control, except as provided for in Rule 19, a let shall be called.

26. If a player wins his first point, the score is called 15 for that player; on winning his second point, the score is called 30 for that

201 The Singles Game

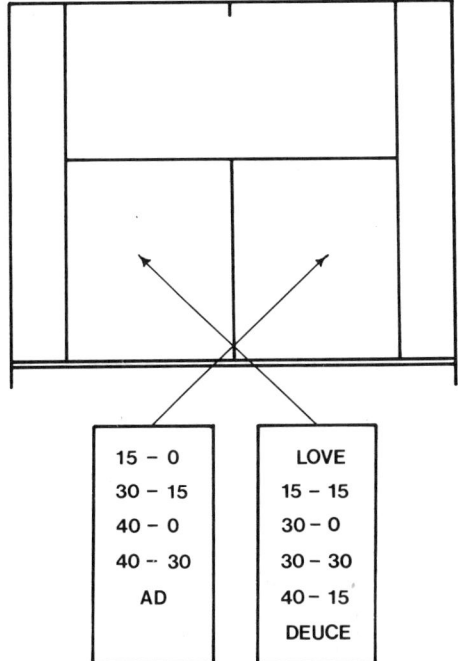

Figure A.6 Scoring procedure.

player; on winning his third point, the score is called 40 for that player, and the fourth point won by a player is scored game for that player except as below.

If both players have won three points, the score is called deuce, and the next point won by a player is scored advantage for the player. If the same player wins the next point he wins the game; if the other player wins, the score is again called deuce, and so on, until a player wins the two points immediately following the score at deuce, when the game is scored for that player.

27. A player (or players) who first wins six games wins a set, except that he must win by a margin of two games over his opponent and where necessary a set shall be extended until this margin be achieved.
28. The maximum number of sets in a match shall be 5, or where women take part, 3.
29. Except where otherwise stated, every reference in these Rules to the masculine includes the feminine gender.
30. In matches where an umpire is appointed, his decision shall be final, but where a referee is appointed, an appeal shall lie to him from the decision of an umpire on a question of law, and in all such cases the decision of the referee shall be final.

In matches where assistants to the Umpire are appointed (linesmen, net cord judges, foot fault judges) their decisions shall be final on questions of fact, except that if in the opinion of an umpire a clear mistake has been made, he shall have the right to change the decision of an assistant or order a let to be played. When such an assistant is unable to give a decision he shall indicate this immediately to the umpire who shall give a decision. When an umpire is unable to give a decision on a question of fact he shall order a let to be played.

In Davis Cup matches or other team matches where the referee is on court, the decision of an assistant to the umpire, or of the umpire if the assistant is unable to make a decision, can be changed by the referee, who may also authorize the umpire to change the decision of an assistant or order a let to be called.

The referee, in his discretion, may at any time postpone a match on account of darkness or the condition of the ground or the weather. In any case of postponement the previous score and previous occupancy of courts shall hold good, unless the referee and the players unanimously agree otherwise.

31. Play shall be continuous from the first service till the match be concluded, provided that after the third set, or when women take part, the second set, either player is entitled to a rest, which shall not exceed 10 minutes, or in countries situated between latitude 15 degrees north and latitude 15 degrees south, 45 minutes; and provided further that when necessitated by circumstances not within the control of the players, the umpire may suspend play for such a period as he may consider necessary. If play be suspended and not resumed until a later day, the rest may be taken only after the third set (or when women take part, the second set) of play on such later day, completion of an unfinished set being counted as one set. These provisions shall be strictly construed, and play shall never be suspended, delayed, or interfered with for the purpose of enabling a player to recover his strength or his wind, or to receive instruction or advice. The umpire shall be the sole judge of such suspension, delay, or interference, and after giving due warning he may disqualify the offender.

> *Notes:* (a) Any nation is at liberty to modify the first provision in Rule 30 or omit it from its regulations governing tournaments, matches, or competitions held in its own country, other than the International Lawn Tennis Championships (Davis Cup and Federation Cup).
> (b) When changing ends a maximum of one minute shall elapse from the cessation of the previous game to the time players are ready to begin the next game.

32. During the playing of a match in a team competition, a player may receive coaching from a Captain who is sitting on the court only when he changes ends at the end of a game, but not when he changes ends during a tie-break game. A player may not receive coaching during the playing of any other match. The provisions of this rule must be strictly construed. After due warning an offending player may be disqualified.
33. In cases where balls are changed after an agreed number of games, if the balls are not changed in the correct sequence the mistake shall be corrected when the player, or pair in the case of doubles, who should have served with the new balls is next due to serve.

The Doubles Game

34. The above Rules shall apply to the doubles game except as below.
35. For the doubles game, the court shall be 36 ft (10.97 m) wide, i.e., 4.5 ft (1.37 m) wider on each side than the court for the singles game, and those portions of the singles sidelines which lie between the two service lines shall be called the service sidelines. In other respects, the court shall be similar to that described in Rule 1, but the portions of the singles sidelines between the baseline and service line on each side of the net may be omitted if desired.
36. The order of serving shall be decided at the beginning of each set as follows:

    The pair who have to serve in the first game of each set shall decide which partner shall do so, and the opposing pair shall decide similarly for the second game. The partner of the player who served in the first game shall serve in the third; the partner of the player who served in the second game shall serve in the fourth, and so on in the same order in all the subsequent games of a set (Figure A.7).
37. The order of receiving the service shall be decided at the beginning of each set as follows:

    The pair who have received the service in the first game shall decide which partner shall receive the first service, and that partner shall continue to receive the first service in every odd game throughout that set. The opposing pair shall likewise decide which partner shall receive the first service in the second game, and that partner shall continue to receive the first service in every even game throughout that set. Partners shall receive the service alternately throughout each game.

204 Rules of Tennis

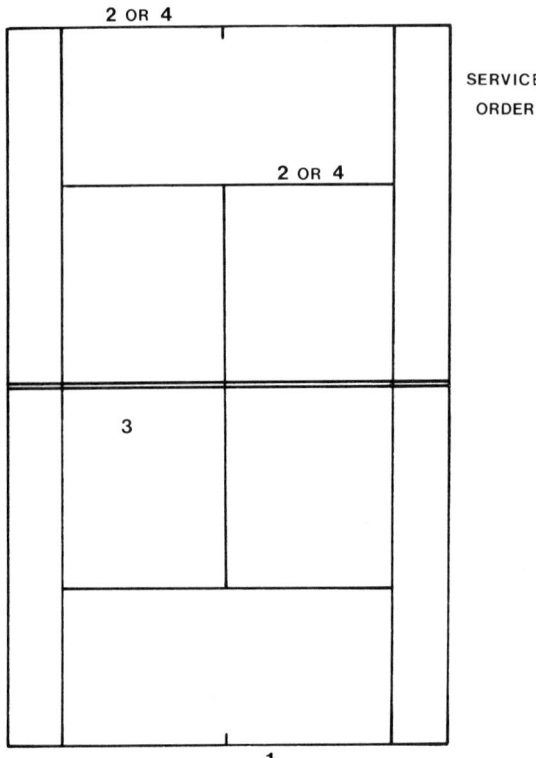

Figure A.7 Serving order in doubles.

38. If a partner serves out of his turn, the partner who ought to have served shall serve as soon as the mistake is discovered, but all points scored, and any faults served before such a discovery, shall be reckoned. If a game shall have been completed before such discovery, the order of service remains as altered.
39. If during a game the order of receiving the service is changed by the receivers, it shall remain as altered until the end of the game in which the mistake is discovered, but the partners shall resume their original order of receiving in the next game of that set in which they are receivers of the service.
40. The service is a fault as provided for by Rule 9, or if the ball touches the server's partner or anything which he wears or carries; but if the ball served touches the partner of the receiver, or anything which he wears or carries, not being a let under Rule 13(a) before it hits the ground, the server wins the point.
41. The ball shall be struck alternately by one or other player of the opposing pairs, and if a player touches the ball in play with his racket in contravention of this Rule, his opponents win the point.

Rules of the Tie-Break System

The tie-break system will operate when the score reaches six games all or eight games all in any set except in the third or fifth set of a three-set or five-set match, respectively, when an ordinary advantage set shall be played in accordance with Rule 25.

The Organizing Committee must decide and announce before the start of any tournament, match, or competition whether the tie-break will operate at six games all or eight games all.

Where a decision is taken to operate the tie-break at eight games all, the Organizing Committee may change this to six games all in one or more complete rounds of any event if, in their opinion, such action is in the best interests of the event.

Note: For indoor events (or events specially sanctioned by the National Association of the country concerned) the tie-break system may also operate in the final set.

PROCEDURE

The following system shall be used in a tie-break game (Figure A.8):

Singles

1. A player who first wins seven points shall win the game and the set provided he leads by a margin of two points. If the score reaches six points all, the game shall be extended until this margin has been achieved. Numerical scoring shall be used throughout the tie-break game.

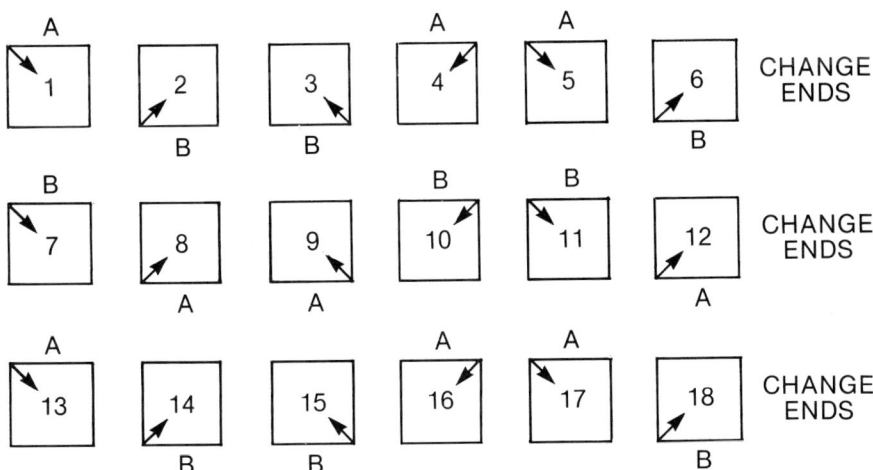

Figure A.8 The tie-break.

2. The player whose turn it is to serve shall be the server for the first point. His opponent shall be the server for the second and third points, and thereafter each player shall serve alternately for two consecutive points until the winner of the game and set has been decided.
3. From the first point, each service shall be delivered alternately from the right and left courts, beginning from the right court.
4. Players shall change ends after every six points and at the conclusion of the tie-break game.
5. The tie-break game shall count as one game for the ball change.

Doubles

In doubles the procedure for singles shall apply. The player whose turn it is to serve shall be the server for the first point. Thereafter each player shall serve in rotation for two points, in the same order as previously in that set, until the winners of the game and set have been decided.

Rotation of Service

The player (or pair in the case of doubles) who served first in the tie-break game shall receive service in the first game of the following set.

No-add Scoring System

This system replaces the traditional terminology by using numbers: 1-love, 1-all, 2–1, 2–2 and so on to 4 points. If the score reaches 3-all the receivers have the option from which side to receive the serve.

APPENDIX B

Glossary of Terms

ace A ball that is served into the correct court and is *not* touched by the opponent.

ad Short for the word "advantage." It is the first point scored after deuce. If the serving side wins the point the score is called *"ad in"*; if the receiving end wins the point, the score is called *"ad out."*

advantage court The left service court, so called because the "ad" score is served there.

aerobic The production of energy with oxygen. Although the intensity of tennis and the length of rallies suggest that it is an anaerobic game, oxygen plays an important role in facilitating recovery between rallies.

all An even score; 30-all, 4-all, and so on.

all-court game A player's ability to hit all tennis strokes competently, feeling equally confident at the baseline and at the net.

alley The area on either side of the singles court that increases the width of the court for doubles play (also called "tramlines").

American twist A service technique in which the ball is tossed over the server's head in such a way that the upward trajectory of the racket imparts topspin and a little sidespin to the ball.

anaerobic The production of energy without oxygen. This is the main system of energy production for the competitive tennis player.

approach shot A shot behind which a player advances to the net.

backhand The stroke used to return a ball hit to the left side of a right-handed player or to the right side of a left-handed player.

backhand court The left side of the court for a right-handed player.

back-scratch position A point during the service swing at which the racket head is looped down the back.

backspin Rotation of the ball in a manner opposite to the direction of travel. It is caused by either a downward (chopping) racket path with a near-vertical racket face or a horizontal racket path with an open racket face.

backswing The first phase of any stroke. This prepares both the racket and the body for the forward-swing phase of the stroke.

baseline The boundary line located at each end of a tennis court.

baseline game The type of strategy preferred by a player who enjoys hitting groundstrokes and therefore plays from the baseline.

base of support The placement of a player's feet with respect to the location of the body.

break service To win an opponent's service game.

bye A walkover; a player given the right to enter the next round of a tournament without having to play a match.

center mark The mark that, by bisecting the baseline, defines one of the limits for the service position.

center of percussion The sweet spot; the central location on the racket face where the impact between the ball and the strings produces optimal rebound velocity and minimal vibration.

center service line The line that is perpendicular to the net and divides the two service courts.

change of pace A tactical maneuver whereby a player alters the speed of the return.

choke To grip the racket up toward the head or to become so tense or nervous that fluency is lost from stroke production.

chop stroke A stroke that hits the ball with a downward movement of the racket face, thus imparting backspin to the ball.

circular backswing The backward movement of the racket whereby a semicircle is described before the forward swing.

clay A general term used for courts composed of clay, dirt, or loose pebbles.

closed racket face The forward face of the racket is turned forward from the vertical position toward the court.

closed stance The standard approach used to hit a tennis ball, in which the player approaches the ball side-on, with the front foot forward, causing the shoulders to be perpendicular to the net.

cocking the wrist Extension of the hand at the wrist.

continental grip One of the grips used in tennis. The "V" formed by the thumb and forefinger should be on top of the handle and the fingers comfortably spread.

continuous training The form of running training that should highlight the off-season preparation. The player engages in continuous running for up to one hour (builds an aerobic base).

cross-court shot A stroke that moves the ball from one side of a court to the diagonally opposite side.

deep shot A stroke that hits the ball deep into the opponent's court, landing close to the baseline.

default Failure to complete a scheduled match.

deuce A score of 40-all in any game.

dink A softly hit shot that goes over the net by a small margin and bounces close to the net.

double fault Failure of both the first and second service attempts to go into the proper court. This results in the loss of the point.

doubles A game of tennis played between four players.

down the line The ball is hit in a line parallel to and close to the sidelines. A right-handed player hitting to a right-handed opponent would play a backhand drive to the forehand of the other player.

drop shot A softly hit shot that barely travels over the net (see "dink").

draw sheet A sheet that shows whom players will compete against in a tournament.

drop volley A shot similar to the drop shot except that it is played from a volley.

eastern forehand A grip used to play balls on the forehand side of the body.

eastern backhand A grip used to play balls on the backhand side of the body.

error A point that ends because of a player's mistake.

Fartlek training A form of running training that falls between the longer continuous running and the more specific interval training. The runner engages in short sprints of about 65 to 87 yards (60 to 80 meters) throughout the continuous training effort.

fault A ball that is served using an inappropriate technique, from the wrong court location, or that does not land in the correct service court.

flat service A service action during which no spin is imparted to the ball.

follow-through The completion of the stroke after the ball has been contacted.

foot fault A fault on serve caused by one foot touching the baseline, the court, the center mark, or the sideline prior to the ball being hit.

forward swing The forward movement of the racket before ball contact.

forehand The stroke used to return a ball hit on the right side of a right-handed player or the left side of a left-handed player.

frame A racket without strings.

game That part of a set that is completed when one player or side wins four points or wins two consecutive points after the score of deuce.

grass (lawn) A type of court surface. This term can also be used to describe a type of strategy; "grass court player" indicates an attacking serve and volley style of play.

grip The method of holding the racket handle. Also, the material covering on the racket handle.

groundstroke A stroke played after the ball has bounced on the court.

gut A type of string used in the racket.

half-volley A ball hit just after it has bounced. Technically it is a groundstroke, not a volley.

handle The part of the racket that is gripped in the hand.

head (of the racket) The part of the racket used to hit the ball. It includes the frame (but not the shaft or handle) and the strings.

hold service The game is won by the player, or team, serving.

in A ball that lands on the line or inside the legal playing area.

in play A ball is "in play" during a rally.

interval training In this training the player engages in short sprints followed by a period of recovery before repeating the initial effort (work-to-recovery ratio normally is 1:3).

isokinetic exercise In an isokinetic contraction a muscle shortens as tension is developed through a full range of motion performed at constant speed.

isometric exercise In an isometric contraction the muscle develops tension but does not change length.

isotonic exercise In an isotonic contraction the muscle shortens as it develops tension. The angle between adjoining bones therefore either increases or decreases.

kill shot An attacking shot played with power to achieve an outright winner.

lactic acid The waste product that accumulates in muscles when energy is produced in the absence of oxygen.

let A call to replay the point. A let is called because of interference to play, uncertainty by the umpire, or when a serve that hits the net lands in the correct service court.

lob A ball hit high enough in the air to pass over the head of an opponent standing at the net.

love A score of zero.

match A contest decided in favor of the first player or team to win two or three sets, as decided by the tournament committee.

match point The state of the game when a player or pair of players requires one point to win the match.

mixed doubles A game of tennis in which opposing pairs each consist of a man and a woman.

net The netting placed across the middle of the court.

no man's land A mid-court location from approximately 1 yard (1 meter) in front of and 2 yards (2 meters) behind the end service line where a return is likely to bounce at the player's feet.

not up A player fails to reach the ball on the first bounce.

offensive stroke An aggressive shot played in an attempt to hit a winner or force an error from the opponent.

nylon A type of string used in the racket.

on the rise The ball is played as it is coming from the ground before it reaches its full height.

open racket face The forward face of the racket is turned from the vertical position toward the sky. This will cause the ball to be hit on more of an upward trajectory, with underspin.

open stance A shot is played with the chest facing the net.

overhead A ball hit with a smash or high volley when it is over the area of the head.

passing shot A ball that passes the opponent, who is standing at the net.

percentage tennis A strategy based on the theory that playing the correct shot at the right time enhances the chance of success.

placement A shot placed so accurately that an opponent cannot reach it (not from a serve).

poach A situation occurring in doubles, when a player moves across the court to intercept a return stroked towards the other player.

point The smallest scoring unit given to the winner of each rally.

psyched-up Keyed up through peak mental preparation for a particular match or tournament.

racket The implement used to hit the ball.

racket face The strings of the racket.

racket head The racket face and the material surrounding it.

rally Continuous strokes hit over the net before a point is scored.

ready position The correct stance adopted by a player in waiting for the opponent to hit the ball.

receiver The player who is receiving the serve.
referee The person who is in charge of the entire tournament (see also "umpire").
round robin A type of tournament in which every player competes against every other player.
seeding A system that permits the top players in a tournament to avoid playing each other in the early rounds.
serve The method of starting each point. The person serving is called the server.
service break Winning an opponent's serve.
service line The line that outlines the back of the service court; it is parallel to the baseline and 7 yards (6.4 meters) from the net.
set That part of a match that is completed when one player or side wins at least six games and is ahead by at least two games, or has won the tie-breaker at six games all.
set point The state of the game at which a player or pair of players requires one point to win the set.
shaft The part of the racket between the handle and the throat.
sideline The line at each side of the court that marks the outside edge of the playing surface. The inner set of lines marks the singles court, and the doubles court sidelines are 4.5 feet (1.37 meters) wider on both sides.
singles A game of tennis between two players.
singles stick A stick used for denoting the limits of the singles court when a singles match is played on a doubles court. These are placed 3 feet (0.91 meter) outside the singles sidelines.
slice service A service technique in which the racket imparts sidespin to the ball.
smash An overhead shot hit with a service action.
spin Rotation of the ball either forward (topspin), backward (underspin), or sideward (sidespin).
straight sets To win a match without losing a set.
strap Material placed in the center of the net to hold the net taut.
stroke The act of striking the ball with the racket.
throat The enlarged part of the racket between the shaft and the head.
tie-breaker A scoring system that comes into operation when the score is six games all. The tournament committee decides on the sets in which a tie-breaker scoring system will operate.
topspin A forward rotation of the ball relative to its direction of travel. This is usually achieved by hitting the ball with a forward swing that flows from low to high with a vertical (or slightly closed) racket face.
tramlines See "alley."
umpire The official who controls an individual match (see also "referee").
volley A ball played before it hits the ground (except in serving).
warm-up The physical preparation immediately preceding a match. It is recommended that all tennis players complete a warm-up routine before going onto the court for a period of stroke practice. The warm-up program before hitting should involve both stretching exercises and a calisthenic circuit designed to warm up all body areas.
western A grip used for the forehand drive (also known as the "frying pan" grip).

APPENDIX C

Tennis Etiquette

The following points of etiquette should be emphasized by coaches, club officials, and experienced players to all new club members, particularly young players. The observation of these practices will improve court behavior and, as a result, enhance everyone's enjoyment of the game.

Before Play

1. Players should observe court rules with reference to the rules of play. If the maximum time of play is one hour and other players are waiting, this time limit should be honored. If singles play is permitted only when some courts are vacant, players should form doubles teams quickly once it becomes clear that a pair is waiting to play.
2. Those not playing should not distract players by talking or hitting balls close to where a match is in progress.
3. A person should never walk through a court on which a rally is in progress and should make sure that all gates are closed after he or she enters the court area.
4. All foreign objects (clothing, bags, extra rackets, and so on) should be placed near the net post, never at the back of the court.
5. Players should introduce themselves to anyone they do not know and introduce any new player(s) to those they do know.
6. The net should be checked prior to the hit-up.
7. To decide from what end of the court the match should be started, it is a good idea to spin a racket.

8. During the hit-up, players should take turns playing from the baseline and the net.
9. Players should practice serving in cooperation with their opponents.

During Play

10. Balls from other courts should be returned to the correct area at the end of the rally. If a ball from another court distracts a player during play, he/she should ask for a let immediately. It is not a good idea to play out the rally and then refer back to the incident in question.
11. At the end of each point, any balls in the receiver's area should be returned to the server.
12. Players should control their feelings at all times, no matter how upset they may become.
13. Players should never abuse or annoy their opponents.

If No Umpire is Available

14. Each player is responsible for all decisions involving balls on the half of the court occupied by that player. A player should be honest and precise with all calls, but if in doubt, he/she should either call for a let to be played or check to find if the opponent saw where the ball landed. If a player asks for an opponent's opinion, then the opponent's answer should be heeded.
15. A player should never catch or deflect a ball he/she assumes will land out of court.
16. A player should refrain from returning an obvious service fault.
17. A player should always attempt to observe the foot fault rule.
18. If a shot is out, the person on that end of the court should call very clearly, "Out." If a shot is good, however, no call should be made.
19. A player should never assume that the opponent will keep the point and game score.

If an Umpire is Available

20. A player should accept and play on the umpire's or linesperson's decision, whether it is for or against him/her.
21. A player should never talk to the umpire, linesperson, or opponent during play.

At the End of Play

22. A player should thank his/her opponent for the match and be restrained in acceptance of victory or defeat.
23. The balls should be collected and returned to their correct location.
24. The players should thank the umpire.

Index

Note: f denotes figure reference; t denotes table reference

Activity principle, 150
Administration of tennis, 155–164
Adult program
   for advanced club play, 183–184
   for intermediate club play, 175–183
Aggressive player, 75–76
Aerobic and anaerobic tests, 103–106
Analysis of game, 99–103
Analysis of stroke production, 99
Anxiety, 88–89
Approach shot, 36–40
Arm stretch, 123, 124f

Back stretch, 123, 124–125f
Backhand drive, 19–25, 21f
   one-handed or two-handed, 140–141
Backswing
   approach shot, 38
   backhand drive, 20–22
   drop shot, 57
   forehand drive, 6–7
   half-volley, 59
Bad calls, 66
Ball toss for service, 30
Behavioral goals, 87
Biofeedback, 86–87
Body-mind integration, 86–87
Borg, Bjorn, 84, 100–102, 143

Calf stretch, 123, 124f
Camp. *See* Tennis camp for children.
Cardiorespiratory conditioning, 111–112
Children's tennis program, 149–152
Coaching theory, 91–93
Combination drill, 126, 127f
Competitive principle, for children, 151
Concentration, 64–67
Consistent play, 67–68
Controversies, 136–147
Coordinated movement, in doubles, 80–82, 81f
Corrective techniques
   approach shot, 38–39
   backhand drive, 24
   drop shot, 58
   forehand drive, 12
   half-volley, 61
   lob, 55
   return of service, 35
   service, 31–32
   smash, 52
   volley, 44
Court conditions, 74
Court positions, 69–70, 77–78, 78f
Court surfaces, 74
Culmination games
   baseball tennis, 17–19, 20f

Culmination games (*continued*)
  champion, 17
  cross-court to cross-court, 16, 16f
  eleven-up, 16, 18f
  eleven-up swing, 33
  Mug's Alley, 17, 19f
  one-on-one, 15–16, 16f
  service golf, 33, 33f
  twenty-one-up, 33
  two-on-one, 16, 17f
Culmination games for individual strokes
  backhand drive, 24–25
  forehand drive, 15–19, 16–19f
  half-volley, 62
  lob, 56
  service, 33–34
  smash, 53
  volley, 47–49

Defensive player, 74–75
Developmental principle, 150
Drop shot, 57–59, 58f

Energy systems, aerobic and anaerobic, 110–111
Environmental conditions, 66, 74, 90
Equipment, 188–191
Etiquette, 212–214
Evaluation
  of player performance, 98–108
  of training, 114

Feedback from coach, 85–86
Firmness of grip, 138
Fitness. *See* Physical fitness.
Fitness appraisal, 187f
Flexibility training, 121–126, 122f, 124–125f
Fluid intake and replacement, 133
Follow-through
  approach shot, 38
  backhand drive, 23
  drop shot, 57
  forehand drive, 10
  half-volley, 61
  service, 30–31
  smash, 50
  volley, 43
  reason for, 142
Food intake, 133
Forehand drive, 6–18, 7f
Forward swing
  approach shot, 38
  backhand drive, 22–23
  drop shot, 57
  forehand drive, 8–9
  half-volley, 60
  volley, 41–42
Frequency of training, 114

Grip
  continental, 3–4, 2f
  eastern backhand, 3, 2f
  eastern forehand, 1–2, 2f
  "frying pan," 4
  western, 4, 2f
Grip, for individual strokes
  approach shot, 37
  backhand drive, 20
  drop shot, 57
  forehand drive, 6
  half-volley, 59
  lob, 53
  return of service, 34
  service, 26, 26f
  smash, 50
  volley, 41
Grip, time for change of, 138–139
Groin stretch, 123, 124–125f

Half-volley, 59–62, 60f
Hamstring stretch, 123, 124–125f
Handicap, 160–162, 161f
Hitting winners, 143

Impact
  ball to racket, 136–137
  service, 30
Injuries, 152
Isokinetic contraction, 117–118, 117–119f
Isotonic contraction, 118–120, 120f

Lesson evaluation, 96–97, 96f
Lesson plans, 95–97. *See also* Unit structure for teaching.
Lob, 53–56, 54f
  recovery of, in doubles, 81
  used against aggressive player, 76
  used against defensive player, 75
Lloyd, Chris Evert, 74, 149

McEnroe, John, 149
Mobility stretching, 125f
Motivation, 87–89, 114
  for children, 151
Muscle strength and endurance training, 117

Net rusher, 76

Off-court training, 115–126
On-court training, 126–129
One-on-one drills, 128–129, 128f
Overload, 112–113

Peaks in performance, 133
"Percentage tennis," 143
Performance, factors influencing, 84
Performance principle, 151
Personality, 89–90
Personality principle, 151

Physical effects of training on children, 152
Physical fitness, 85–87
Poaching, 80–82
Postitional tactics, 78–80
Preparation for stroke
  approach shot, 37
  smash, 50
  volley, 41
Progression in training, 114
Psychological effects of training on children, 152
Psychology in tennis, 83–90
Purpose
  in doubles play, 77
  in stroke selection, 70

Racket, size of, for child, 139–140
  string type, tension, and flexibility, 191
Racket selection
  for adults, 190–191
  for children, 189–190, 189f
Racket weight, balance, and grip size, 189, 189f
Ready position, 5–6
Regularity of training, 114
Reinforcement, 86
Return of service, 34–36
  strategy, 72
Round robin, 158–159
Rules of tennis, 192–206
Running as training, 115–116

Salt tablets, 146
Scatter drill, 126, 127f
School programs
  for children 8–9 years old, 165–170
  for children 13–14 years old, 170–175
Seeded tournament, 163–164, 163f
Self-handicapping, 159–160
Service, 25–34, 27f, 29f
  flat, 25, 30, 31f
  kicker, 25, 30, 31f, 71, 79
  optimal height for impact, 141–142
  slice, 25, 30, 31f, 71, 79
Service toss, 74
Sex differences in training, 144–145
Sex-role principle, 152
Short ball, 80
Shot selection, 68–69
Side trunk stretch, 123, 124–125f
Singles, preparation and tactics, 73–76
Smash, 49–53, 51f
Social and competitive club play, 155–162
Social interaction, 150
Specificity in training, 112
Spectators, 66
Speed, 143–144

Squad organization for physiological development, 114–132
Squad preparation, 112–114
Stance, 137
  for service, 26–28
Statistical analysis techniques, 100–103, 101–102f
Strategy, 64–67
  for doubles, 77–82
  for service game, 70–72
  for singles, 67–76
Strength. *See* Muscle strength and endurance training.
Stress, 83
Stress, physical, in training, 111–114
Stretch volley drill, 129, 129f
Swing
  lob, 54
  return of service, 34–35
  service, 28
  smash, 50
Switch-partner doubles, 160

Talent identification and development, 153–154, 153f
Tanner, Roscoe, 100–102, 141–142
Teaching drills
  approach shot, 39–40, 40f
  backhand drive, 24
  drop shot, 59
  forehand drive, 12–15
  half-volley, 61–62, 62f
  lob, 56
  return of service, 35–36
  smash, 52
  volley, 44–47, 45–47f
Teaching strategies
  for speed and accuracy, 94–95
  whole-versus-part, 93–94, 95f
Tennis appraisal, 187f
Tennis camp for children, 184–187
"Tennis elbow," 146–147
Tests
  energy requirements for speed and stamina, 103–106, 105f
  flexibility, 106–107, 106–107f
  physical characteristics, 103, 104f
  strength, 108, 108f
Tips
  approach shot, 38
  backhand drive, 23
  drop shot, 57
  forehand drive, 10
  half-volley, 61
  lob, 54
  return of service, 35
  service, 31
  smash, 52
  volley, 43–44

Topspin for forehand drive, 10–11
Tournament organization, 163–164, 163–164f
Tournament preparation, 132
Training programs, 110–135
Training schedule, 130
Training time, 117
Trunk rotation, 123, 124f
Trunk stretch, 123, 124f
Two-on-one drill, 126, 128f

Unit structure for teaching, 165–187. *See also* Lesson plans.
Verbal abuse, 66
Video systems for stroke analysis, 99
Volley, 40–49, 42–43f

Warm-up, 73–74, 130
Weakness, opponent's, 70
Weekly training schedule, 129–132
Weight training for women, 145
Will to win, 87–89

796.3422　　　　　　　　　　84-4659
Eℓ58a
　Elliott
　The art and science of tennis.

LIBRARY
ATLANTIC CHRISTIAN COLLEGE
WILSON N C